ENGLAND'S "PRUSSIAN MINISTER"
Edwin Chadwick and the Politics of Government Growth, 1832–1854

Sir Edwin Chadwick. Courtesy of The Bettmann Archive/BBC Hulton

ENGLAND'S "PRUSSIAN MINISTER"

Edwin Chadwick and the
Politics of Government Growth,
1832–1854

Anthony Brundage

"...we must be beware not to lose the cooperation of
the country. They will not bear a Prussian Minister to
regulate their domestic affairs, so that some faults must
be indulged for the sake of carrying improvements in
the mass."

—Lord John Russell to
Edwin Chadwick (1836)

THE PENNSYLVANIA STATE UNIVERSITY PRESS
University Park and London

Library of Congress Cataloging-in-Publication Data

Brundage, Anthony, 1938–
  England's 'Prussian minister'.

  Bibliography: p.
  Includes index.
  1. Chadwick, Edwin, Sir, 1800–1890. 2. Great
Britain—Officials and employees—Biography. 3. Health
reformers—Great Britain—Biography. 4. Great
Britain—Politics and government—1837–1901. 5. Public
health—Government policy—Great Britain—History—19th
century. I. Title.
DA565.C38B78 1988   354.410084'092'4   87-29220
ISBN 0-271-00629-3

Contents

Acknowledgments

I am most grateful for the kind and expert assistance rendered by the staffs of the numerous archives and libraries where the primary sources I consulted are located. Special thanks go to the staff of the Watson Library at University College, London, the repository of the Chadwick Papers. Their unfailing patience, courtesy, efficiency, and expertise helped make the research for this book a most pleasant experience.

I would also like to express my gratitude to Professors D. Cresap Moore, Richard Davis, and Ian D. C. Newbould for reading all or part of the manuscript and offering helpful advice and encouraging words.

And once again, as in my previous scholarly endeavors, my wife Martha and daughter Catherine proved immensely supportive and understanding.

1 Introduction: Bentham, Chadwick, and the Philosophic Radicals

On June 9, 1832, a few days after the passing of the Great Reform Act, an extraordinary gathering took place at the Webb Street School of Anatomy and Medicine in London. Those in attendance were mostly young, middle class, and intellectual, and entered the hall with a mixed air of curiosity and reverence. They had come for the last rites of Jeremy Bentham, the philosopher who had devoted most of his eighty-four years to producing scathing indictments of England's political, legal, and administrative institutions. Scornful of tradition and aristocratic misrule, Bentham had devised elaborate codes for the wholesale reorganization of English government according to the canons of reason, efficiency, and utilitarianism. Highly eccentric in personal manner and inclined toward reclusiveness, he had yet been able to inspire both affection and a dedication to his principles among some of the best and brightest of succeeding generations. Many of them were there on June 9, and knew that the departed sage had left the most minute instructions for his own services. Since no opportunity to advance human knowledge should ever be allowed to pass, he had directed that his body was to be dissected, with an anatomy lecture and eulogy to accompany the procedure. The man given the honor of performing these functions was Thomas Southwood Smith, a Unitarian minister turned medical doctor and one of the inner circle of Benthamites. In spite of an electrical storm raging dramatically outside, Southwood Smith discharged his task with consummate skill and coolness.

While this memorable event was a celebration of a long and distinguished life, it no doubt also inspired concerns for the future. How would the movement, which even while the master was alive had shown markedly divisive tendencies, be held together? In spite of the powerful reforming impulses of the previous two years, the only solid achievement was a partial reform of Parliament. The ramshackle structure of administration and justice, without order, symmetry, or efficiency, remained untouched. Social problems created or exacerbated by industrialization and urbanization could not be addressed until the corrupt aristocratic dominance of government at all levels was removed. Pondering the magnitude of the tasks that lay ahead were men as diverse as the leading intellectual figure of the movement, John Stuart Mill, the "radical tailor" Francis Place, the wily M.P. Joseph Hume, and a thirty-two-year-old lawyer-journalist named Edwin Chadwick. These, and dozens of others who considered themselves Bentham's followers, determined to do what they could to promote reform, or at least that particular segment of it that seemed most pressing to each individual. This did not necessarily entail an attempt to follow Bentham's blueprints exactly. The essential thing was to maintain Bentham's rigorous, critical analysis of even the most hallowed institutions and practices, and foster this spirit amongst the public as well as in the corridors of power, so that the inertia of the ruling elite could at last be overcome. An evaluation of the success of this undertaking is one of the chief aims of this book.

Assessing the influence of ideas on history is an enterprise noted for its pitfalls, and the question of the impact of Bentham's ideas is no exception. He himself disliked the term "Benthamism," because it emanated from Whig and Tory critics and because it implied a slavish devotion to his doctrines. The alternative terms "Utilitarians" and "Philosophic Radicals," both coined by John Stuart Mill, allow a little more room for heterodox opinions, but do not dispose of the problem of Bentham's influence. Some of the questions that persist are: What were the essential points of the doctrine, and how are the ambiguities and inconsistencies to be resolved? How homogeneous was the movement, and what other ideas and motives influenced his followers? How successful were the Benthamites in implementing the master's blueprints? How important were non-Benthamite ideas and values in the complex political, social, and administrative reforms that punctuate the century and a half since the master's death? Those familiar with the scholarly debate on the "nineteenth century revolution in government" are aware that these questions are much in dispute, and that Benthamism has been vigorously challenged as the prime motive force by such other factors as paternalism, evangelicalism, or simply "intolerability."[1] The debate has lapsed into quiescence, and it is not my intention to revive it, at least on the old terms. Nonetheless, important questions raised in the controversy remain unresolved, including those listed above. It is hoped that this study will help to provide some answers, or at least point to some new directions in developing them.

The writing of another biography on Chadwick, in spite of the existence of the two excellent ones by S. E. Finer and R. A. Lewis,[2] can be justified by noting that both were published in 1952, and Chadwick's career needs to be reconsidered in the context of the numerous studies of Benthamism and reform published since then. Furthermore, Lewis's study was confined to Chadwick's involvement in the public-health movement, and Finer's, while spanning the entire life, tended to ignore important episodes of Chadwick's career like the Towns Improvement Company. Even such central activities of Chadwick's life as the poor-law and public-health campaigns, which Finer treated so fully and so well, are in need of a new look. The result is a substantially revisionist account that sheds new light on the relationship between the theory and practice of governmental reform. A biographical approach has been turned to good account by William Thomas in his book *The Philosophical Radicals.*[3] Unfortunately, Thomas decided not to write a chapter on Chadwick, largely because "there seemed little point in repeating a story which Professor Finer has told so well."[4] This misses the point, both because even the best-told story does not preclude major reinterpretation and because a gaping hole is left in Thomas's otherwise excellent study by the omission of the man Ursula Henriques has aptly characterized as "the arch-Benthamite."[5]

Edwin Chadwick was born January 24, 1800, at Longsight, near Manchester, the eldest son of James Chadwick, a leading figure in the intellectual and cultural life of the area. His father, intoxicated with the French Revolution and the Rights of Man, became an outspoken radical, Francophile, and follower of Thomas Paine. Andrew Chadwick, Edwin's grandfather, had also taken a prominent, if far less radical, part in public affairs. A friend of John Wesley, Andrew is credited with having founded the first Methodist Sunday Schools in Lancashire. His grandson Edwin described him as "a pious unostentatious promoter of measures for the improvement of the condition of the population."[6] Andrew's probity caused him to spurn the making of a fortune in real-estate speculation, with the result that James and his family were forced to struggle for a number of years. Shortly after Edwin's birth, James suffered the loss of his wife along with economic misfortunes, and took his family to London in 1810 to pursue a career in journalism. His economic and professional position improved when he became editor of the *Statesman* in 1812. A further advancement occurred in 1816 when he took over the editorship of the *Western Times*. This marked the end of Edwin's close involvement with his father. James remarried in Exeter and began raising a second family. In 1837 or 1838 he emigrated with his family to New York City, where he pursued his journalistic career, with indifferent success, until his death at age eighty-five in 1863. Edwin did maintain contact with some of his American relations, especially his brother-in-law Andrew Boardman, an attorney. And in later years, he displayed considerable fraternal pride in the exploits of his half-brother Henry Chadwick, a leading American sportswriter and a key figure in the development of professional baseball.

When his father moved to Devon, it was decided that sixteen-year-old Edwin would remain in London to complete his education and map out a career.[7] Having been instructed at home by his father and by private tutors, Chadwick developed a lifelong disdain for what he considered the wasteful practices and frivolous curriculum of most schools and universities. This attitude of resentment and jealousy of the classically educated elite was due in part to his own restricted educational opportunities. Deprived of his mother in childhood and the guiding hand of his father in adolescence, Chadwick had to chart his own course, striving to succeed in a social world that cast a cold, indifferent eye on a provincial middle-class youth without money or connections. Mastering his insecurities and overcoming the obstacles that lay in his path created a hard-driving, combative, and essentially humorless personality that exhibited its softer side only in the presence of close friends and family. It also seems unlikely that Edwin received much in the way of formal religious instruction, given James's radical, freethinking disposition. He thus entered adulthood unencumbered by any strong sense of religious tradition, but with a sense of mission and purpose acquired from his grandfather's Methodism and his father's radicalism.

At the age of eighteen he entered an attorney's office to begin preparation for a modest career in law. But after five years, his ambition to attain the prestige and potentially greater income of a barrister led him to give up his apprenticeship as an attorney. This meant starting over, and in 1823 he was admitted to the Middle Temple to begin the seven years' preparation that would culminate in his being called to the bar. His residence at Lyon's Inn was admirably situated for him to observe all that was most exciting and most appalling in the London of the 1820s. Study of the law at the Inns of Court was largely a private affair, leaving Chadwick ample time to develop numerous acquaintances among the medical and legal students of the district. Like many students, he helped support himself as a "penny-a-liner" for a number of the metropolitan newspapers, a useful preparation for a career in which powers of observation and description were to be so crucial. His medical contacts gave him his first glimpse of the enormous cost of human suffering created by poverty and an unhealthful environment, and opened up vistas of an exciting set of challenges that lay beyond the legal sphere. These contacts also introduced him to the invigorating world of the Philosophic Radicals. In 1824 he met Dr. Thomas Southwood Smith and then John Stuart Mill. Although he remained at the fringes of the group (or rather groups) for several years, through reading, conversation, and attendance at lectures and debates, he developed his knowledge of Benthamism. An important mark of acceptance came in 1828, when the *Westminster Review* published his first article, an impressive analysis of insurance and Friendly Societies.[8] In it he stressed the positive role of government and the need for accurate statistics, so as to "direct the public exertions in removing those circumstances which shorten life, and in promoting those under which it is found to attain its greatest duration."[9] To this Benthamite emphasis on accurate information as the basis for preventive action was added an attack on the complacent belief that "the existing practice, whatever it be, is the best possible."[10]

Like most Benthamites, Chadwick also absorbed Ricardian economics. While at first blush the insistence on laissez-faire in Ricardo's work might seem at odds with the espousal of an active government, for Chadwick and others the hands-off posture was to apply to trade, rent, profits, and wages—economic factors pure and simple. Government intervention was necessary, however, to create and maintain free-market conditions where these did not exist, and even to promote vigor and efficiency, hence economic productivity, by ameliorative measures. It was this that tended to set most Ricardians apart from the Malthusians. The latter, obsessed with the grim "population principle," were apt to consider any amelioration temporary, delusive, and ultimately productive of even greater suffering. In spite of the dismal sound of Ricardo's "iron law of wages," the Ricardians were not necessarily pessimists on the question of improving the human condition. Everything turned on increasing the stock of capital faster than population. Provided the economic forces were unfettered, some combination of technological advance, a more vigorous labor force, and more efficient institutions could enhance productivity and with it the stock of capital and human happiness. Particularly when operating in harness with Benthamism, Ricardian economics was thus an "optimistic" creed, and Chadwick never ceased to disparage the fatalism of the Malthusian pessimists.

The most important friendship he developed among the economists was with Nassau William Senior, with whom he was later to cooperate in the forging of the 1834 Poor Law. When Senior and another economist, Richard Whateley, later Archbishop of Dublin, founded a new journal called the *London Review,* they asked Chadwick to write an article for the first number. Chadwick had something already at hand—a lengthy analysis of the problems of crime and policing, which he had tried in vain to bring to the attention of Robert Peel and the House of Commons Select Committee on the Police of the Metropolis. It is clear from this attempt to gain recognition from the country's political leaders that Chadwick's ambition was increasing along with his experience and confidence. While he was unable to make any contribution to the Metropolitan Police Bill of 1829, the interest and controversy created by the bill's passage made it an ideal time for his article to appear. Published under the title of "Preventive Police," it recommended a greatly expanded concept of policing along Benthamite lines.[11] In this article Chadwick displayed considerable writing skill. His ability to accompany a lucid description of principle with vivid anecdotal material to illustrate it proved most effective in the writing of government blue books.

In his police article, he quoted long passages from the autobiography of a thief, a man who kept returning to criminal associations in spite of being able to command high wages as a skilled workman. Chadwick used this individual as an example of his assertion that crime arose chiefly from greed and flawed character, not dire necessity:

> It is a fact, established from observation of the course of life and characters of those who appear as criminals in our penal courts, that in by far the greater number of cases the motive to depredation is not necessity or poverty, in the common acceptation of the term, but, as in the instance we have quoted, the "easy guinea", — an impatience of steady labour, an aversion to the pains of exertion, a proportionally strong appetite for the pleasures of ease.[12]

The solution to the problems lay not in draconian punishments for the few who were apprehended, but in a pervasive, intrusive police mechanism coupled with a well-regulated indigence-relief system to remove the plea of necessity. This done, Chadwick claimed, it would be possible to operate according to the principles of Seneca,

> where he represents the governors of kingdoms in the amiable light of parents. The subject, as well as the child, should be left without excuse before he is punished: for in that case alone the rod becomes the hand either of the parent or the magistrate. All temptations, therefore, are to be carefully removed out of the way; much less is the plea of necessity to be left in the mouth of any.[13]

This endorsement of an authoritarian, tutelary state, along with his insistence on police being both preventive and performing a wide range of services, was a foretaste of the policies he was to promote as a public official in the late 1830s. It also attracted favorable notice from the Benthamites. Francis Place wrote: "You have done this so well anything I can do will seem plagiarism, and must in reality be so to a considerable extent."[14] His growing reputation led to his being asked to open a debate on the poor laws at the London Debating Society in November 1829.[15] By the beginning of 1831, he was on terms of growing intimacy with Joseph Hume, who introduced him warmly as "a man of talent and of the best political principles."[16] Finally, he was brought to the attention of the great Bentham himself, and by 1831 had left his lodgings at Lyon's Inn to take up residence at Queen Square as the philosopher's secretary.

Bentham's invitation was a great honor, and Chadwick did not hesitate to accept it. His new position would certainly augment his prestige among the Philosophic Radicals and perhaps among certain circles of the ruling Whig party as well. Moreover, Bentham brought Chadwick in specifically to assist him with the drafting of the *Constitutional Code,* and this offered an unparalleled opportunity to refine his understanding of the principles of government. Still, Chadwick was his own man, with a developing reputation as a journalist. His first two articles had been acclaimed as the work of a writer of great promise, and he had recently been taken on by Albany Fonblanque as sub-editor of the radical *Examiner.* Although there is no indication that he was ever anything but respectful and diligent at Queen Square, there must have been times when he chafed at the demanding and eccentric ways of the reclusive sage. And while Bentham's isolation grew largely out of his bitterness at the rejection of his Panopticon scheme in the bruising world of politics, Chadwick longed to enter that world. He must have felt restive at continued immersion in theories of reform while there beckoned opportunities for fame and power in their actual implementation. For this reason Chadwick turned down the tempting offer of a comfortable annual pension in return for becoming the official expositor of Benthamism for the rest of his life, although he did accept a smaller annuity from Bentham's estate that had no strings attached.[17]

Since Chadwick worked on the *Constitutional Code,* it would be appropriate to inquire how closely the administrative structures he was to fashion in such fields as poor law, factories, and public health resemble Bentham's blueprints. Helen Benyon has pointed out how widely Bentham's disciples, including Chadwick, departed from his code.[18] When we consider only the new central government organs, the resemblance seems closer, as in the case of the Poor Law Commission, which calls to mind Bentham's Indigence Relief Minister, or the General Board of Health, which can be taken as the counterpart of Bentham's Minister of Health. While these were boards that Bentham had always denounced for their tendency to function as "screens" for corruption and inefficiency,[19] Chadwick too always argued for "single-seatedness" in the executive body. When we turn to the details of the administrative system, the differences are greater. Bentham did not really provide for an inspectorate as such, and Ursula Henriques is correct that the details worked out by Chadwick and others in the 1830s "owed more to the exigencies of the situation than to Bentham's blueprint."[20] Bentham considered a royal commission "an instrument of monarchical tyranny,"[21] while much of Chadwick's influence stemmed from his participation in royal-commission inquiries. On the remuneration of officials, Bentham argued for putting offices up to public bidding, accepting the qualified person willing to accept the lowest salary. He defended his economy-minded proposals against Burke,[22] while Chadwick quoted Burke on the need for high salaries for officials.[23] There is also a contrast between Bentham's endorsement of democracy[24] and Chadwick's fundamental antipathy to enfranchising the masses. Recognizing these and other departures from the master's principles, it is nonetheless obvious that Chadwick had drunk deep from the well of utilitarianism and shared Bentham's disdain for history and tradition, contempt for inefficiency and ignorance, and passion for a new order. John Roach's opinion on this point is compelling: "His legal studies, his knowledge of poverty in London no doubt taught him a great deal, but the architecture of his mind, the broad design of his approach to policy was Benthamite, and it is difficult to believe that they would have been the same had he not known Bentham and worked on the Constitutional Code."[25]

Another similarity between the two men can be discerned by considering Bentham's Panopticon scheme. The Panopticon was Bentham's name for his ingenious all-purpose public institution that could be used for prisons and workhouses as well as for schools. It was designed on a radial plan, with the inmates isolated in rooms or cells around the periphery. From a central inspection lodge they could be kept under constant surveillance—or rather threat of surveillance, for

Bentham devised it so that the inspection lodge would not be visible from the cells. Not only would criminals and paupers be reformed, but Bentham promised major reductions in expense from the existing inefficient and often barbaric public facilities. He proposed to contract with the government to provide incarceration and reformation, with his expenses and a modest profit to result from the fruits of the inmates' labor. When Parliament at last declined to act after two decades of fitful consideration of the scheme, Bentham lashed out at George III and the entire political establishment.

Historians, as Gertrude Himmelfarb has noted, have tended to be reluctant to discuss this episode, finding the totalitarian implications of Panopticon distasteful and out of keeping with Bentham's image as a benevolent and visionary pioneer of the welfare state.[26] But a knowledge of the Panopticon plan is necessary to grasp the nature of Benthamism, and it is also crucial to an understanding of Chadwick and his policies. It is not that Chadwick shared his master's obsession with precise architectural details, but rather that his concept of a tutelary state, as he developed its details in the 1830s and 1840s, came to resemble Panopticon in its thoroughness, tidiness, and intrusiveness. The authoritarian tenor of Benthamism, seen so clearly in Panopticon, was embraced wholeheartedly by Chadwick. This "Prussian" tendency (as his contemporaries were apt to characterize it), a compound of his own personality and the Benthamism he espoused, ultimately created overwhelming opposition to him and his reforms.

If Chadwick and Bentham were, on the whole, ideological soul mates, there is one important distinction that needs to be appreciated before turning to the details of Chadwick's career. Thanks to a sizeable legacy, Bentham had the lifelong security and leisure to devote his full time and energy to the demanding tasks he had set for himself. His wealth and position were a significant factor in gaining a hearing for his ideas and acquiring a following among men of rank and station. His decided peculiarities of manner and temperament tended to be treated as delightful eccentricities that rendered him all the more attractive. No such indulgences were granted to an obscure, penniless figure like Chadwick; he would have to make his way on his merits and willpower. And though he was relatively indifferent to creature comforts, he could never afford to be cavalier about money. A burning ambition and the necessity of devising strategies to realize that ambition were as much a part of Chadwick's being as his Benthamism. This is best appreciated by returning to the eulogy delivered at that rather bizarre memorial service on a stormy June day in 1832. Concerning Bentham's attitude toward the world of affairs, Thomas Southwood Smith declared:

> That he might be in the less danger of falling under the influence of any wrong bias, he kept himself as much as possible from all personal contact with what is called the world. Had he engaged in the active pursuits of life — money-getting, power-acquiring pursuits — he, like other men so engaged, must had have prejudices to humour, interests to conciliate, friends to serve, enemies to subdue; and therefore, like other men under the influence of such motives, must sometimes have missed the truth, and sometimes concealed or modified it.[27]

When these words were uttered, Chadwick had been involved for several months in the poor-law inquiry undertaken by the government. Success in this would open exhilarating prospects of power — along with the pitfalls described by Southwood Smith.

2 Chadwick, the Whigs, and the Role of Government: The Poor Law and Factory Inquiries

When Earl Grey's mostly Whig ministry took office at the end of 1830, it was committed to a program of "peace, retrenchment, and reform." Considering the excited mood of the country, it was quite natural that the last of these would take precedence. For the next two years, the cabinet, denounced from the right for subverting the constitution and from the left for ignoring the people's will, struggled mightily to fashion a viable measure of parliamentary reform. When, in spite of the fulminations of political unions and die-hard Tories alike, and in the face of serious outbreaks of popular violence, the Reform Act was passed in 1832, it might seem that the bulk of the government's labors were at an end. Peace and retrenchment, the remaining two elements of the reform ministry's triad, did not seem to require an extensive legislative program. Yet in the ensuing seven years, the Whigs presided over one of the most extraordinary periods of government growth in British history. Reforms in such areas as factories, the poor laws, education, and police all involved the growth of central government—new structures, new procedures, and new kinds of interference with localities and individuals. Did these innovations reflect some additional "reform agenda" beyond that of parliamentary reform, or were they simply pragmatic responses to new and pressing social evils? Were governmental solutions to these evils inherent in Whig ideology, or did the government have to turn in desperation to the Benthamites? What sort of compromises were necessary in order for the social and administrative reforms of the 1830s to reach the statute book? What role did Edwin Chadwick, as the Benthamite "point man," play in this process? The remainder of this chapter will consider these questions by examining the royal-commission investigations that culminated in the Factory Act of 1833 and the Poor Law Amendment Act of 1834.

Before turning to these two royal commissions, it is useful to inquire into the attitudes toward social problems and the role of government apt to be held by leading Whigs in the 1830s. It scarcely needs mentioning that we look in vain for a "typical" Whig thinker or politician. The Whigs were both a party and a tradition. Their beliefs did not constitute a rigid ideology, but rather a loosely held set of principles, not all of which would be endorsed by every Whig. If there was a core belief held by all, it was a commitment to liberty, as that concept had been developed by Fox and others during the long period of political and intellectual repression that began in the 1790s. During their forty years in the political wilderness, the Whigs had not been pressed to implement this concept with actual measures. At any rate, some of their libertarian thunder had been stolen by the liberal Tories during the period 1822–30, when most of the repressive legislation had been repealed. Thus when power was thrust upon the Whigs unexpectedly in 1830, the concept of liberty was not likely in itself to take them very far. It was another pervasive Whig belief, the reform of Parliament, that brought them to power and occupied most of their time and energies for the first two years. To understand the reforming impulses that helped shape the various social and administrative reforms after 1832, we need to look at newer elements that had been added to the basic beliefs in liberty and parliamentary reform.

The two intellectual systems that were widely accepted among Whig leaders were classical economics and Benthamism. As we have seen in the first chapter, these systems seemed closely interrelated, thanks in part to the master's ardent endorsement of the principle of laissez-faire. Only with the implementation of the reforms of this period would the tensions between the two systems begin to reveal themselves. Many Whig leaders had more than a nodding acquaintance with the tenets of political economy. Such key figures of the ministry as the Marquess of Lansdowne, Viscount Palmerston, Lord Brougham, Lord John Russell, and Francis Jeffery had learned them

firsthand from Dugald Stewart at the University of Edinburgh.[1] Lord
Althorp, the Chancellor of the Exchequer and a key figure in the
factory and poor-law acts, belonged to the Political Economy Club,
election to which required adherence to Ricardian economics. There
Althorp, along with C. E. Poulett Thompson and Francis Baring of
the Board of Trade, discussed the issues of the day with economists
and Benthamites like Nassau Senior, J. R. McCulloch, and Chadwick.[2]
Moreover, a number of young Whigs like Charles Villiers and Thomas
Hyde Villiers, sons of the Earl of Clarendon, were introduced to the
works of Bentham and James Mill at Cambridge in the 1820s.[3] This
process of transmitting Benthamite ideas to the Whigs, described by
S. E. Finer as one of "irradiation," is seen by him as crucial in setting
the stage for the reforms of the 1830s: "The result was to introduce
Benthamite precepts and example to a wide circle of influential
people: aristocrats who had ministerial patronage, merchants and
bankers who were often MPs, and a swarm of humbler persons who
were later deployed to fill vacancies in an expanding civil service."[4]

It is important, however, to ask how far these "irradiated Whigs"
can be truly considered Benthamites. This is not merely or even
primarily a question of the degree of attachment they may have had
to the principles of the master. It is much more fundamental to
examine how far their progressive views were attenuated or transformed
by a value central to all Whigs, namely paternalism. David Roberts is
surely correct to view paternalism as the most pervasive and powerful
principle in early Victorian England. Roberts defines a paternalist as
"one who believes that society can be best managed and social evils
mitigated by men of authority, property and rank performing their
respective duties toward those in their community who are bound to
them by personal ties of dependency."[5] As men of authority, property,
and rank, the Whig peers and gentry participated as enthusiastically
in paternalism as their Tory counterparts. It must also be stressed
that, for most Whig magnates, paternalism was to be exercised at the
local as well as the national level. Peter Mandler has claimed that the
Whigs "were paternalists more as governors in the capital than as
landowners in the country."[6] There is an element of truth in this—
Whig grandees certainly tended to be a good deal more cosmopolitan
than most Tory squires, with their fierce local pride and distrust of
central government. But the Whigs, too, were owners of landed

estates and as such were part of the natural ruling elite of the countryside. With their sense of continuity, family pride, and attachment to a locality, they did not hesitate to take an active part in local government—as Lord Lieutenants, magistrates, and, after 1834, as poor-law guardians.

It is true, as David Roberts claims, that even an ardent Benthamite like Chadwick had "a small, but still dogged, streak of paternalism."[7] But for middle-class intellectuals like Chadwick, paternalism was a very abstract concept and therefore not incompatible with an abstract model of centralized government. For the Whigs, on the other hand, paternalism always carried a highly specific connotation—something meant to be exercised by themselves and those like them within traditional, hierarchically structured, and rather static communities. This concept of paternalism gave the Whigs a vastly different view of the role of central government. They were open to the necessity of government growth when a strong case could be made for it but were determined that whatever new organs were created would not be hostile to the continuing dominance of local government by traditional elites. They were willing to experiment, innovate, and even restructure, but only with an eye to maintain or strengthen the role of the country's natural leaders. Another important difference is that middle-class utilitarians like Chadwick looked on Benthamism as a potential vehicle for acquiring power, position, and prestige, while the Whigs already had these things. Power was their birthright. They were born, bred, and educated to it, and assumed it at both the national and local levels with an air of patrician confidence that many insecure and ambitious middle-class Benthamites deeply resented.

If the Whigs' social position and role as local magnates are vital to understanding what Benthamism meant to them, they also help us to understand why the Whigs undertook poor-law and factory reforms. During the first two years of Grey's government, violent protests by the workers erupted in many parts of the country. In the towns, the threat or use of force often accompanied protests, demands, and strikes by political unions, trade unions, and short-time committees. As men of property and as the professed allies of the middle class, Whig ministers were disposed to consider measures beyond the reform bill that might restore urban tranquility. The rural disturbances were even more alarming. As country gentlemen, the Whig leaders naturally felt an immediate and pressing concern about the threat to property and the social order represented by the Captain Swing riots of 1830–31. Rick-burnings and other assaults on property and persons struck fear into many parts of the countryside. The Whigs were determined to take action, not as Benthamites but as leaders of the propertied order. As the Lord Advocate, Francis Jeffery, put it in January 1831: "The real battle is not between Whig and Tories, Liberals and Illiberals and such gentlemen-like denominations, but between property and no property—Swing and the law."[8] The Swing riots would be frequently cited by government leaders over the next several years in relation to their major program to restore the rural social order: amendment of the poor laws.

The Swing riots were by no means the sole cause of the government's undertaking a poor-law inquiry. Laborers were not the only restive segment of the agricultural population in 1830. There had been a loud outcry by squires and farmers for years about the burden of taxes and rates, which together with low prices constituted "agricultural distress." Since poor rates were an important component of this distress, poor-law reform was an obvious solution. In June of 1831 the ultra-Tory Earl of Winchelsea asked government ministers if they had any plan for affording relief to the agricultural interest. Lord Melbourne, the Home Secretary, gave a noncommittal reply, but Lord Brougham, the Lord Chancellor, promised a poor-law reform during the next session.[9] The highly eccentric Brougham, who was estranged from most of his former Benthamite colleagues as well as from his fellow cabinet ministers, may have surprised everyone by his declaration. It is unlikely that the cabinet wished to undertake a poor-law reform at that time. It would be nearly eight months later, at the start of the 1832 session, that the topic was again broached by a cabinet minister. This was the declaration by Lord Althorp on February 1, 1832, that a royal commission would investigate the topic, after which ministers would "determine whether they would propose any measure on the subject."[10]

There was certainly nothing new about a government agreeing to investigate the poor laws with a possible view to legislating. During the preceding decades numerous inquiries had been held in an attempt to devise a solution to runaway poor rates and pauper insubordination. But opinion, within and outside Parliament, varied widely, from preservation of the parochial status quo to outright abolition of the poor law. Consequently, the only significant legislative fruits had been the optional Select Vestries Acts of 1818 and 1819, which weighted the right to vote in the parish vestry according to rateable value. The idea behind this statute was to establish rigorous, less generous poor-relief policy by removing power from inefficient and sometimes corrupt parochial small-fry. As a voluntary act, however, its impact had been limited. If the Whigs thought they might succeed in passing a thoroughgoing reform, it was because of the profound shock created by Swing along with the anguished cries of agricultural distress. Why, then, did they not simply follow earlier practice by utilizing a parliamentary select committee? A royal commission, while by no means a new device, was a startling and, in some quarters, alarming choice. A panel of extra-parliamentary experts, granted under royal seal sweeping powers in gathering evidence, traveling around the country to investigate firsthand, raised the hackles of many defenders of local and individual rights. Cries of unconstitutionality were not uncommon. Furthermore, the use of expert, nonpartisan investigations as a prelude to legislation is rightly seen as a feature of Benthamism. This led some contemporaries, as well as subsequent historians, to conclude the government ministers, confronted with problems beyond their understanding, were turning in desperation to experts for the solutions.

But the Whig leaders, with their understanding of economics and acquaintance with the more sophisticated methods of analysis of the day, were not apt to feel baffled by the poor laws. In addition to this expertise they had acquired a close knowledge of poor-law administration from their involvement in local government. Finally, their own air of supreme confidence did not render them vulnerable to feelings of desperation regarding governmental problems. A more persuasive explanation of Whig motives is offered by Clokie and Robinson in their history of the origins and uses of royal commissions:

> Where no issue of policy was involved, the Government desired expert inquiry of a nonpartisan type which would produce results they could accept. On the other hand, when the Government did possess a policy which must be preceded by inquiry, they desired to have the investigation made by men who, even if not openly partisan (on their side), were at least

sympathetic and not irreconcilable. Select committees could not always provide these conditions. Royal Commissions, on the other hand, could be made definitely expert or impartial when needed or they could be "packed" to any degree desired.[11]

Thus the motive was more straightforwardly political. From the cabinet's point of view, royal commissions were much more reliable and manageable, even if there was a price tag in terms of the opposition to their use on constitutional grounds. Because of their obvious political utility, royal commissions were the inquiry vehicle of choice for the rest of the century, with select committees being avoided as much as possible.

But the further question that is suggested by this interpretation is: Which of the two uses set forth by Clokie and Robinson applies in the case of the royal commission of the poor laws? Did the government already have a specific measure in mind, or were they waiting for the commission's report to decide what course to adopt? The evidence is both scanty and inconclusive. To begin with, the idea of using a royal commission came in a letter of January 19, 1832, from Thomas Hyde Villiers to Lord Howick, the son and heir of the Prime Minister. Villiers, secretary to the Board of Control, whose premature death later that year would cut off a promising political career, was a friend of John Stuart Mill and, according to the Webbs, "one of the channels through which much Benthamism reached the minds of ministers."[12] But Villiers, a younger son of the Earl of Clarendon, was also a Whig, and his Benthamism was most likely subject to the important modifying factors discussed earlier. Moreover, as a minor member of the ministerial team, he was prone to view a royal commission in a political light. The one piece of evidence that does strongly suggest that the government already had a measure in mind is a letter from Sir James Graham, who, before his defection from the cabinet on church policy, was First Lord of the Admiralty. Several years later he told Peel that "the Government . . . contemplated and sought a specific change, and had the commission as a Pioneer for their measure."[13] On the other hand, Lord Lansdowne, the Lord President of the council, expressed a belief in needing the commission to investigate before any measure could be framed. He wrote to Lord Brougham in 1833 that the report would enable them "to come to the session with minds made up as to the extent of remedial interference necessary by amendment in the law itself."[14] It is quite possible, of course, that Brougham, who was on the outs with his cabinet colleagues, was kept in the dark about the preconcerted ministerial measure. But regardless of whether or not poor-law reform was preconcerted, or whether every minister knew of it, no one in the government was willing to allow policy to be determined by a royal commission.

Of the five men suggested by Villiers to serve on the royal commission, only two were closely connected to the Benthamite circle—James Mill and the political economist Nassau Senior. The cabinet accepted Senior, whose Benthamism was problematic, but declined to appoint Mill.

Senior himself suggested three more names, of which only one, the barrister and journalist Walter Coulson, was a Benthamite. There were originally seven commissioners appointed, three of whom were on neither Villiers's nor Senior's list. Of these latter, two were important: Bishop Blomfield of London, who was to work closely with Chadwick on the poor law and other reforms over the next two decades; and William Sturges-Bourne, chairman of the 1818 committee that fashioned the Select Vestries Acts (or Sturges-Bourne's Acts, as they were called).[15] Twenty-six assistant commissioners were appointed to carry out the fieldwork. Chadwick was the most important of these, and received his position through Senior.[16] R. A. Lewis has commented aptly on this appointment: "It was no civil service fledgling, docile, well-bred, and ignorant . . . that Senior thus introduced, but an assertive, rather crude, lawyer-journalist, with habits of mind already fixed, who for years had been elaborating theories of positive Government action and was eager for the opportunity to put them into practice."[17]

Chadwick quickly proved to be the most skillful, resolute, and industrious of the twenty-six assistants. His original district for investigation was the north and east of London, to which was added Berkshire. Since he was not appointed to the central commission until after the inquiry had been under way for more than a year, he had no part in devising the procedures. While Senior had wished to send the assistants forth with only a simple injunction to investigate, others on the central commission insisted on very detailed instructions, which together indicate the targets of the reform and give some hint as to possible remedial measures. For example, the assistants were to report on the prevalence and ill effects of the allowance system, the labor rate, and the roundsman system—devices that reformers had attacked for years for stimulating pauperism and population growth and undermining labor discipline. They were also told to inquire into the feasibility of putting local poor-law administration in the hands of well-to-do ratepayers by a plural voting system. Since this was a device associated with the Select Vestries Act, that particular instruction was probably the work of William Sturges-Bourne.[18] And since plural voting was to be a vital component of the constitution of boards of guardians under the New Poor, it reinforces the impression that the measure was to some extent preconcerted.

Chadwick, eager to distinguish himself in his first official post and to help shape an important reform of government, worked furiously at his report. His dispatches were considerably more extensive than those of the other assistants. No one had foreseen quite how voluminous the combined dispatches would be and how this would delay the writing of the commission's report. Even in the excitement of the first general election under the Reform Act, the cabinet began to grow restive at the protracted poor-law inquiry. Anxious to have some fruits of the investigation in print to prepare Parliament for legislation, Melbourne ordered the commission to ready a volume of "Extracts."[19] This illustrative material was rushed into print in February 1833, and the lengthiest and most impressive of the condensed reports was Chadwick's on London and Berkshire.[20] In it he called for a central authority "with extensive powers," a workhouse test, and simplification of the law of pauper settlement.[21] The high visibility and favorable notice that Chadwick attracted for his zeal as an assistant commissioner led to Senior's getting him added to the central commission in April 1833 to help work up the remedial measures.[22] At almost the same time, the government appointed him chief central commissioner on the newly created royal commission on factories. From April to July 1833, when the factory commission issued its report, Chadwick was actively engaged on two royal commissions, each concerned with some of the most pressing social problems of the day.

Like the poor laws, factory conditions had been the subject of periodic investigations for a generation. These had resulted in the acts of 1802, 1819, and 1831, which, though well-meaning, foundered because of the absence of any effective enforcement mechanism.

From the Grey government's perspective, however, there were some important differences. As landed leaders they felt less compulsion to act than with the poor laws, which were a primarily rural problem. As believers in the basic tenets of political economy, they were loath to interfere in the "free market" of factory labor, while interference in the tangled and demoralizing affairs of poor relief seemed necessary in order to establish a free labor market. Furthermore, ministers disdained to adopt a reform that was being demanded by trade unions and short-time committees, particularly when these demands were sometimes accompanied by threats. To act would be to capitulate to intimidation by the lower orders. On the other hand, the demand for action was not confined to the workers or radicals. Ever since the famous "Yorkshire Slavery" letters by Richard Oastler appeared in 1830, the Ten Hours Movement had captured the sympathy and support of a wide segment of society. Many Evangelical Tories supported the movement as a means of expressing their own pious brand of paternalism as well as a weapon against the triumphant Whigs and the insidious and unfeeling principles of political economy they seemed to champion.

There were numerous Ten Hours supporters in Parliament as well, and they rallied to the support of the bill introduced in December 1831 by the Evangelical Tory manufacturer Michael Sadler. The government knew that the move to limit workers under eighteen to ten hours a day was in fact designed to limit adult hours as well, since children and adults were teamed together on the various textile machines. Unwilling to countenance such a drastic repudiation of economic dogma and in response to the outcry of the threatened manufacturing interests, the ministers sought to sidetrack the bill by compelling Sadler to submit it to a House of Commons select committee. This strategy backfired, however, when the committee, directed by Sadler himself, produced devastating evidence of the manifold physical and moral evils inflicted upon factory children. The likely passage of the Ten Hours Bill was forestalled by the final dramatic stages of the passing of the 1832 Reform Act and the necessity of a general election. The election of December 1832 both enlarged the number of Whig supporters in the House and eliminated Sadler, who, in contesting the new constituency of Leeds, lost to Macaulay. But Sadler's bill was still there even if he was not, and was now in the hands of that most dedicated of Evangelicals, Lord Ashley. This was the work of the Oastlerites, who insisted on a ten-hours measure and a Tory sponsor, even though there was a greater likelihood of passing an eleven-hours bill introduced by the Whig M.P. for Yorkshire, Lord Morpeth.[23]

It was thus in the context of intransigence on the part of the Ten Hours Bill's parliamentary supporters, backed up by continuing public clamor, that the cabinet agreed to a royal-commission investigation. This had been suggested by the manufacturers as a way of telling the "other side of the story" and revealing the alleged distortions and biases of the Sadler committee report. The motion for a royal commission was made by a representative of the manufacturing interest, Wilson Patten, on April 3. Thomas Spring Rice, the financial secretary to the Treasury, acknowledged that the ministry's acquiescence might lead some members "to think that the government had particular feelings in the matter, and that the Commission might be prejudiced." He then attempted to reassure the House with a rhetorical question that doubtless had the opposite of its intended effect: "What interest could the Government have but that of the country?"[24] The motion passed by the narrowest of margins, 74 to 73. Not only were many M.P.s unconvinced about the propriety of a royal commission, but the public outcry intensified. The Whig ministers were viewed in some quarters as mere tools of the manufacturers. They were linked in a conspiracy to defeat the Ten Hours Movement and continue the exploitation and brutalization of small children. The royal commissioners also came in for their share of execration, and Chadwick began to receive his first taste of public hostility, even before he commenced his investigations.

Unlike the royal commission on the poor laws, where Benthamites were decidedly in the minority, all three of the factory central commissioners were Benthamites. Besides Chadwick, there were Dr. Southwood Smith and Thomas Tooke. The Whigs were willing to appoint such doctrinaires to this particular inquiry because they were known to be absolutely sound on the issue of non-interference with adult labor. Also, as cool and dispassionate analysts, they could be relied upon to counter the emotionally charged tone of the Sadler Report. Finally—and this characteristic applied primarily to Chadwick —their zeal and industry would make it possible for them to get their report into print before the end of the session, thus allowing the government to take the offensive against the Ten Hours Bill. Indeed, of all the official inquiries Chadwick was to direct over the next two decades, this was by far the most rushed. Appointed in April, the commissioners were expected to report before the end of June. This would have been exceedingly difficult even if they had been given the fullest cooperation by the factory operatives and others from whom they required evidence. In fact, the Ten Hours Movement leaders in the north organized a hostile reception for the commissioners who carried out the fieldwork, with the hottest area being in the West Riding of Yorkshire, Richard Oastler's bailiwick.

For five weeks in the spring of 1833, Alfred Power and the other commissioners confronted mass meetings, protests against the exclusion of the public from the hearing rooms, and threats of violence.[25] As a central commissioner, Chadwick was spared the immediate anxiety of physical assault, but he came in for a fair measure of verbal abuse. When his written instructions to the commissioners in the field were made public, *The Times* commented acidly: "Such a mass of impotent and stupid verbiage it has seldom been our fortune to face, or so much pomp and pretension combined with such vagueness and insincerity of purpose."[26] Among the instructions is one that indicates a plan that was in Chadwick's head before the inquiry and that was to become one of the most controversial points of the report and bill—restricting children's working hours in such a way that two relays could be used with each set of adult workers.[27] If Lord Melbourne displayed a certain impatience with the poor-law inquiry, where there was no alternate legislation to forestall, he would brook no delay whatever with the factory commission, for the Ten Hours Bill was coming up for its second reading.[28] Accordingly, Chadwick rushed the report to its conclusion, and it was ready for presentation on June 25, barely fifteen weeks after the royal commission was established.

The Factory Report is significant for a number of reasons. To begin with, in spite of the frantic pace, Chadwick did not confine himself simply to the question of working hours. He insisted on a wider investigation that embraced all the major environmental aspects of the workers' health and well-being. In a passage that clearly adumbrates his "sanitary idea," he set forth some of the "concurrent circumstances" that needed to be considered:

... the situation of the factory, the state of drainage about the building, the size and height of the workrooms, the perfect or imperfect ventilation, the degree of temperature, the nature and quantity of the effluvia evolved, whether necessarily or unnecessarily, in the different processes of manufacture, the conveniences afforded to the workpeople for washing, and changing their clothes, on leaving the factory, and the habitual state of the factory and of the operatives as to cleanliness.

Larger factories were deemed to be greatly superior to smaller ones in regard to these characteristics.[29] The same point was made concerning the cruelty issue, which the Sadler committee had featured so prominently. Chadwick declared that the evidence indicated great improvements in recent years, with such ill-treatment as was still to be found existing "chiefly in the small and obscure factories...."[30] On the central issue of restricting hours, the report stole a march on the Ten Hours Movement by deriding Ashley's bill for not providing sufficient protection. Since children were not free economic agents, Parliament was justified in intervening, and the evidence on disease or physical degeneration pointed to an eight- rather than a ten-hour-a-day maximum.[31]

The recommendation of an eight-hour working day for children was based on more than medical evidence. First of all, it would permit the use of relays, a topic that was developed in detail in the report,[32] thereby avoiding limitations on adult working hours. Of equal importance, however, was Chadwick's strong antipathy for the Ten Hours Movement and trade-union leaders. Increasingly mistrustful of popular radicalism and still smarting from the invective hurled at the factory commission, he denounced union leaders as "that class of men who entitle themselves, unfortunately with some truth, the delegates of the workpeople, whom the repeal of the combination laws released from all restriction in the disposal of their own property (labour), and who now seek to impose restrictions equally vexatious on the disposal of the property of others." He went on to claim that those "who have placed themselves at the head of the agitation of this question are the same men who in every instance of rash and headlong strikes have assumed the command of the discontented members of the operative body, and who have used the grossest means of intimidation to subjugate the quiet and contented part of the workpeople."[33]

If trade unions were one of the great obstacles to the creation of a free economy, the poor laws were another. Involved as he was on both inquiries simultaneously, Chadwick did not miss the opportunity of pointing out the links between the poor-relief system and factory labor. The parochial settlement laws, which entailed a "population penned up in petty districts," led to a profligate waste of labor accompanied by moral degeneracy:

> ... the children of paupers are kept in indolence, which unfits them for steady industry as adults, whilst in other districts the demand for the labour of children appears to be such as to occasion them to be worked beyond their powers, and to impair their capacity and well-being as adults. The fact that the general wages of children and youths in the manufacturing towns are double the wages of children and youths in the agricultural districts, whilst in the latter the workhouses are full of unemployed persons, affords an indication of the working of the system. Yet the certainty of an adequate unrepulsive parochial allowance, happen what may, impairs the habits of economy of those of the manufacturing classes in the towns who receive such high wages as would enable them to provide against temporary cessations of employment, and the casualties of sickness and superannuation, for which they now claim provision from their parishes.[34]

Thus a drastic overhaul of the poor laws would restore a wholesome discipline both to the underpaid, languishing rural laborer and to his overpaid, intemperate urban counterpart. In addition to the important economic point he was able to make in this passage, Chadwick also stressed it for another reason. It was being said, even by some of his colleagues on the commission, that the relay system would not work because of the shortage of children. By freeing up stagnant pools of child labor in the countryside through elimination or overhaul of the laws of settlement, this obstacle would be overcome. And indeed, one of the first tasks Chadwick would undertake when he became Secretary of the Poor Law Commission in 1834 was the establishment of a Migration Agency to facilitate such transfers.[35]

The other recommendations in the report are best considered in conjunction with the Factory Act, or Althorp's Act, as it came to be called. When Ashley insisted on proceeding with the second reading of the Ten Hours Bill on June 17, Althorp did not oppose it. He did, however, indicate that parts of Ashley's bill did not go far enough, while others were excessive. When pressed, Althorp revealed that the heart of the measure he approved would restrict to eight the hours for labor of children nine to thirteen, with no night work.[36] This was, of course, the limitation recommended by the royal commissioners, whose report would not be in print for over a week. What followed, when the House went into committee in July, was the total reconstituting of Ashley's bill into one that conformed in its essentials to the commission's report. A limitation of nine hours per day and forty-eight hours per week for those aged nine to thirteen was inserted. Ashley's motion to keep a full restriction on hours up to age eighteen was beaten soundly by a vote of 238 to 93.[37] The vitally important provision for an independent inspectorate under central supervision was also added. A late addition to the bill definitely not to Chadwick's taste was the creation of a new category of "young persons" aged fourteen to seventeen, whose hours were restricted to twelve per day and sixty-nine per week. To Althorp and the cabinet this seemed a sensible compromise and was designed to dampen the clamor out of doors. To Chadwick, however, this concession made a mockery of the carefully worked-out demonstrations in his report that with puberty came full economic independence plus an ability to withstand the rigors of protracted labor.

The other change that deeply disturbed Chadwick was the gutting of the educational clause by the House of Lords. Considerable stress was laid on education in the report. American factory workers, it was claimed, were disinclined to adopt rancorous attitudes toward their masters or engage in strikes, thanks to universal education.[38] Besides, by requiring proof of daily schooling, the law could not be evaded by having a child work two jobs. Chadwick got Althorp to insert a clause empowering the factory inspectors to establish schools where there were none, deducting no more than one penny in the shilling from each child's wage, with the remainder to be raised from a levy on the manufacturers. The latter were to be permitted to deduct the assessment from their poor rates. In the upper house, this provision encountered the powerful opposition of the Marquess of Salisbury, who secured its defeat.[39]

Thus defective in Chadwick's view, the bill received the royal assent on August 29. The shortcomings of Althorp's Act (3 & 4 Will. IV, c. 103) are well known. A tiny, overworked inspectorate, unsatisfactory appointments to the corps of sub-inspectors (superintendents), widespread evasion, falsification of age certificates, lack of schools and schoolmasters, foot-dragging by hostile magistrates, and a somewhat indifferent government, all made for partial compliance at best. Nonetheless, the statute stands as the first significant piece of social legislation in Britain based on a major (if foreshortened) inquiry by experts entailing interference by the central government in labor relations, supervised by agents of central government. In the making of the Factory Act, Chadwick experienced relatively few difficulties working with the Whigs (at least compared to subsequent reforms), since he saw eye-to-eye with them on the central economic issues. But what is important to realize is that in neither his case nor theirs did an acceptance of laissez-faire economics preclude paternalist interference. The point of this can be grasped if we compare Chadwick's attitude to that of Nassau Senior, who steadfastly opposed all attempts to regulate either adult or child labor. "To enforce ventilation and drainage," he wrote, "and give means and motives to education, seems to me all that can be done by positive enactment."[40]

Even Thomas Tooke, Chadwick's Benthamite colleague on the factory commission, was more narrowly orthodox in economics. Chadwick had inserted in the report a rather sweeping statement on the need for employers' liability in cases of industrial accidents. This passage escaped the notice of both Southwood Smith and Tooke at this time, but when it was cited by an inspector in the mines inquiry eight years later, Tooke sent an icy letter to Chadwick saying that had he noticed the passage he would have "perceived the unsoundness of the doctrine applied as it is to the case of adult workmen as well as to that of children properly so called."[41]

Thus Chadwick was rather more disposed to interventionism than most of the other Benthamites (this certainly would include Hume and Place) and decidedly more so than most political economists. Nonetheless, Chadwick remained implacably opposed to state regulation of adult working hours and to trade unions, which he continued to see as the sinister force behind the Ten Hours Bill. When that measure began to show signs of likely passage in 1846, he wrote to Robert Peel that if Parliament "which is now legislating for the freedom of Trade shall legislate for the restriction of adult labour and wages, it should beware that it does not make itself an agency for trades unions, in all other trades and on other matters."[42]

When the Factory Report was completed in June 1833, Chadwick was able to redirect his full attention to the poor-law inquiry, now as one of the central commissioners. Incredibly, even in May, during the most intensive phase of drawing up the Factory Report, he somehow found time to give to poor-law matters. He told Denis LeMarchant, Brougham's secretary, that he had examined witnesses and written and sent to his fellow commissioners "notes of heads of a bill" which he believed they were ready to endorse. He would have accomplished more, he added, but for "the necessity of fagging at the factory commission."[43] Chadwick had been appointed to the central board, at Senior's urging, for the purpose of drawing up the remedial measures. He immediately consulted the solicitor John Meadows White, who would be appointed the legislative draftsman for the measure early in 1834, for advice on drafting the bill. White's response, dated May 25, 1833, shows how developed Chadwick's ideas for poor-law reform were nine months before the report was finished. The clauses of the bill, White advised, must be arranged

> so as to follow almost of necessity out of the next preceding clause. Thus on having all power transferred to you, you would naturally look for a power to make new laws and constitutions. On all poor being put under your superintendence, all existing acts would be at your disposal and this would carry control over officers—and officers over funds and funds would give power to assess and this would carry power to distrain and impose penalties. A repeal of the right of parishes to unite would give the power to effect unions to the Board—this would introduce workhouses and this the classification and separation in one or more houses of a man and his family—this extensive power would require a power to commit. . . .[44]

Besides the almost dizzying effect of this litany of new central-government powers, White's letter shows Chadwick entered upon his role as a central commissioner with his mind already made up on the main features of the Poor Law of 1834: the powers of the new central agency, the reliance on rigorously administered workhouses, and the grouping of parishes into unions. Having the basic legislative plan in mind, it was a question of arranging the massive evidence to support it. This was no easy task, and when he was being pressed six months later to complete the report, he explained to Brougham that "the difficulties in the way of digest and exposition of a plan founded *on evidence* I do assure you are very severe."[45]

It may be asked how Chadwick's fellow royal commissioners reacted to his legislative plan and what modification it underwent before finally being submitted to the cabinet. On the first point, the only other commissioner who seems to have developed a remedial scheme was Nassau Senior, and it was far more centralized. As he explained it to Brougham in January 1833, it would entail three central inspectors presiding over a corps of two hundred paid and centrally appointed magisterial inspectors, each with authority over a district averaging seventy parishes.[46] This plan was rejected by the other royal commissioners and was disapproved following a debate at the Political Economy Club.[47] It was ever after Chadwick's boast that, when Senior's "very different plan had been set aside," his was adopted and he was made a member of the central commission "as they could not in honour invest themselves in my plumes, or accept of services belonging to a principal unless I were made one."[48] His vital administrative contribution, he claimed, was the principle of "the combination of the parochial means in Unions, and of the combination of the principles of central control with local action";[49] that is, he provided for local government while Senior did not. Finer is no doubt correct that Chadwick's motive in rejecting Senior's extreme centralization was that it had no chance of being enacted because of the enormous expense involved.[50] While willing to make this concession, however, Chadwick was hopeful that the discretionary powers of the local authorities could be restrained if not eliminated—a vain hope, as we shall see.

Chadwick's idea of vesting local administration in bodies elected by the localities rather than in agents of central government was obviously important, but it had yet to be shaped into specific form. Seeking advice from Alfred Power, one of the field commissioners for the factory inquiry and a future assistant poor-law commissioner, he was warned that the government was likely to appoint unqualified aristocrats to the central board, with the result that "the poor laws would have little chance of undergoing any improvement as regards their administration."[51] This possibility made the constitution of the local boards critical. William Day, another future assistant poor-law commissioner as well as a country gentleman, urged Chadwick to insure that "the votes are taken according to the Vestry Act, and that the qualification of the Guardians is made sufficiently high to secure their respectability."[52] Yet another man subsequently to receive a poor-law assistant commissionership, Charles Mott, warned him that, while the upper classes would welcome the intervention of a central board, "a different reception would await the proposal from the *small Housekeepers* and *persons interested in the present system.*"[53]

The combined force of this advice propelled Chadwick in a direction he was already disposed to travel—toward the adoption of the heavily weighted property franchise employed in Sturges-Bourne's Act. This provision duly found its way into the later versions of Chadwick's bill, compounded by making resident magistrates poor-law guardians ex-officio.[54] This favoring of property over numbers found no favor with his fellow Benthamites, most of whom had inherited the ardent democracy of the sage's later years. Place, Hume, and Grote all opposed the plural voting provision.[55] Adding magistrates to the boards of guardians was doubly galling—as further enhancing the power of property and utilizing that element of the old constitution the Philosophic Radicals had long denounced as "the great unpaid." This disagreement did not, however, lead to the sort of sharp rupture Chadwick experienced when Albany Fonblanque forced him to resign his post at the *Examiner* for his "partial arguments against the people."[56] Democracy was, after all, only one element of the Benthamite creed. Chadwick clearly considered it not just inessential, but positively dangerous. Even though Hume, Place, and others parted company with him at this point, they still looked hopefully to him as the person most strategically placed to effect the wholesale reform of English government according to the canons of rationality, efficiency, and the felicific calculus.

Another likely reason there was no rupture with the Benthamites was their apparent belief that the more obnoxious provisions of the bill were forced on Chadwick by the government. This was a belief Chadwick did nothing to discourage, as when he complained later that the drafting of the bill was turned over to "an Attorney and three counsel."[57] This was true, but also quite beside the point, since the technicalities of the drafting process did little to alter the bill, and at any rate the draftsman employed by the government was John Meadows White, who had been recommended by Chadwick himself.[58] Chadwick also helped foster misleading impressions regarding his attitude toward magistrates. Most of his contemporaries (as well as later historians) derived these from the Remedial Measures of the 1834 Poor Law Report, which castigates magisterial interference in an essentially Benthamite manner. But in his "Notes of Heads of a Bill" these same magistrates were deemed worthy to become members of the boards of guardians. And in his report as an assistant commissioner, which was published several months after the report, the magistracy was lauded and their active participation in the new system eagerly anticipated.[59] Whatever favorable impressions the Benthamites derived from perusing the anti-magistrate sections in the Remedial Measures, Chadwick was anxious that the cabinet not consider these his real views. He wrote to Brougham in January 1834, assuring him "that we intend no mischief to the magistrates and shall adopt no measure that has not the sanction of some of the most eminent of their number." And he strongly denied that the royal commission would "recommend that a legion of new and paid functionaries should be established throughout the country to supersede the unpaid."[60]

There is more than a touch of deviousness on Chadwick's part in this business, and it is to be explained as something more than a simple attempt to maintain good relations with the Benthamites while simultaneously currying favor with the landed magnates. He did believe strongly that men of property were the safest element to trust with local administrative power, and their control was to be assured through the plural voting system. Magistrates were also men of property, and thus adding them to the boards would enhance the respectability and responsibility of these bodies. This is not incompatible with his criticism in the report, which was based on their interference *as magistrates,* particularly when acting alone and with little or no information on the poor-relief cases in which they meddled. As ex-officio guardians of the poor, they would function as part of a well-informed corporate entity—the regime of property in the district whose poor they were charged with supervising. Furthermore, Chadwick anticipated that the discretionary powers of the boards of guardians would be severely limited. With a strong central authority mandating the use of the workhouse test to the able-bodied and their families, the system would be largely self-acting. In the letter to Brougham quoted above, immediately following the statement that the reform of the poor laws would not "supersede the unpaid," Chadwick added: "We profess to adhere to the statute of Elizabeth, and render the services of the unpaid unnecessary."[61] Here, he thought, was the way to square the circle. If keeping magistrates in the new system would help pass the reform, it was a necessary, politically astute move. If it also earned him the gratitude of the Whig cabinet and secured his appointment to the new central authority, this too was necessary. Few others had the knowledge and dedication to direct the new national system of poor relief. Given his relatively limited experience of government and the ways of men of power, Chadwick could not know that his calculations were to be proved erroneous.

3 A Frustrating Taste of Authority: The Implementation of the New Poor Law

With the publication of the Poor Law Report in February 1834, Chadwick turned his attention to cultivating a favorable public reaction, doing what he could to secure the bill's passage and positioning himself for an appointment to the central board. Characteristically, he considered it to be "his" report, even though Nassau Senior told Tocqueville that "three fourths of it was written by me, and all that was not written by me was re-written by me."[1] As we have seen, Chadwick did write the remedial measures and devised the local administrative system of unions of parishes presided over by boards of guardians. The workhouse test, on the other hand, was a standard feature of much of the reform literature of the previous generation, and it was a central part of Senior's plan. But Chadwick, drawing upon Bentham's Panopticon scheme, gave it greater definition and, by linking it to the concept of "less eligibility," invested it with the appearance of a scientific principle. The icy logic of the report was enlivened and made more readable by the ample use of quotations and case studies, an approach that Chadwick followed in all his official reports. As he explained to Brougham: "I have always found that little popular impression can be made by general statements, unless they are made concrete by exemplifications of the particular cases."[2]

The brisk sale of the Poor Law Report was due in part to Chadwick's fine journalistic sense. His ability to render dry, difficult subjects vivid and personal caught the public imagination, although of course many readers denounced the report's harshness toward the poor. The report was bound to be controversial, attacking as it did deeply ingrained local practices like the allowance system (grants of outdoor relief by parishes that increased with the size of the laborer's family) and the labor rate (assessing each farmer according to his rateable value and the total cost of supporting all the laborers in the parish, minus the amount he actually expended in wages). Land allotments to agricultural laborers were also denounced in the report. Chadwick's attack on allotments involved the suppressing of considerable evidence that pointed to their effectiveness in reducing pauperism.[3] His distaste for allotments derived in part from the fact that they were a favorite device of Tory paternalists like Michael Sadler, who had proposed a bill in 1831 that would have provided quarter-acre allotments with government-subsidized housing.[4] More fundamentally, Chadwick opposed allotments because they inhibited the development of a mature agrarian capitalism with a totally wage-dependent work force. A peasantry even partially insulated from market forces by the possession of allotments would retard economic development, particularly the large-scale enterprise which Chadwick believed to be the most productive. His views in this regard were parallel to those in the Factory Report, in which he had pronounced in favor of large factories over small. This view was also compatible with those of Whig ministers and indeed of most members of Parliament. Whatever the paternalist pretensions of these men, they were capitalists who preferred the larger profits and greater efficiency that came with increased scale. It was not a question of abandoning paternalism. As they saw it, paternalism was being destroyed by some of the very devices that were thought to reflect it. The allowance system, adopted for the best of motives, had produced a work-shy, rebellious peasantry. Chadwick's strong medicine promised to restore labor discipline and the "natural affections" with which laborers should regard their masters. The Poor Law Report thus struck a responsive chord with most of the country's leaders.

The generally favorable reception of the report, however, did not redound to Chadwick's immediate benefit. He felt shunted aside as Senior and Sturges-Bourne were given the task of working out the details of the bill with a cabinet committee. This was no mere formality.

There was obviously a determination to go over the measure in great detail, and the entire cabinet turned up for the first three-hour meeting on March 17.[5] Senior successfully resisted some significant changes suggested by cabinet ministers, although he was unable to prevent the emasculation of the central commission's power to order the building of workhouses without local consent. Chadwick was called in to head off Althorp's plan to exempt all parishes with a population of more than seventy thousand. This was aimed especially at assuaging metropolitan opposition to the bill, but Althorp was convinced by Chadwick's written argument to offer no exemptions.[6]

In spite of the opposition of *The Times* and a host of Tory and Radical papers, it was clear from the outset that the bill would enjoy lopsided majorities during its passage. After the second reading in the House of Commons passed a vote of 319 to 20, the bill's opponents in both houses had to content themselves with attacks on some of the more vulnerable sections of the measure, such as the bastardy clauses.[7] But they were able to accomplish relatively little, rendering the task of cabinet ministers an easy one. One important change was made by Lord Salisbury, who persuaded the Upper House to strike out the clause that would have prohibited all outdoor relief to the able-bodied the following July. This followed an unsuccessful attempt by Chadwick to dissuade Salisbury,[8] who a year before had succeeded in wrecking Chadwick's factory-education scheme. Chadwick was also active in lobbying for the bill with the metropolitan vestries, and even in encouraging Alfred Power and others to work up some "caricature illustrations of the poor law" which might "help in getting the laugh on our side."[9]

During the second reading in the House of Lords, Chadwick was warmly praised by Brougham, but took no satisfaction from it. The trouble was that Brougham's speech was a remarkably vituperative blast against the poor, with frequent references to the wisdom of Malthus. The linking of Malthus with Chadwick completed the villainous portrait of the latter that had been forming in the minds of the New Poor Law's opponents. Ever after, it was charged against Chadwick that he was the architect of a "Malthusian" poor law, that he had really wished to abolish poor relief altogether, but being unable to effect that, drove the poor to the dismal choice of death by starvation or incarceration in a "Bastille." This was particularly galling to Chadwick, who, throughout the inquiry and the writing of the report, had taken great pains to refute the Malthusian-inspired movement to abolish the poor law altogether. He had insisted on inserting in the report, against the wishes of Nassau Senior, a critically important anti-abolitionist statement:

> If we believed the evils stated in the previous part of the Report, or evils resembling or even approaching them, to be necessarily incidental to the compulsory relief of the able-bodied, we should not hesitate in recommending its entire abolition. But we do not believe these evils to be its necessary consequences. We believe that, under strict regulations, adequately enforced, such relief may be afforded safely and even beneficially. In all extensive communities, circumstances will occur in which an individual, by the failure of his means of subsistence, will be exposed to the danger of perishing. To refuse relief, and at the same time to punish mendicity when it cannot be proved that the offender could have obtained subsistence by labour, is repugnant to the common sentiments of mankind; it is repugnant to them to punish even depredation, apparently committed as the only resource against want.[10]

Chadwick justified this to Brougham as "keeping windward of the humanity mongers,"[11] but there is no reason to doubt that it represented his genuine convictions.

For the rest of his career, Chadwick would chafe under the unfairness of the charges and the grotesque caricature of himself that took root in the minds of many. A. P. Donajgrodzki has most compellingly drawn together the separate strands of the "repressive" Chadwick and the "benevolent" Chadwick under the rubric of "Social Police." Under this concept, the state was to perform an active, ameliorative, and tutelary role.[12] The problem was that in the Poor Law Report it was the voice of the "repressive" Chadwick that dominated. The "benevolent" Chadwick was scarcely heard at all, the ameliorative measures being consigned to that part of his evidence that was never published.[13] A glimpse of his "Social Police" approach can be seen in his evidence before a House of Commons select committee on drunkenness in 1834:

... I would submit, as an opinion, that more would be done by educating by the substitution of innocent for gross and noxious modes of excitement; by facilitating cheap and harmless modes of amusement, than by legislative restrictions, although the proof of absence of self-control constitutes a case for legislative interference, and restricted measures might be resorted to concurrently with other measures to influence the habits.[14]

That the balance between repression and amelioration implied in this passage is absent from the Poor Law Report might be explained in part by the haste with which the report had to be promulgated. But if haste is the explanation, a choice had nonetheless to be made, and that choice clearly had been to give priority to repression. In that sense, the public's perception of Chadwick was perhaps not so wide of the mark as he insisted it was. At any rate, whether it was justified or not, he was well on his way to becoming the most visible symbol of the New Poor Law's alleged inhumanities.

Having produced a report and the outlines of an administrative scheme that found favor with the government, Chadwick hoped to be rewarded with one of the three Poor Law Commissionerships, each of which carried a salary of £2,000. He was aware, however, that the cabinet was apt to make the appointments on the basis of birth and wealth rather than talent. Thomas Whately, the depauperizer of the parish of Cookham and himself an aspiring candidate, complained to Brougham of rumors that the posts would go to men of "rank and station," adding that "*one* such man as Mr. Chadwick, would be worth an *hundred* of those I allude to. . . . "[15] Someone close to Chadwick considered a prime candidate in certain quarters was Francis Place, who, however, had also heard the rumors and scoffed at the notion of the Whigs appointing a "Radical Tailor." It was, he insisted, "an office for a man who has *name* and connections."[16] Place was evidently not considered qualified even for the corps of Assistant Poor Law Commissioners (of which there were at one point a maximum of twenty-one, each earning £700 plus expenses), despite Fonblanque's insistence that "for very shame it could hardly be refused."[17]

Chadwick's social standing could hardly be said to be much higher than Place's, but he apparently had few misgivings. He stood in public estimation as the most qualified and resolute candidate. With his extensive knowledge, determination, and zeal, he would be indispensable to the new Poor Law Commission. Just in case the cabinet might be disposed to bypass Chadwick, Nassau Senior sent a lengthy memorandum to Melbourne suggesting five men.[18] Chadwick's name was set apart from the others, since his appointment was said to be imperative, and the cabinet was to select two of the other four men on the list. The cabinet did follow Senior's advice relative to the other four names, selecting George Nicholls, the depauperizer of Southwell, and Thomas Frankland Lewis, a Tory country gentleman who had served on Sturges-Bourne's select committee fifteen years before. But the "indispensable" Chadwick was set aside, with J. G. Shaw Lefevre, the protégé and former bailiff of Lord Althorp, getting the third post. Aristocratic "jobbery" had triumphed over considerations of merit, and Senior was as aghast as Chadwick at this travesty. Even the cabinet began to realize the magnitude of their blunder. With the possible exception of Nicholls, none of the three commissioners would have much idea about how to implement the new system. Something had to be done to bring the deeply offended Chadwick aboard after all, a task which fell to Lord Althorp. Since the three positions on the board were filled, Chadwick had to be persuaded to take the £1,200 post of secretary. He at first indignantly refused, but when Althorp promised he would be a virtual "fourth commissioner" and would in fact have more direct supervision of the system than the other three, he finally gave in.[19] But none of this was put in writing or even communicated to the three commissioners—a source of infinite vexation and frustration for Chadwick in the ensuing years.

Operating at first in the old offices of the factory commission in Whitehall Yard, the Poor Law Commission moved into Somerset House at the end of September. The break-in period was particularly hectic—furniture and stationery had to be procured, clerks hired, and office procedures established. On top of this, the commission was inundated with requests for advice from overseers and magistrates throughout England and Wales. Replies had to be drafted, circulars prepared, memoranda to other government departments dispatched. The bulk of these manifold labors fell on Chadwick, yet these were the happiest days of his long tenure at Somerset House. The sense of real executive authority was a heady one, but also an illusion, for as the commissioners became acquainted with their duties and an office routine was established, Chadwick would find himself increasingly excluded from major decision-making. But for the first few months, he was very much the man in charge, a position symbolized by the many requests for patronage that were sent to him. Some of these came from his Benthamite friends. Place wrote to secure a clerkship for a former employee of the *Westminster Review,* while John Stuart Mill put forward his cousin for the post of matron at the Saffron Walden workhouse.[20] Joseph Hume, involved in the establishment of the *Constitutional,* a radical paper that was published between September 1836 and July 1837,[21] wrote Chadwick in the hopes of getting "a share of the advertisements of the Poor Law Commission" and offering to make the paper "an advocate for the poor laws."[22]

The Benthamites also wrote to him in the hopes of influencing policy. Hume, as a Benthamite democrat as well as a metropolitan M.P., strongly disliked the plural voting system for boards of guardians. The system, he warned Chadwick, was "prejudicial to the popular power, on which you may depend on it, your power must eventually rest. . . ."[23] He also urged Chadwick to see that the assistant commissioners acted "with great moderation and forbearance" and that a "prudent and conciliatory course" would leave "no doubt of complete success."[24] Place, on the other hand, wanted Chadwick to press the full vigor of the law, with an unsparing application of the workhouse test. After describing the profligate relief policies that prevailed in some London parishes, Place concluded:

> This ought not to be, so pray lay your precious paw, in your quiet smooth way upon them, and compel them to adopt the Workhouse; and do it perfectly—never mind their howling— the more they howl the more you must squeeze them, make them take into the house all the pauper's family—"Father, Mother and Sue"—don't let them take some in and leave some out, and then, but not until then, will the matter approximate even, to what is wholesome.[25]

Whether they counseled harsh or moderate policies, his correspondents assumed that Chadwick was in a policy-making position, and this was increasingly less true. His role at Somerset House became more circumscribed as the policy was adopted of having the commissioners communicate directly with the assistant commissioners, poor-law officials, and magistrates. The eclipsing of Chadwick by this policy led *The Times* to ask mockingly whether he did not "find his nothing to do so oppressive that he cannot bear any addition to it?"[26]

This was a gross exaggeration—even when stymied by such procedures, Chadwick was not without a considerable amount of work and influence at Somerset House for the first five years. In addition to supervising a large clerical establishment, he was frequently consulted by two of the commissioners (Lefevre and Nicholls) and a number of the assistant commissioners. Many of his correspondents were magistrates, guardians, and local poor-law officials, who found his advice most valuable. Chadwick also had the chief responsibility for preparing the annual reports of the Poor Law Commissioners, which explained to the public the principles of the measure and the progress of its implementation. He placed a considerable emphasis on the reduction of outdoor relief and poor rates, to the extent that Hume told him years later that "he erred in the early reports in making the pecuniary saving too prominent as the result of the new act, and that the *Self dependence* ought to have been the leading topic in all the reports."[27] Wishing to infuse the reports with a detached, official tone, he insisted on editing the assistant commissioners' dispatches and even returning them for a rewrite. One exasperated assistant commissioner, submitting his revised report to Chadwick, commented: "I have availed myself of your suggestions and *rewritten* my report, carefully abstracting all that was *learned* and *poetical.* I am certain it will now be stupid enough, and prosy enough too."[28] He freely altered content as well as style, as when he insisted on deleting from Assistant Commissioner Alfred Power's report a description of the surplus population in Berkshire, something that was incompatible with Chadwick's anti-Malthusian views.[29] Chadwick also used the first annual report to publicize the labor-migration scheme, which he had helped develop during the factory inquiry, though a recent study has shown the scheme to have been more successful in stimulating northern resistance than providing jobs to southern laborers.[30] Lord John Russell, who pronounced the first annual report "exactly what he wished to receive,"[31] also found Chadwick useful to have on hand for advice when poor-law matters were being debated in Parliament. Even in the midst of compiling the first annual report, Chadwick told Brougham, he spent his evenings after office hours "at the house of commons to meet an attack of Fielden and also to prepare against three petitions threatened from Buckinghamshire together with much other annoying business."[32]

Although the commission's annual reports were Chadwick's major literary undertaking during these years, he by no means neglected non-official channels of publication. From the start, he planned a pro-poor-law article for one of the major reviews. But he was beaten to the punch by Major Francis Bond Head, the most flamboyant and eccentric of the assistant commissioners. Head managed to get the Tory *Quarterly Review* to publish a highly favorable account of the act's implementation in Kent,[33] but Chadwick found fault with the article's somewhat flippant and satirical tone. He admitted to Macvey Napier, the editor of the Whig *Edinburgh Review*, that the *Quarterly* article had "created a considerable impression," but cautioned him "that it would not be befitting the Edinburgh Review to notice the subject in a jejune or hastily written article."[34] Instead of satirical sniping at the act's opponents, Chadwick sought to win them over in his own article by insisting that the New Poor Law was not really a centralizing measure. He told Napier he would show

> that what the government has done does not supersede, but on the contrary strengthens and systematises the local government, and gives greater power to the representatives of the people, in other words to the people themselves against narrow and petty oligarchies. It appears to me to be of some importance to a Liberal government that something should be said to meet the wild outcries on the subject.[35]

This was indeed the principal theme of Chadwick's article, which was published in July 1836.[36] He developed this point further in his testimony before a House of Commons select committee on the highway acts in 1838, in which he recommended placing highways under the control of boards of guardians.[37] The New Poor Law, he declared, was "a measure by which strong local administrative bodies of representatives have been created over the greater part of the country, where nothing deserving the name of systematised local administration has heretofore existed."[38] Chadwick sent his evidence before the committee to Russell, urging him to use this argument against those Tories who raised the cry of centralization against the New Poor Law.[39]

This was an argument that Russell had already used to good effect in the House of Commons,[40] and Chadwick's reiteration of it was meant to convince the cabinet that he was not a zealous Benthamite centralizer and could be safely appointed to a full poor-law commissionership. In spite of his efforts to promote his image as a defender of local government, it is clear that Chadwick yearned to enhance the powers of central government and to reduce or eliminate the discretionary authority of local bodies. A portion of his evidence before the highway-act committee that he did not send to Russell reveals his thinking:

> Those who raise the indiscriminate cry of centralization as a new arrangement in this country, might be asked whether they question the benefits of centralized administration of justice, a centralized post, a centralized army, or a centralized navy, governed by central authorities exercising subordinate legislative powers, or legislating by general orders.[41]

Government ministers were not deceived; they recognized the expediency of Chadwick's protestations of reverence for local government and realized how sharply he would curtail it if given the opportunity. This is the chief reason he was never appointed to the board of commissioners, in spite of the promises made to him in 1834. There was, of course, the social factor — that, as Earl Spencer (formerly Lord Althorp) finally explained to him in 1841, his "station in society was not as would have made it fit that he should be made one of the Commissioners."[42] Nonetheless, he might have been found acceptable were it not for the perception of him as an ardent centralizer who would interfere with the large measure of independence enjoyed by boards of guardians, an independence the Whigs considered both natural and politically expedient. As Spencer explained to Russell in 1838, Chadwick was "clearly in ability and knowledge quite fit to be a

Commissioner but in such an appointment you have many other things to take into consideration." He concluded by urging that Russell "not appoint any one who is likely to make any alteration in or to impede in any way the present working of the Law."[43]

The Whigs' liking for "the present working of the Law" derived from their attachment to the ethos of a locally oriented paternalism. As I have demonstrated at length in *The Making of the New Poor Law*, the act's implementation, in most rural areas, saw the active involvement and cooperation of peers and gentry. The assistant commissioners, operating under the instructions of their superiors at Somerset House, invariably consulted with and often deferred to the local magnates in their districts on such vital matters as the drawing of poor-law union boundaries, the building of workhouses, and the best means for curtailing outdoor relief. The result of this process was that many poor-law union boundaries were drawn to delimit estates or politically harmonious clusters of communities, with scant reference to the rational, scientific criteria that Chadwick set forth in the first annual report.[44] Within these new districts, the leading part in the initial affairs of the union usually fell to the ex-officio guardians, with the major resident magnate becoming chairman. The majority of the elected guardians typically were tenants of the chairman and the other ex-officios, making the board an accurate reflection of the local social and economic hierarchy. In such districts, the New Poor Law thus enhanced a sense of community as well as the leadership of traditional elites. The regular meetings of the guardians in the board rooms of the new workhouses functioned as an important ritual of solidarity for the local regime of property. It also confronted pauper supplicants with a much more formidable obstacle than the easily intimidated parish overseer or kindly "poor man's magistrate," who between them constituted the soft underbelly of the Old Poor Law.

Such proud new assemblies were not disposed to function as mere executors of policies made in London. They insisted upon a wide range of discretionary authority, turning for advice only when necessary to the Poor Law Commissioners. The latter understood well that they needed to exercise their modest powers with the greatest restraint and sensitivity. They began to issue outdoor-relief prohibitory orders to boards of guardians in 1835, but these were riddled with exceptions.[45] Subsequent orders allowed the substitution of an outdoor labor test for the workhouse test for the able-bodied.[46] Even protracted unemployment did not necessitate the offer of the workhouse. Commissioner Lefevre replied to a query on this subject from a guardian that the fifty-second clause of the act automatically provided a loophole, "so that any special exception for such cases in our Rules became unnecessary."[47] Chadwick was aghast at such laxness, and vehemently protested, incurring the undying enmity of Thomas Frankland Lewis.[48] Nothing underscored his impotence and isolation as his inability to get his way on the prohibition of outdoor relief. It is evident that the commissioners' soft-pedaling of the workhouse test was in harmony with the views of the government as well as with the vast majority of guardians. This is not to say that the local boards disliked the workhouse test. Most of them showed neither a reluctance to incur the expense of building workhouses nor an unwillingness to utilize them against selected segments of their able-bodied pauper population. Unregenerate or rebellious workers could expect to taste the full rigor of the new law, while the humble, diligent, and deferential might be favored with a benevolent grant of outdoor relief. The guardians insisted on taking an applicant's character into account in making their decision, whereas Chadwick conceived the workhouse test to be "self-acting"; that is, it would automatically distinguish between the genuine and spurious applicant. The former notion, rooted in the traditional paternalist ethos, required a permanent local body vested with wide discretionary power. The latter concept would have required only a minimal local authority or, perhaps in time, none at all.

If boards of guardians insisted upon implementing a distinctly non-Benthamite "workhouse test," they were also determined to build the kind of workhouse they wanted. The Poor Law Report had recommended separate institutions for able-bodied males, able-bodied females, the aged and impotent, and children. During the first year of the act's operation, the Poor Law Commission sent out as an instructional letter a proposal by Assistant Commissioner William Day for separate workhouses.[49] Day claimed these could achieve the classification envisioned in the report much more cheaply (by utilizing existing parish workhouses) and avoid offering a single target to rebellious laborers. The instructional letter endorsing Day's views was very likely Chadwick's doing, since his own views were similar and it was the sort of policy he was often able to make on his own during the first year of the commission. It certainly was not the view of Commissioner Lewis, who told Earl Fitzwilliam, the chairman of the Peterborough board of guardians, that there was "no doubt that a central Workhouse is if it can be obtained at a Moderate Cost a Better thing than a Collection of Houses."[50] This view was the one adopted by the great majority of boards of guardians, who took pride in the sight of their forbidding new structures. M. A. Crowther claims correctly that "there is no evidence that Chadwick fought against the general workhouses,"[51] but the proliferation of these institutions did represent a repudiation of his views.

The same could be said for his attitude regarding the introduction of the New Poor Law into the northern counties. Amendment of the poor laws had been a response to the agonized cries of the propertied classes of the rural south against rising rates and the insubordination of the poor. Once the act was passed, the demand for its immediate application came, not surprisingly, from the same region. When the commission decided to commence operations in the rural south, Chadwick protested that the "perfect poor law weather" and gener-ally favorable economic picture in 1834–35 offered an ideal opportu-nity to establish the act in the north.[52] He failed to realize how politically impossible it would have been for the commissioners to have ignored the urgent demands from the rural elites during the protracted period it would take to implement the act in the manufac-turing districts. Furthermore, everyone knew that determined north-ern resistance was to be expected, and it was therefore prudent to introduce the law into regions where the likelihood of success was very high. The more sensitive poor-law officials knew it would be necessary to proceed cautiously. Assistant Commissioner James Kay advocated a "Fabian" policy to his colleague Alfred Power, who was assigned the task of introducing the act in the manufacturing areas.[53] But Power, who had served as one of the field investigators for both the factory and poor-law inquiries, was determined to apply the new law quickly and forcefully. He and Chadwick were well known to each other, and besides being temperamentally similar, shared a common rancor against northern radicals. Both men, remembering the raucous defiance of the factory commission by the Ten Hours Movement, saw the New Poor Law as a salutary instrument of discipline to be used against the insubordinate masses of operatives. The result of Power's crusade was a series of crises and confrontations in many northern textile towns, characterized by mass demonstrations, threats of violence, and refusals to build workhouses or even to elect guardians.[54]

Chadwick entirely supported Power's efforts, but his superiors and members of the cabinet began to have doubts. Russell, the Home Secretary, telling the commissioners it was impossible to force the act upon an "excited community," counseled delay.[55] The minority in the north, willing to incur the odium of fostering the introduction of the law, received scant support from London. The ex-officio guardians at Dewsbury in Yorkshire, the only members of the board willing to act, were informed by Russell that they were virtually on their own.[56] The anti-poor-law movement in the north, an outgrowth of the factory movement and precursor of Chartism, contained many talented, vigorous leaders, capable of a skillful, protracted, and imaginative resistance to the act. One of the most vivid examples of this was the remarkable series of "Marcus" pamphlets, which advocated infanticide and were allegedly written by one of the poor-law commissioners. When this was strenuously denied, the Reverend J. R. Stephens, a prominent anti-poor-law leader, stated that even if this denial were true "there was still Mr. Chadwick himself, his patron Lord Brougham, and his bosom friend Mr. Francis Place, and their female assistant Miss Martineau."[57] Thus Chadwick's "Malthusian" reputation grew in the public mind, in spite of all his protestations. But his insistence that such charges resulted from ignorance or malice showed the width of the chasm that separated him from the law's opponents. To the latter, it was a mere quibble whether Chadwick could accurately be labeled a Malthusian. Anyone who could advocate the harsh, soulless regimen of the workhouse for those who had fallen on hard times was morally no better than an unregenerate poor-law abolitionist — worse, because while professing to retain a public-relief system, he labored to make it so repellent that few would avail themselves of it. To harshness and hypocrisy was added the charge of obstinacy, for failing to admit that the workhouse system was not only inapplicable to manufacturing areas generally, but hopelessly unable to cope with the mass unemployment that hit the area from 1837 on.[58]

Chadwick's failure to grasp the strength of northern resistance and make corresponding adjustments and compromises was part of his general political insensitivity. It carried over in his attitude toward parliamentary politics. Because the act had been passed by overwhelming majorities, he tended to assume that there was little to fear from that quarter. He was right insofar as the possibility of repealing the New Poor Law was concerned, but this by no means disposed of the problem. Cabinet ministers, ever attuned to subtle shifts of mood as well as the possibility of larger swings of opinion, observed and adjusted carefully. Russell could be a difficult colleague, but it was he who insisted on moderation in the northern campaign, recognizing that protracted violent resistance in such a vital region could adversely affect Whig fortunes at the next election. He was also aware that many Tories, in spite of their own active participation on their local boards of guardians, were likely to use the New Poor Law's unpopularity to enhance their electoral prospects. With the onset of a depression, disputes within their own party, and wrangles over Ireland and Church matters, the Whigs knew they were vulnerable at the next general election. They thus sought to shield themselves from charges of being doctrinaire or cruel in poor-law administration. When even the ordinarily "sound" Brougham declared in the House of Lords in 1835 that it was never intended that married couples be separated in the workhouse, Power, Chadwick, and the other hardliners were aghast.[59]

It was with such considerations and strategies that the election of 1837 was fought. In the 1835 contest, the government had suffered considerable losses. Reading this, correctly, as a shift of the electorate to the right, the government was disinclined to push any further reforms. In 1837 Russell made his famous "Finality" speech, foreclosing the possibility of further reform of the parliamentary franchise and creating a crisis for those radicals who wished to continue the alliance with the Whigs. If further legislative innovations were ruled out, so was provocative administration of the recent enactments, including the New Poor Law. Thus even before William IV's death in 1837 necessitated a new general election, the government had already switched to a passive mode. It is difficult to decide how much of a factor the anti-poor-law cry was at the polls. Certainly *The Times,* the Tory press in general, and Conservative election agents pulled out all the stops, to the extent that even the realistic Russell complained that the "cry against the Poor Law exceeds anything in Tory profligacy known before."[60] Still, the Home Secretary agreed with Chadwick that the anti-poor-law cry had probably been responsible for only one or two of the twenty-three seats lost by the government.[61] More ominous was the shunning of the New Poor Law by some Whig candidates who, according to Power, had "spoken of the law not being applicable to the north."[62] The election was eventful for Chadwick in a personal sense, as Earl Fitzwilliam had promised him the reversion of the family borough of Malton in Yorkshire. To his chagrin, Fitzwilliam's heir, Lord Milton, lost in Northamptonshire and had to fall back on Malton. This was the first of several efforts by Chadwick to gain a seat in the House of Commons, all of them unsuccessful. It is hard to imagine what he expected to accomplish in Parliament. He might have associated with the dwindling, demoralized band of radical M.P.s or attached himself to Lord Morpeth or some of the other progressive Whigs. Either way, there was little prospect of heading a vigorous reform movement from the House. His lack of wealth, position, cultivation, and political savvy, coupled with an abrasive personality and doctrinaire cast of mind, would most likely have made his parliamentary career one of protracted agony. That he was willing to hazard such a fate testifies to his driving personal ambition as well as to the frustrations of his administrative career.

Besides the general election, there was another event of great significance in 1837: the appointment of a House of Commons select committee to inquire into the operation of the Poor Law Amendment Act. From the outset, the law's opponents in Parliament had kept up a steady attack, presenting petitions, probing the act's vulnerable provisions, and even moving for total repeal. While the latter was always voted down by large majorities, many supporters of the act sympathized with some of the petitions on such matters as bastardy, workhouse dietaries, and the separation of married couples. Encouraged by *The Times* and other papers, plus a large number of clergymen and Tory gentry, it was clear the criticism would not subside. The government, therefore, deemed it prudent to accede to the demand for a select-committee investigation. An inquiry would show the Whigs were not insensitive to the cruelty issue, and with a packed committee it would be possible to fashion a report vindicating the law and the government responsible for it. Still there were risks involved: severely damaging evidence might be introduced, and even the pro-poor-law majority on the committee might prove vulnerable to the pressure of newspapers, public opinion, or their own consciences. When John Walter, the proprietor of *The Times* and M.P. for Berkshire, moved for a select committee in February 1837, Russell agreed to it, but insisted on an amendment that the investigation be confined to poor relief "under the orders and regulations issued by the Commissioners. . . . "[63] This had the effect of shielding boards of guardians and throwing the spotlight on Somerset House.

Since the Poor Law Commission was thus placed in a position of possible scapegoat, Chadwick knew that he was in a particularly vulnerable position, given the adverse publicity that had come his way. In the event, no damaging revelations were made, and the packed select committee succeeded in defusing most of the worst evidence.[64] Chadwick, who worried that the law would not be ably defended by Russell on the committee, was kept busy locating "industrious labourers" who would testify to the improvements created by the act.[65] Aside from lining up an array of favorable witnesses and testifying ably himself, there was little he could do to affect the outcome. His fears about the inquiry's encouraging further laxness in administration were well founded, and made worse by the general election following the death of the king in June. This brought more pressure on committee members, sometimes quite directly in their constituencies. Even Russell was not immune. Berated by anti-poor-law hecklers at Stroud, he declared himself willing to accept any change that "would render the condition of the poor less uncomfortable."[66] Chadwick not only minimized the significance of the anti-poor-law vote, but claimed that some of the act's opponents lost because of their stance. John Walter, he told Russell, decided to withdraw as a candidate after a canvass revealed that "the determination to vote against him on account of his conduct on the Poor Law Question was so extensively prevalent that he stood no chance of being returned."[67]

Because of the sudden dissolution of Parliament and the ensuing election, the select committee had to hastily draw up an interim report, leaving further inquiry for the following session. As Chadwick feared, the report gave aid and comfort to the New Poor Law's enemies, calling for the prevention of cruelties and granting outdoor relief freely. The practice of admitting children into workhouses without their parents, a violation of the Poor Law Commission's order, was mentioned but not condemned. There was an insistence on granting even greater discretionary powers to boards of guardians, which were declared to "bring to the consideration of cases connected with circumstances and character of the poor, a degree of intelligence and experience unknown before, except in rare instances."[68] This endorsement of taking an applicant's character and circumstances into account in deciding on the type and amount of relief was an especially galling repudiation of the "self-acting" workhouse test, carrying as it did the imprimatur of the House of Commons. Chadwick lamented to Lord Howick that the select committee's report "has revived the hopes of the abettors of the allowance system; and in many of the unions in Berks, Bucks, Kent, and Gloucester a tendency to an increase in expenditure is now manifested."[69] And to the Duke of Richmond, he described the report as "a severe blow."[70]

Chadwick knew that it was not only boards of guardians that would be encouraged to water down the "principles of 1834"—his superiors would do the same. In August 1837 the commissioners issued a new draft circular spelling out and expanding the exceptions to the ban on outdoor relief to the able-bodied, and sanctioned the practice of taking children into the workhouse without their parents. The commissioners declared they felt "more confident" in allowing exceptions to the rule because of the committee's report.[71] Much of the pressure to sanction the admission of children into the workhouse without their parents had come from William Miles, Tory M.P. for Somerset, chairman of Quarter Sessions, and a powerful member of the select committee. Chadwick had attempted to get the Somerset and Gloucestershire boards of guardians to publicly oppose Miles's resolution, but Assistant Commissioner Robert Weale, knowing Miles's influence in the region, had refused.[72] Chadwick was more successful in appealing to Russell. In a lengthy and well-argued memo to the Home Secretary, he claimed that the exemptions constituted a return to the abuses of the Old Poor Law and asked whether the commissioners had "the right to extend the practice of giving relief in aid of wages to persons who do not use an ordinary and daily trade of life to get their living by?"[73] Russell was sufficiently impressed by this memo to order the commissioners to suspend issuing the new circular.[74] This turned out to be only a reprieve for Chadwick and other adherents of strict administration. The select committee resumed its inquiry in the fall of 1837, and their second report promised to be more damaging than the first. Their attention was directed this time to the implementation of the act in the manufacturing areas, thus providing a field day for opponents, since the anti-poor-law movement, galvanized by Power's northern crusade, was in full swing. When the report was issued in August 1838, it declared the act's implementation to be successful only to the extent that harsh rules had been relaxed when necessary. The report endorsed taking children into the workhouse while their parents received outdoor relief, substituting outdoor labor for the workhouse test, and other practices abhorrent to strict constructionists.[75]

In addition to trying to minimize the havoc wrought by the two reports of the select committee, Chadwick had two other concerns. One was to secure the long-promised position as one of the Poor Law Commissioners; the other was to insure the passage of legislation to continue the commission when its five-year term came to an end in 1839. In July 1838, when Nicholls was dispatched to Dublin to implement the Irish Poor Law, Chadwick sent a twenty-eight-page letter to Russell setting forth his claims to fill the vacancy and disparaging the system of administrative boards. He asserted that two commissioners would be better than three and one better than two: "Board management or management by numerous coordinate functionaries is falling into disrepute." After a similar letter a week later,[76] on July 27 he sent Russell a proposal for very substantial savings that could be effected by eliminating eight or nine assistant commissioners.[77] Using this memo as a basis, Russell refused the commissioners' request to appoint additional assistants, since the corps was "at present rather larger than necessary."[78] But he also refused to appoint Chadwick to the board, leaving only two commissioners at Somerset House to oversee the English Poor Laws. Ironically, this was in harmony with Chadwick's letter of early July impugning the efficiency of boards, but of course what Chadwick had in mind was that he would become a chief commissioner with one or two junior colleagues.

If the refusal of the government to appoint Chadwick when Nicholls was sent to Ireland was frustrating, an even more flagrant denial of what he considered his rights occurred a few months later, upon the retirement of Thomas Frankland Lewis. On this occasion the Whigs compounded the insult by giving the appointment to George Cornewall Lewis, who shared his father's contempt of Chadwick. Although it should have been clear by this time that he would never receive an appointment, Chadwick persisted in his application, alternating between rehearsing the unkept commitments and promising money-saving reforms at Somerset House if he were "placed in a position to move them as a member of the Board."[79] The final indignity from the Whig government regarding the appointment came with Lefevre's retirement in 1841. When he heard the rumor of the pending appointment of Sir Edmund Head to the post, Chadwick fired off the usual protest, telling Russell that, "irrespective of my own claims," Head was one of the worst of the assistant commissioners and heavily implicated in the return of the allowance system to many poor-law unions.[80] The Whigs were not able to proceed with the appointment, as Melbourne's feeble ministry was tottering to its fall. When Peel's government took office, Chadwick applied to the new Home Secretary, Sir James Graham. He can have had but few hopes for this application, since Graham had always treated him coldly and was at any rate a close friend of George Cornewall Lewis. Graham replied curtly that "I contemplate a different arrangement and that I must discourage any such expectation on your part."[81] Shortly afterwards, the appointment of Sir Edmund Head was announced.

The government's refusal to consider Chadwick for a commissionership was based in part on his lack of social standing but also, as suggested earlier, because he was viewed as an inflexible doctrinaire and a political liability. Considering the Melbourne government's shaky tenure during the period 1837 to 1841, it is not surprising the Whigs wished to avoid assuming another electoral liability. Moreover, they were concerned about the bill to renew the Poor Law Commission in 1839. There was no chance of the total repeal of the New Poor Law, but many of its supporters would have cheerfully abandoned the central commission, which was believed to have done its work, leaving the administration of relief entirely to the boards of guardians. During the passage of the renewal bill, this sentiment was raised repeatedly, and overcome only by assurances that the "safe" men on the central board would continue to operate with restraint and in fact allow even greater discretion to local boards.[82] To have appointed Chadwick would have negated the moderate, conciliatory image the

Whigs needed to project. Besides, they too wished the boards of guardians to continue exercising wide latitude in the granting of poor relief. Chadwick had conjured up the new system of local administration, little realizing the independence these new bodies would insist upon and their tendency to operate under traditional leadership and tolerate a certain level of traditional poor-relief abuses. One Philosophic Radical who did realize what had happened was John Stuart Mill. Years later, Mill wrote to Charles Dupont-White concerning the latter's recently published *Centralisation:*

> Vous croyez peut-être que l'administration de la charité publique est réellement centralisé chez nous depuis la loi de 1834. Eh bien, il n'en est rien. L'immense abus qu'on avait fait du pouvoir local avait tellement effarouché le public qu'il est devenu possible de fair cette loi; mais il n'est pas été possible de l'executer; le pouvoir local a fini par regagner sa prédominance sur le pouvoir central; et celui-ci n'a pu conserver ses attributions qu'en les exerçant avec une réserve si excessive qu'elles sont restées plutôt une resource pour des cas extrêmes qu'un ressort régulier d'administration. Il en sera ainsi pour longtemps de tout ce qu'on tentera chez nour dans le sens de la centralisation. On admettra bien l'intervention du pouvoir central comme remède héroique et passager; on ne l'admettra pas comme régime.[83]

4   New Concepts of Order, Old Structures of Authority: Creating a Rural Police

Chadwick's first few years with the Poor Law Commission made him fully aware of the many obstacles that confronted his own advancement as well as the cause of sound poor-law administration. He therefore attempted to move around the obstacles by undertaking police reform. Chadwick initiated the rural police inquiry in 1836 partly as an escape from the frustration of his position at Somerset House. He was seldom happier than when in the midst of a full-scale investigation. Not only was it an activity ideally suited to his talents, but it rendered him relatively free from interference, carping criticisms, and distortions of his work, at least up until the point his report was presented. When that time came, he knew that he would have to wage a political battle to implement his suggested reforms and insure they were properly administered. He had been forced to do that with the New Poor Law, and however badly that measure was being mismanaged, he still had hopes of gaining a seat on the Poor Law Commission and setting things right. Indeed, with a successful police inquiry, his chances of gaining the commissionership would be enhanced. Moreover, there was a direct link between poor-law and police matters, as the numerous disturbances that greeted the New Poor Law's introduction throughout the country showed.

In addition to the necessary connection with poor-law administration, police reform had been an interest of Chadwick's for a number of years. In his 1829 article on "Preventive Police," it will be recalled, he had amplified Bentham's preference for prevention over punishment and had also called for a "combination of services." Not only would policemen be engaged in helping cleanse streets, apprehend vagrants, and remove road obstructions, but police magistrates would be given a wide array of judicial functions. Such consolidation would help avoid the "multiplication of establishments" and "entanglement of jurisdictions" that Chadwick declared was "the vice of the French system of judication and of police."[1] This anti-French note was rather a departure from Bentham's admiration for French administrative institutions. In his *Constitutional Code,* Bentham envisaged a French-style police centralization with the country divided into districts supervised by "Local Headmen" (the equivalent of French prefects) under the control of a Minister of the Preventive Service.[2] In fact this was not a repudiation of Bentham, for in most of his other early writings on police, Chadwick followed the French system closely.[3] The anti-Gallic tone of the 1829 article is due to Chadwick's desire to get the attention of Robert Peel, whose Metropolitan Police Act of that year was passed in the teeth of opposition charges that it would unleash a "French gendarmerie" upon the country. For possibly the same reason, Chadwick's article had very little to say about new administrative structures. Thus he had achieved a prudent detachment from some of the more radical and unpopular Benthamite nostrums, yet had retained the admiration of the master and his disciples by his endorsement of the preventive principle. This studied avoidance of following Bentham chapter and verse on the police question paid off when he secured an appointment as a member of the royal commission on a rural constabulary.

The genesis of this inquiry and the subsequent Rural Constabulary Act of 1839 has attracted little scholarly attention. Some historians who have inquired into the origins of the act have focused on the immediate threat posed by the Chartist movement. This connection was stressed by Jenifer Hart and amplified by F. C. Mather.[4] Others have concentrated on the influence of the reformers. Finer sees Chadwick as the architect of the act,[5] but Charles Reith insists that Chadwick's role has been exaggerated and points to Col. Charles Rowan, the head of the Metropolitan Police as well as a member of the royal commission, as the real formulator of the organizational basis of the new police.[6] In a recent essay, Hart is in agreement, pointing out that Chadwick showed very little interest in the organizational scheme.[7] She also notes that Lord John Russell contemplated a rural police bill even before the appointment of a royal commission. It is unfortunate that Hart does not pursue this link to the Home Secretary, for it is only by examining the policies of Russell and his colleagues that the genesis of the rural police and Chadwick's part in it can be properly understood.

Writing to Russell in August 1836, Chadwick reminded him that the Poor Law Report of 1834 had stressed the need for a rural police and that the Poor Law Commissioners were receiving numerous requests for such a force. The best way to effect the reform, Chadwick continued, was by a royal commission, which could be expected to operate as it had with the poor-law inquiry: "By sending circulars asking for opinions, as well as for information to the petty sessions as well as to Parishes, a great proportion of the public were brought as it were to a council and enlisted in support of measures which appeared to be and in some degree were the results of their deliberations." He had "no material difference of opinion" with the Metropolitan Police Commissioners on the principles of a measure, and could write the report virtually single-handedly by devoting a couple of hours a day to it for several months. The inquiry would not interfere with his labors at Somerset House; indeed the success of the New Poor Law itself required a professional rural constabulary. Finally, Chadwick saw the police function as integrally connected to the work of the boards of guardians, "in respect of casual poor or mendicants and vagrants, the pursuit and apprehension of runaway parents, the punishment of refractory paupers, the suppression of tumults connected with the administration of relief."[8]

Russell's reply is of particular interest because it shows that cabinet ministers had turned their attention to the subject even before Chadwick's suggestion:

> I have already got the outline of a plan for the purpose which was chiefly drawn up by the Duke of Richmond. He proposes, which I think is essential, that in the event of constables not being appointed by the Boards of Guardians, the Justices should name them.

He also told Chadwick that he and Col. Rowan should be on the royal commission, while the third should be a country gentleman, preferably Charles Shaw Lefevre, whose attendance would hardly be required "more than a few days, as the labour would in fact fall upon yourself and the paid Clerks."[9] Charles Lefevre, a Whig M.P. for Hampshire and the brother of the Poor Law Commissioner, was perfectly acceptable to Chadwick but at first declined the appointment, pleading the pressure of other business.[10] Chadwick thereupon pressed for the appointment of Henry Bickersteth, an eminent lawyer connected with the Benthamite circle who had just been created Baron Langdale and appointed Master of Rolls. Chadwick was candid about wanting Langdale: " . . . from the terms in which he has spoken of some of my labors I am perhaps justified in assuming that he would feel confidence in whatever draught of a report I might submit to him."[11] Russell, however, was in no mind to add a Chadwickian yes-man to the royal commission and replied curtly: "The Commissioner wanted is a country gentleman and not a Lawyer or Londoner. I have some thoughts of asking the Duke of Richmond."[12] Chadwick was appalled at the prospect of having on the commission someone decidedly unorthodox in poor-law administration, as was shown by his earlier espousal of the labor-rate system. Nor would he be a pliant colleague: "His Grace is also said to be military in his habits, and not disposed to be patient of lengthened reasonings or long investigations but more disposed to cut knots than untie them."[13]

Chadwick bent every effort to convince Lefevre to change his mind, and at last succeeded. But Lefevre complicated matters by urging Russell to appoint Richmond as head of the commission. He pointed out that Rowan would naturally be considered by the public to want a constabulary patterned after his Metropolitan Police, while "Mr. Chadwick will be suspected of being too well inclined to connect the new Constabulary with the Poor Law Guardians."[14] When the Duke declined the appointment, Chadwick was no doubt greatly relieved, but as Russell still refused to appoint Langdale, he was left without a Benthamite colleague on the commission.[15] He tried at least to insure that the secretary to the commission was ideologically congenial, and lobbied hard for the appointment of his protégé, the young barrister S. H. Gael, who offered to serve "in any way which would do service for you, myself and to the memory of Bentham."[16] Chadwick, fully expecting Russell to sanction the appointment, had Gael perform a number of the preliminary labors for the royal commission. Finding that the Home Secretary was in no mind to appoint one of his followers, Chadwick protested stiffly: "If I have been premature in this matter I must plead as my excuse that in each of the Commissions under which I have acted the Commissioners have chosen the Secretaries. I believe the public service has in all these cases been promoted by that course."[17] Russell was adamant, however, and insisted upon appointing Samuel Redgrave, one of the Home Office clerks.[18] Gael, who had been assured by Chadwick that the post was his, declared himself unoffended, but could not resist adding that "in my humble opinion you and your Brother Commissioners were badly treated by Lord John Russell."[19]

It is clear that a good deal more was involved in the affair of the secretaryship than the Home Secretary's desire to confer a bit of patronage on one of his clerks or to refuse it to one of Chadwick's followers. Russell was determined to confine Chadwick to the role of an investigator and writer of a report that would simply provide an impressive compilation of evidence for a plan that Russell had already decided upon. Whenever Chadwick tried to step beyond this function, Russell was quick to put him in his place. At almost the same time he was insisting on appointing Redgrave over Gael as secretary, Russell delivered a stern lecture to Chadwick concerning the latter's desire to subject prison dietaries to the "less eligibility" principle:

> I wish your paper could be made less controversial, as there is matter enough without making it so. There is one thing always to be kept in mind. We are endeavouring to improve our institutions. Hitherto they have been loose, careless, wasteful, injudicious to an extreme, but the country governed itself, and was blind to its own faults. We are busy in introducing system, method, science, economy, regularity, and discipline. But we must beware not to lose the co-operation of the country. They will not bear a Prussian Minister, to regulate their domestic affairs, so that some faults must be indulged for the sake of carrying improvements in the mass.[20]

The list of qualities Russell claimed the government was seeking to instill in the country was virtually identical with those qualities espoused by any Benthamite, but the caveats show the vast gulf between Whiggish political sensibilities and the abrasive, impatient approach of doctrinaires like Chadwick. And even though Whigs and Benthamites agreed on the qualities they wished to infuse into the country's institutions, they tended to differ dramatically as to the administrative structure in which these should be applied. The Benthamites pursued an abstract model of government. The Whigs, on the other hand, as men of wealth, rank, and landed property, wished to see "system, method, science, economy and regularity" applied within an administrative structure compatible with the existing social hierarchy.

Even if Russell had been disposed to allow Chadwick a free hand in fashioning the report and drawing up a centralizing bill, Rowan and Lefevre were on hand to constrain him. Both his colleagues played an active role on the commission, and their ideas were in sharp conflict with Chadwick's. Furthermore, they served as a conduit for the ideas of the Duke of Richmond, who, in spite of his refusal of Russell's offer, functioned as a virtual fourth commissioner. Lefevre, as the country gentleman on the commission, proselytized in behalf of moderate police reform in the countryside while simultaneously attempting to dissuade Chadwick from pushing extreme or unpopular measures. He had originally urged Richmond's appointment in the belief that for police reform to succeed the commission must "send it out to the country with the sanction of Men of High Station and Character. . . . " And he was able to report a successful meeting with his neighboring gentry: "I dined yesterday in company with divers Squires of strong Tory Politics—and I led them to the discussion of the advantages of an improved rural constabulary—in which they all agreed—and I suspect we shall have more opposition from the out and out Radicals than from any other Quarter."[21] Like Russell, Lefevre warned Chadwick about the dangers of giving offense—in this case regarding the tone of the queries that were being circulated to rural magistrates.[22] He also kept well informed of the testimony being taken in London, and at one point rebuked Chadwick for injecting one of his pet projects into the inquiry:

> I see you examined one witness with respect to the Expedi-
> ency of establishing Local Courts—with paid Judges. I doubt
> the policy of this for if we attempt too much we shall only add
> to the number of our Objectors—and render the Task of the
> Government who attempt to carry any measure we may rec-
> ommend still more difficult.[23]

Col. Rowan was also a very active royal commissioner and frequently consulted the Duke of Richmond regarding police reform.
The two men had been close friends since serving together in the
52nd Regiment during the Peninsular campaign, and it was altogether natural for Richmond to invite Rowan to Goodwood for
consultations.[24] In January 1837 Rowan wrote to ask the Duke his
views on the organizational structure of the new rural police, particularly "how far you would be for leaving the immediate direction of it
either with the Magistrates in Petty Sessions or with the Guardians of
the Poor." He concluded with a skeptical comment on Chadwick's
belief "that with plenty of power entrusted to proper hands, crime as
well as pauperism might be driven from the land. . . . "[25] A few months
later Richmond submitted a lengthy manuscript setting forth his
views on police reform. Rowan replied that "a great deal of it coin-
cides with my own views and I shall think not far off Lefevre's still
subject however when the whole of the information has been well
digested." He promised to send the manuscript to Lefevre.[26]

Although Richmond's manuscript is not extant, it is clear that the
views expressed were at odds with Chadwick's and were more or less
in line with Rowan's and Lefevre's. There was thus a natural tendency
for the two commissioners to close ranks against the extravagant
schemes of their Benthamite colleague. This collusion is revealed in
a letter from Lefevre to Rowan in September 1837:

> It is time we should be doing something with regard to the
> Rural Constabulary—and with a view to bringing our delib-
> erations *to a point*. I have sent you a rude sketch of the plan of
> which I hinted to you some of the leading features when I
> had the pleasure of seeing you in London. If you think it
> feasible pray forward it to Chadwick—altho' I do not expect it
> will satisfy his appetite for centralization. We have seen in the

> evidence already collected quite enough to convince us that a
> host of prejudice will be roused against any plan which
> possesses too centralizing a character—and I have therefore
> endeavored to contrive that a portion of the force shall ema-
> nate from the Government i.e. from yourself without exciting
> the jealousy of the Inhabitants of Counties and remote pro-
> vincial districts.[27]

He went on to propose placing the rural constabulary under the
control of new county councils, which had been recommended by the
Royal Commission on County Rates, on which Lefevre had served.
This commission, in its final report in 1836, endorsed the recommendation of Sir C. E. Smith, a Hertfordshire justice and chairman of the
Hertford board of guardians, that each council be composed of
representatives from the boards of guardians, with county magistrates,
or some portion of them, having ex-officio seats. The county-rates
commission explicitly repudiated Joseph Hume's plan for new county
financial boards elected directly by the ratepayers.[28] At the very start
of the constabulary inquiry, Hume had written to Chadwick: "I think
you will do a great good by getting the unpaid removed from their
present power of doing mischief."[29] It is clear that Lefevre, by calling
for county councils composed of representatives from boards of guardians plus county J.P.s sitting ex-officio, was determined to leave the
"unpaid" very much in control. Since most rural boards of guardians
were dominated by resident magistrates and the most active elements
of Quarter Sessions would sit on the new boards, supervision of the
new constabulary would be securely in the hands of landed leaders.
Such control would in fact be little different from that of Quarter
Sessions.

While Rowan and Lefevre were thus determined to thwart a centralized organizational structure, they were willing to give Chadwick a
relatively free hand in conducting the inquiry and writing most of
the report. He was receiving both solicited and unsolicited advice
from various quarters, much of it confirming his own preference for
vesting local control of the constabulary in the boards of guardians.
Three assistant poor-law commissioners who considered the subject
all endorsed this scheme. James Kay reported that in East Suffolk,
where serious anti-poor-law disturbances had necessitated calling in

the Metropolitan Police, all the members of Quarter Sessions approved the idea of a poor-law police. Kay himself was quite enthusiastic, pointing out that by having the union head constable resident in the workhouse he could be maintained cheaply, work closely with the guardians, protect the relieving officers, and be kept "separated from the mass of the people.... "[30] From the north, W. J. Voules wrote to recommend dividing each poor-law union into police districts and requiring every constable "to attend the weekly meeting of the board and to deliver in written answers to certain questions, framed so as to extract the utmost possible information, respecting the state of each police district, and to give any verbal explanation which may be called for by the Guardians.... "[31] Edward Gulson addressed himself to some important political constraints, particularly the vexing question of centralization. After consulting with several Conservative peers, he reported they all favored a rural police bill, but he warned Chadwick:

> Of course the Tories would be very averse to the existing Government having in *their* hands so formidable an engine as a general police—The Duke of Rutland—Earl Winchelsea— The Duke of Newcastle—and all the Tories object to *any* Government having the control of such a force—and I think very justly—these will be points for you to work out—and upon which to steer as clear as possible of *party* power. If you can do this you will have their support.[32]

These pro-poor-law, pro-police peers were no more willing to accept central supervision of a new constabulary than they were to tolerate interference in the running of their boards of guardians. Therein lay Chadwick's central dilemma.

The organizational structure of the constabulary could be deferred while he concentrated on the inquiry itself. The amount of labor involved quickly surpassed his early estimates. Detailed queries had to be drafted and circulated to towns, boards of guardians, and rural magisterial divisions. The results then had to be compiled, tabulated, and analyzed. While not quite on the scale of the poor-law inquiry, there were also no assistant commissioners to carry out the local investigations. Chadwick himself conducted fieldwork, using his holiday in the autumn of 1837 to take a swing through Cheshire, Lancashire, Staffordshire, Warwickshire, Hertfordshire, and Somerset.[33] He also utilized the services of his friend W. A. Miles, the Charity Commissioner, who received only traveling expenses for conducting some of the fieldwork. Miles provided some of the evidence against the Cheshire Constabulary,[34] a paid force established in 1829 that Chadwick was to criticize in the report for being untrained and too much under the control of the county justices. He also had Assistant Poor Law Commissioner R. Digby Neave provide him with material to use against the Cheshire police.[35] It soon became clear that Chadwick's early estimate of a few months' labor in the evenings was hopelessly optimistic. Partly this was due to the scope of the inquiry and the necessity of carrying out most of the investigations himself. Furthermore, the start of the inquiry coincided with the implementation of the New Poor Law in the north, and the entire Somerset House establishment was kept fully occupied by the intense opposition. Also, the Poor Law Commission was under close scrutiny by Parliament in 1837 and 1838, and much of the work of defense fell on Chadwick.

A further reason the inquiry was protracted more than two years beyond Chadwick's original estimate was his unwillingness to confine it to the incidence of ordinary crime in the countryside. Instead, he focused on time-consuming investigations concerning the "migratory depredations" of criminal gangs issuing forth from the cities, the plundering of storm-wrecked cargo vessels, and the evils of trade unions. By emphasizing migratory bands of criminals, Chadwick was setting up the case that crime was not a local problem and hence could not be effectively countered by purely local institutions. And by frightening the public, it might be possible to pass a more sweeping measure. He was supplied with a good deal of information on migratory crime by W. A. Miles, who seems to have had something of an obsession with "trampers," and recommended at one point:

> Every Lodging House is a link in the chain of crime—and I would have them all licensed—their doors should be open to the Police at all hours—and they should be compelled to make a daily return of the number of customers, their names —or nicknames (which latter when known would be the more desirable) together with a description of their persons.[36]

Chadwick also had Miles gather information on the plundering of wrecked vessels by dispatching him to Lloyds of London.[37] Trade unions came under investigation in 1838 when Chadwick sent identical detailed queries to the Lancashire manufacturers R. H. Greg and Henry Ashworth and the Factory Inspectors Leonard Horner and Robert Saunders. They were asked specifically to provide evidence about "the need of a police and of legislative provisions for the protection of Capitalists and workmen against the interference of third parties namely the Trade Unions."[38] Nor did Chadwick ignore his scheme of a "preventive police" performing a wide range of services. This concept was incorporated in the questionnaire he sent to borough magistrates, which contained queries about the role of local constables in such functions as paving, cleansing, and lighting the towns, and in the removal of nuisances, care of fire engines, and inspection of weights and measures.[39]

By extending his investigations in this fashion, Chadwick sought to produce a more interesting and impressive report, and thus win over more adherents to his police-reform plans. His royal-commission colleagues, however, began to grow impatient, and at any rate their concept of policing was rather more prosaic than Chadwick's. In 1838 a somewhat exasperated Lefevre urged him on by observing how ready the gentry were for reform:

> Crime is making very rapid strides in the rural districts—and gentlemen begin to feel their pockets and possessions exceedingly insecure. Pray work at the Report, because I verily believe something might be done during the present Session if it could be brought out in time.[40]

Chadwick had in fact already amassed a wealth of data and anecdotal material and was busily writing portions of the report. In May he was able to forward partial printed proofs to Russell, explaining that the press of poor-law business and the extended scope of the police inquiry had entailed many delays. He predicted that "in interest and importance the whole report will equal or be second only to the Poor Law report of inquiry."[41] But Russell's response to his extensive recommendations for a preventive police was hardly encouraging:

> How far the country is prepared to adopt any measure to pre-
> vent crime I know not—it appears from the evidence you have
> taken that the thieves were generally protected by the kind-
> hearted landlady and let off by the good-natured Magistrate.[42]

Such homely skepticism from the Home Secretary did not bode well for the preventive principle.

Apart from the concept of a preventive police, the other contentious item that had to be faced at this juncture was the organizational structure. Chadwick sought to place the constabulary under the superintendence of boards of guardians, in the belief that they offered the best potential for centralized control as well as for tying police and poor-relief functions closely together. It must be remembered, too, that he still hoped to gain an appointment to the Poor Law Commission, which would have gained a degree of authority over the police had his scheme been adopted. The Duke of Richmond's plan, described earlier, also gave preference to vesting control in the boards of guardians, and it may be wondered how this differed from Chadwick's plan. It is important to understand that Richmond's idea of a board of guardians was very different from Chadwick's. The Duke and other landed magnates did not conceive of the boards of guardians as administrative units within a centralized system. They saw the boards as proud, independent local-government bodies that strengthened their control over the residents of their estates and neighboring villages. The Duke of Richmond, an active and vigorous chairman of the Westhampnett Union in Sussex, brooked no interference with his own board.[43] Not all boards, however, conformed to this magnate-dominated pattern. Some poor-law unions, because of the paucity or inactivity of resident gentry, were more susceptible to central direction. Others incorporated both town and rural parishes, an arrangement that would result in higher rates for the latter should police functions be assigned to boards of guardians. On the whole, therefore, it seemed far more satisfactory for the landed interest to have the new forces directed by the justices, as Richmond had suggested as an alternative to control by the guardians.

It was precisely this arrangement that Chadwick fought desperately to prevent. He directed Redgrave, the royal commission's secretary, to scour the parliamentary debates for arguments against magisterial superintendence. Redgrave found some supporting material in the debates on the Irish Constabulary Act of 1836:

> I have extracted Sir R. Peel's opinion on the appointment of the Irish Police by Magistrates. In the same debates Lord Morpeth and another member, arguing upon the impolicy of leaving the appointment of the Irish Police in the hands of the Magistracy, stated that the Magistrates themselves were so well aware of the difficulty of exercising such a power without local prejudice that in several counties they had voluntarily resigned the appointments to the District Inspectors.[44]

It was doubtful how compelling the example of Ireland might prove to be, but Chadwick was not able to find much additional evidence beyond the alleged inefficiency of the magistrate-controlled Cheshire police. He used this material in the draft of the commission report to bolster his assertion that it would be unwise to lodge direct authority with the justices. Boards of guardians, he asserted, were ideal because they contained elected middle-class members as well as magistrates, and their poor-relief functions were sure to decline when the full rigor of the workhouse test was applied. He further recommended that poor-law union constables make regular reports to the boards of guardians, and even that petty sessions be held at the workhouses.[45]

None of this material ended up in the published report, due to the insistence of the other two royal commissioners, especially Lefevre. While they were not disposed to amend the purely descriptive material that constitutes the bulk of the report, they were unwilling to accept the recommendations on boards of guardians. In March 1839 Chadwick sent proofs of the report simultaneously to Russell, Lefevre, and Rowan, hoping to forestall amendments by his colleagues. But Lefevre refused to acquiesce:

> I have just received the last proof of our Report which I will read this Evening—but I for one cannot consent it being sent to Lord John Russell until we have seen it put together. I wish you would direct a perfect copy to be sent to me forthwith—and Rowan should have another, and we will then meet

together on the earliest possible day and settle what course it
will be best to pursue.[46]

Lefevre's intervention created a most embarrassing predicament for
Chadwick, who had to tell the Home Secretary "to consider the draft
not received."[47] The meeting demanded by Lefevre took place later
that day or sometime the next, with the result that the recommendations were altered to give control to the county magistrates rather
than to the poor-law guardians. Chadwick evidently had no choice
but to capitulate on this key issue. Informing Russell of the change on
March 5, he put as good a face on it as possible by claiming that when
the recommendation to vest control in the boards of guardians was
first drawn up,

> the Magistracy appeared less disposed to any alteration than
> at present and it was thought desirable that examples of the well
> working of the Police System tho' in small districts should be
> introduced; now however the Commissioners believe that
> opinion is more matured in favor of the general measure and
> consider it more conducive to its efficiency and arrangement
> that its introduction should be limited to districts not less
> than a whole County, except in Yorkshire and Lincolnshire.[48]

A few weeks later, Lefevre achieved a further enhancement of magisterial control when he insisted that Police Superintendents be made
removable by Quarter Sessions, "or it will appear as if we wished to
place the Superintendents without the *judicial supervision* alias *control*
of Her Majesty's Justices."[49]

The magnitude of the alteration can be seen by comparing the
relevant passages of Chadwick's draft report with those in the published report. The draft declares, in regard to the justices, that it
would not be advisable to

> secure to them an undue share of the attention of the new
> force. We think it desirable that the constabulary should also
> have an interest in giving attention and satisfaction to indi-
> viduals of a lower rank whose persons or property stand in
> need of protection. We consider that the new Boards of Guard-

ians supply a convenient and effectual means of accomplishing this object. . . . It is perhaps the first administrative body pervading the whole kingdom, having a staff of paid officers, acting under systematised rules.[50]

When boards of guardians are discussed in the published report, however, there is a dramatic reversal of the earlier optimistic assessment:

> We have no doubt that the management by such Boards would be deemed good amidst districts where nothing could easily be worse; but our chief objections to such an arrangement consists of the stated objections to the management of a police by committees, or by numerous bodies; to local appointments, to untried and practicably unchangeable constables, to uncombined and conflicting management, and the absence of securities for efficiency or of unity in general action.[51]

Thus the published recommendations endorsed the principle of control by a traditional organ of administration that incorporated the power of the landed elite. But even if Chadwick had managed to get his way on the report, it is doubtful that the cabinet would have adopted it as the basis of a legislative measure. Fully two months before the completion of the report, Russell had taken the initiative with county magistrates throughout the country in a manner that clearly reveals his preference. On February 2, 1839, the Home Office circulated to the chairmen of Quarter Sessions in England and Wales a resolution adopted by the Shropshire Quarter Sessions:

> That in consequence of the present inefficiency of the Constabulary Force, arising from the great increase of population and the extension of trade and commerce of the country, it is the opinion of this Court, that a body of constables appointed by the magistrates, paid out of the County Rate, and disposable at any point in the Shire where their services may be required, would be highly desirable, as providing in the most efficient manner for the prevention as well as detection of offences, for the security of persons and property, and for the consequent preservation of the Public Peace.[52]

Each chairman was asked to submit this resolution to the justices for their opinion. Of the thirty-six Courts of Quarter Sessions responding during the next two months, nineteen expressed approval and eight registered disapproval, with the remainder deferring judgment.[53]

It is noteworthy that the Home Office circular was in the form of a referendum on placing Quarter Sessions in charge of the constabulary, rather than a questionnaire with alternatives such as control by boards of guardians. And the results of the survey, while hardly an overwhelming endorsement of the proposal, were sufficiently positive for Russell to proceed with a bill. The royal commission was pressed by the government to get its report into print. When Lefevre dropped by the Home Office at the end of March, he was told by Russell that "he must have the Constabulary Report to lay before the House before the adjournment for the Holidays."[54] Since Russell, Lefevre, Richmond, and Rowan had seen to it that the report recommended a system congenial to many landed leaders, the nature of the government's bill was scarcely in doubt. Forwarding a copy of the report to the Duke of Richmond at the beginning of April, Rowan pointed out that they sought to "*permanently* meet the mischief that arises out of the present state of things under a state of society in the country so different from everything in former times. We felt that nothing less comprehensive, or containing less of organization than what we have ventured to propose, would do so."[55] Rowan also took it upon himself to urge Russell "to give the power absolutely of Dismissal (of constables and superintendents) to the Magistrates,"[56] a provision that was duly incorporated in the bill.

Whatever frustrations and disappointments Chadwick felt about his defeat on the organizational basis of the new police, it did not detract from his excitement over the publication of the report. Ever the journalist and publicist, he relished the prospect of presenting copies to the country's leaders as well as the spirited discussion that was sure to take place in the press. Rowan reported that Peel took his copy of the report with him to the Lord Mayor's banquet and read it in the carriage.[57] Chadwick sent a copy to Lord Brougham with the observation that it was "next to the poor law report of inquiry one of the most imports that has been published" but that he feared it was "likely to be much neglected."[58] His concern over the likely neglect of his report was due to the feebleness of the Whig government and the preoccupation of the country with Chartism. To overcome this, more than three thousand copies of the report were distributed to individuals and newspapers.[59] Chadwick had Redgrave send a copy to every county paper in the country.[60]

Much of the press comment was of course unfavorable. *The Times* had been opposed from the very start of the inquiry, and the Chartist papers fulminated against the report and the bill.[61] The *Morning Herald,* under the heading of "Extraordinary Exposure," gleefully reported a meeting of Middlesex magistrates furious about Chadwick's unflattering description of the House of Correction at Cold Bath Fields. It was shown that he had relied upon a six-year-old letter from a prisoner describing conditions that had since been changed. The justices voted unanimously in protest against "reports got up in such a way" and forwarded a printed copy of their report to the Home Secretary.[62] In spite of the outcry, Chadwick remained deeply attached to this report for the rest of his life. He exulted in responses like that of Dr. John Simon, who, after reading a copy of the report given to him in 1850, pronounced it "as good as a novel."[63] As late as 1860, more than twenty years after its publication, Chadwick was still disseminating his report. He sent a copy to Florence Nightingale, telling her that, as her liking for novels was well known, she might find the report "amusing reading."[64]

The evidence in the report is indeed highly readable. A brief history of policing in England since the thirteenth century is followed by a wealth of vivid and colorful anecdotes of wrongdoing, along with numerous case histories of criminals. The emphasis throughout is on the "migratory depredators" issuing forth from the towns to plunder the countryside. Considerable attention is also paid to violence and intimidation by trade unions. In an oblique reference to recent Chartist disturbances, trained police were deemed to be vastly superior to the military in quelling riots. In spite of Chadwick's earlier insistence on the connection between poor-law administration and police, there is virtually no discussion of it beyond a terse opinion: "Crime is caused by dissipation and not by want."[65] Chadwick probably avoided the topic because an explicit linking of poor law and police would have been impolitic if not inflammatory. The Chartist movement was at its peak and drew much of its energy from hatred of the New Poor Law. It was also a critical year for the Poor

Law Commission, which faced extinction unless Parliament passed a renewal bill during the session. Whatever the reason for the omission, it was not because Chadwick had changed his mind on the relationship between the poor law and police. Years later he told Macvey Napier that the Scottish poor law would not work well because "you have in Scotland no rural police worth the name to apply coercion with one hand whilst the workhouse doors are held open with the other for the really destitute."[66]

The bill which Russell introduced in July incorporated the royal commission's major recommendations, but there were a couple of important omissions. The report called for the government to pay one-fourth of the expenses of any county force, but the anti-centralizers in the House of Commons succeeded in striking this from the bill.[67] This brought the bill in line with the resolutions of the Shropshire Quarter Sessions described earlier. The royal commission's recommendation that the Metropolitan Police train and appoint the members of county forces was also eliminated. Thus emasculated, the bill was brought in very late in the session and hurried to its passage with little discussion. Disraeli made impassioned speeches against it during the first and third readings, accusing ministers of making war against their fellow countrymen.[68] The only other attempt at opposition came during the committee stage from a small band of radicals and Irish led by Joseph Hume and Thomas Attwood. Hume urged the creation of ratepayer-elected county boards to supervise the constabulary, but his motion to delay the bill was defeated 85 to 14.[69] The bill produced scarcely a ripple in the House of Lords. Earl Stanhope, that doughty anti-poor-law campaigner, denounced the bill as "a stepping stone to an organized centralized police force throughout the whole of the country."[70] But his was the only protest, and the bill received its third reading on August 23.

For Chadwick, the results of his three years' hard work were disappointing, to say the least. Instead of a comprehensive network of police forces under some form of central direction, there was a permissive statute (2 & 3 Vict., c. 93) with virtually no central government control. There was no provision that the new forces would be properly trained. Not only would there be policed and unpoliced counties adjacent to one another, but the borough forces were kept as separate establishments. Chadwick drew up an angry indictment, which began by denouncing the obvious and necessary fact that the government had been guided by "what it considered the popular opinion, or what would be acceptable to parliament."[71] He went on to predict that the separate town and county forces would "conflict with and impede each other." As he had done in the report, Chadwick pointed to the inefficiency of the Cheshire constabulary to show the evils of an untrained force. And the ill effects of having independent, untrained forces would be compounded by placing them under the control of the magistrates.

It does not appear that Chadwick sent this critical document to anyone, perhaps out of fear of cutting himself off from all hopes of preferment at the hands of the Whigs. Instead, he adopted another strategy—fostering the belief that the 1839 report was only a first installment and was meant to be followed by a report concerned with means of preventing rather than merely repressing crime. He persisted in this campaign for many years. Forwarding a copy of the report to Jelinger Symons in 1844, he described it as simply a preliminary report:

> We were to enter into the means for the *prevention,* as well as those described in the report of the means of *repression* of crime by the agency of a police. The evidence as to the means of prevention was not published, indeed the draught report then in progress was suspended.

He illustrated his point by citing the evidence in his 1842 Sanitary Report (to be described in the next chapter) on the tendency of overcrowded housing to stimulate crime.[72] He badgered Charles Shaw Lefevre to resume the inquiry, telling him twenty years later that there were still funds in the royal commission's account. The exasperated Lefevre (now Lord Eversley) replied that he had always considered the commission terminated in 1839 and that if there was any money left "the sooner it is returned to the Treasury the better."[73]

Chadwick's charge that the royal commission's labors remained incomplete and that the government had supinely capitulated to the anti-centralizers must be treated skeptically. There is no surviving evidence to support the first claim. Nowhere in the official correspondence of the commission is there any mention whatever of a follow-up report to deal with prevention as distinct from repression. Possibly Russell's insistence on having the report published in time for the introduction of the bill forestalled the inclusion of a "preventive" report, though the Home Secretary's impatience after three years is altogether understandable. There is an incomplete "Second Report" dealing with prevention in the Chadwick papers,[74] but this does not seem to have been brought to the attention of his commission colleagues. As to the charge that cabinet ministers allowed the bill to be fatally weakened, it is true they acquiesced in the elimination of a Treasury grant and supervision by the Metropolitan Police Commissioners. But these were politically necessary steps, and Russell declared in Parliament in 1840 that he had wanted to keep both provisions.[75] Moreover, the government could hardly be blamed for the permissive nature of the statute, which had been recommended in the report itself, or for the separation of county and borough forces. In regard to the latter, new forces were already being established in a number of towns under the provisions of the Municipal Corporations Act of 1835 (5 & 6 Will. IV, c. 76). The government would have brought down a storm of protest upon its head by attempting to snatch back from the towns a power so recently granted as part of the reform agenda. At any rate it was Chadwick and his colleagues who, by failing to address the issue in the report or even to define the word "county," insured that county and borough forces would remain separate.[76]

And so, in Chadwick's eyes, another of his reforms had been botched by an aristocratic government. Men of rank and station, impatient of prolonged inquiry and the zealous search for guiding principles, had taken the path of least resistance. In both poor law and police, government ministers passed what they believed were workable reforms by fitting them to the existing social system or administrative structure. This was particularly true with the constabulary, in which the Courts of Quarter Sessions were given control. Even the boards of guardians, which Chadwick had devised for the poor law and tried to use for the police, were all too often under the thumb of the magistracy. With traditional elites supervising these critical areas of government, how would it be possible to realize a nationally uniform system of efficiency and order? These melancholy reflections were compounded by an awareness that, though he was unable to get the measures enacted that he contemplated, he was nonetheless saddled with their unpopularity. Chadwick's name was becoming a byword for repression, first as the architect of the hated workhouse system, now as the founder of a new police. But with his police inquiry at an end and his poor-law career stalled, Chadwick sought a fresh field of government activity where he might yet establish the preventive principle and escape what he considered his undeserved reputation as an oppressor of the poor.

5   From "Repression" to "Prevention": The Sanitary Idea

Chadwick's biographers regard his entry into the public-health movement as the beginning of the positive or "meliorative" stage of his career. R. A. Lewis treats this development as all but inevitable in light of Chadwick's belief in the environmental causes of disease, expressed in his 1828 article on insurance.[1] Finer points to the reprinting of this same article in 1836, as well as the opportunity presented by the Civil Registration Act of that year.[2] More recently, however, M. J. Cullen has depicted Chadwick as a latecomer to the sanitary movement.[3] Cullen suggests that Chadwick got the idea from one of Southwood Smith's books in 1835, and that he added to the 1836 reprint of his own article "new footnotes which gave a more prophetic look to his earlier views."[4] According to Cullen, Chadwick's main concern with the Registration Act was his unsuccessful attempt to keep the appointment of local registrars out of the hands of the boards of guardians.[5] And even his victory in getting the crucial cause-of-death amendment (requiring the cause of death to be certified by a doctor) inserted in the registration bill was not so much a mark of his dedication to sanitary science as it was a sop to the medical men, with whom he was feuding over the system of poor-law medical service tenders.[6] This step failed, however, to placate the doctors, adding to Chadwick's frustration over the appointment of the first Registrar-General. He tried to secure the post for the mathematician Charles Babbage, only to see it go to T. H. Lister, the brother-in-law of Lord John Russell. Chadwick did succeed in getting the very able William Farr named as Lister's assistant, but Farr proved to be highly independent, refusing to let the Poor Law Commissioners have anything to do with registration. Thus, as Cullen remarks, "Chadwick had lost all round."[7]

It was just such defeats, however, that fortified Chadwick's determination. He may have hit upon the public-health movement relatively late, but he developed its connection with crime, ignorance, and the rest of the reform agenda more thoroughly than others. He also came to realize its potential for restoring movement to his stalled and frustrating career. The opportunity was provided by an audit that disallowed charges for nuisance removal by certain East End boards of guardians during the influenza epidemic of 1837–38. The Home Secretary, Lord John Russell, ordered the commissioners to undertake an inquiry on the connection between an unhealthy environment and pauperism.[8] Frankland Lewis was content to turn the matter over to Chadwick, who in turn secured the services of Doctors James Kay, Neil Arnott, and Thomas Southwood Smith. Since all three were known for their belief in environmental influences on health, it is hardly surprising that their reports, published as supplements to the Poor Law Commissioners' annual report in 1838, endorsed Chadwick's views.[9] Another article by Southwood Smith appeared in the commissioners' next annual report,[10] and it was this document that was cited by Bishop Blomfield in his motion in the House of Lords in August 1839 directing the Poor Law Commissioners "to inquire whether the same destitution did not prevail in other districts of the kingdom, particularly in populous and manufacturing districts. . . . "[11]

Chadwick was no doubt pleased to have a full-scale national sanitary inquiry as a vehicle for his advancement, since the constabulary inquiry was at an end and he was increasingly denied any real authority at the poor-law office. There was, however, a disquieting aspect of the sanitary movement, namely, the prominent role claimed by some of his medical friends. It was, after all, the reports of Arnott, Kay, and Southwood Smith that had caught the attention of public and Parliament. It seemed all too probable that any likely reform measure would vest power in the hands of such men, eclipsing Chadwick once again. Indeed, Southwood Smith had recently urged adding a medical authority to the Poor Law Commission itself.[12]

Southwood Smith's reputation as the rising star of the sanitary movement was enhanced by his appearance as the chief witness before the House of Commons Select Committee on the Health of Towns chaired by R. A. Slaney in 1840. This committee was appointed after Lord John Russell had objected to the wide scope of Slaney's original motion, which was simply to examine "the discontents of the working classes in populous districts."[13] The Home Secretary feared that such an open-ended inquiry, coming on the heels of major Chartist disturbances, "would lead to inquiries into political grievances, and the suggestion of political remedies."[14] He had no objection to an investigation of the "civil condition" of the working classes, however, and thus Slaney found himself chairing a committee on public health. Southwood Smith was the first witness to appear and gave the lengthiest testimony. Furthermore, his report on the prevalence of fever in the metropolis was printed as an appendix to the committee's report.[15] Arnott was among the four other M.D.s to testify, but Chadwick was not invited to appear. The medical slant of the testimony was reinforced by the committee's report, which recommended elected or appointed boards of health in all populous towns. Medical men were to take an active part on these local bodies, which were to be required only to report their proceedings to a central board. While there were to be general acts relating to sewerage and building regulations, no real central government supervision was contemplated.

Although Chadwick found the lack of centralization in the committee's recommendations objectionable, the section on sewers was even worse. The report embraced Southwood Smith's proposal of 1838 that there be a vast extension of the traditional large flat brick sewers, the chief purpose of which was to drain ground water and putrescent matter. To avoid the deadly "miasma" produced by the accumulation of organic refuse in sewers, Southwood Smith suggested its removal "by an efficient body of scavengers."[16] But Chadwick, in the course of his inquiries, had become converted to the radically different concept developed by John Roe, an engineer employed by the Holborn and Finsbury Commission of Sewers. This involved the use of glazed, small-bore, egg-shaped sewer pipes by which refuse from houses and streets would be removed by a constant supply of water. Thus town drainage would become an arterial system, rapidly whisking away a community's organic excretions to the nearest river.[17] There can be no question as to the genuineness of Chadwick's conversion. The new method promised to be healthier, cheaper, more efficient, and more reliable. At the same time, it is clear that it recommended itself to Chadwick for quite another reason — it would tend to divert the sanitary movement away from medical concerns and solutions to one in which the emerging science of civil engineering would play a key role. Just when it appeared that major new powers were about to be vested in medical doctors, Chadwick began championing the new technology in such a way as to demonstrate that no narrow professional specialization, be it medicine or engineering, qualified someone to direct the course of the sanitary movement. The person needed must be knowledgeable in all the pertinent fields and possessed of administrative expertise as well as a sense of the interconnectedness of things. There was only one man in the kingdom so qualified.

Chadwick's major fear at this juncture was hasty action by Parliament before his own inquiry was completed. Indeed, Lord Normanby, who had recently succeeded Russell as Home Secretary, had already introduced a building bill based upon the Slaney committee's recommendations. Chadwick pressed Normanby so hard to withdraw the bill that he was ordered peremptorily to cease his own investigations.[18] It was the manifest weakness of the Whig ministry that saved Chadwick. Dispirited and under increasing attack since 1839, the government was unable to secure a speedy passage of Normanby's bill. The coup de grace was delivered by Peel's successful motion of no confidence on June 4, 1841. The ensuing Conservative electoral triumph put an end to Normanby's measure, for the new Home Secretary, Sir James Graham, declined to introduce any sanitary bills until Chadwick completed his report.

Chadwick turned his reprieve to good account. At the start of the inquiry he had drawn up a set of questions based on the Fever Report of 1838 and sent them to union medical officers and assistant commissioners throughout the country. In addition he made a number of excursions into the provinces to investigate conditions firsthand, sometimes in the company of Dr. Arnott. In 1840 Scotland was added to the inquiry.[19] He was busily engaged through the spring of 1842 in digesting the mass of reports that were flooding in, arranging the evidence to support his new theories, and writing the report. After the first draft was completed, George Cornewall Lewis refused to countenance the report's attacks on existing local sanitary authorities. For once, however, Lewis's opposition worked to Chadwick's benefit, as the report was allowed to be published under Chadwick's name alone.[20] He also sent the draft to John Stuart Mill, who professed not to find "a single erroneous or questionable position in it, while there is the strength and largeness of practical views which is characteristic of all you do." However, Mill went on:

> In its present unrevised state it is as you are probably aware, utterly ineffective from the want of unity and of an apparent thread running through it and holding it together. I wish you would learn some of the forms of scientific exposition of which my friend Comte makes such superfluous use, and to *use* without *abusing* which is one of the principal lessons which practice and reflexion have to teach people like you and me who have to make new trains of thought intelligible.[21]

Two months later Mill was able to pronounce the revised report free of defects other than "occasional ungrammatical sentences."[22]

Chadwick's *Report on the Sanitary Condition of the Labouring Population of Great Britain,* officially presented on July 9, was an almost instant success, outselling every previous government publication.[23] Fully half of it consists of lengthy quotations from the many doctors and poor-law officials Chadwick had consulted. Out of this mass of descriptive material bolstered by statistics drawn from the Registrar-General and other sources, Chadwick made a solid case for the existence of a major urban crisis. The report was artfully crafted to lead the reader from a consideration of the wretched state of the dwellings of the working class to the wider town environment and the shockingly heavy costs, both in money and human suffering, of the existing state of neglect. Most important, the conception of urban communities as organisms with complex arterial systems was clearly developed. Water supply, drainage, paving, and sewerage were seen as integral components of the system. For the elimination of a community's wastes, Chadwick advocated an ingenious solution. Instead of simply flushing organic refuse into the rivers and thus polluting them, this nitrogen-rich material could be conveyed by pipes to fertilize neighboring farms.[24] This "sewer manure" would prove to be one of Chadwick's more controversial schemes, as well as a key component of his ill-fated Towns Improvement Company, which will be discussed in the next chapter.

It is instructive to note Chadwick's treatment of the medical profession in the Sanitary Report. On the one hand he made extensive use of their data and observations, repeatedly citing certain doctors as authorities. But he also berated the profession for concerning itself with fruitless debates over the precise causes of fever, thus distracting attention from the vital task of prevention.[25] The latter was beyond the professional competence of the medical men, or so Chadwick asserted:

> I would submit that it is shown by the evidence collected in the present inquiry, that the great preventives—drainage, street and house cleansing by means of supplies of water and improved sewerage, and especially the introduction of cheaper and more efficient modes of removing all noxious refuse from the towns—are operations from which aid must be sought from the science of the civil engineer, not from the physician, who has done his work when he has pointed out the disease that results from the neglect of proper administrative measures, and has alleviated the sufferings of the victims.[26]

Yet Chadwick was as wary of the engineers as he was of the doctors. As he told Macvey Napier: "The chief remedies consist in applications of the science of engineering of which medical men know nothing, and to gain powers for these applications and deal with local rights some jurisprudence is necessary of which the engineers know nothing."[27]

The impact of Chadwick's critical statements about the medical profession was softened to a degree by his call for establishing within each new medical district a full-time salaried medical officer with wide powers of inspection. Still, the real work of devising and implementing the requisite public works would fall on the district engineer.[28] In a radical departure from the use of traditional parish boundaries, the new medical districts were to be formed on the basis of natural drainage areas. Each was to have a supervisory body on the model of an appointive sewers commission.[29] Beyond this, Chadwick's administrative recommendations appear curiously vague, and there is no mention of any central authority. However, the Benthamite insistence on national uniformity of structure and methods, as seen in such phrases as "doing the same things in the same way" and "calling the same officers, proceedings, and things by the same names," strongly implies the existence of a central coordinating authority.[30] Chadwick's reluctance to deal with it directly perhaps derived from his fear of appearing once again as the power-hungry centralizer, a charge that had been hurled at him repeatedly. The important thing was to gain acceptance for his comprehensive analysis of the public-health crisis. Once this was accomplished, there would follow as a matter of course an administrative machine that only Chadwick could properly direct.

While it might appear that Chadwick had positioned himself well for a leadership role in public-health administration, he continued to keep all his options open and to try every possible avenue of advance. He urged Lord Lansdowne to submit his name for the distribution of honors on the occasion of the Queen's marriage in 1840, but was informed curtly by Melbourne that no distribution of honors was planned.[31] All during the investigation and writing of his public-health report he continued actively to seek a Poor Law Commissionership, in spite of previous rebuffs. He even told Russell that he had plans for saving £5,000 in expenses but that they could not be carried into full effect "unless I were placed in a position to move them as a member of the Board."[32] Told there was no possibility of appointing a fourth commissioner, Chadwick approached Russell again upon Lefevre's retirement from the Poor Law Commission in 1841, this time spelling out part of his salary savings plan: instead of paying each of the three board members £2,000, there was to be one senior commissioner with £2,000 and two junior commissioners at £1,500 apiece.[33] The cabinet, nearing its final moments of power, would not incur the odium of such an unpopular appointment on the eve of a general election, though Chadwick asserted that his reputation for harshness was undeserved.[34]

As a way out of this embarrassing predicament, Normanby made vague promises of some new post, and Chadwick was asked to list alternatives to his present employment. The first items on his list were the factory act and prisons, the inspectors for which "have not the direction and control which was expected and intended by the legislature."[35] He then suggested a position as special counsel to the Home Office (like James Stephen at the Colonial Office or Rowland Hill at the Treasury), since he had already developed considerable expertise in a number of fields falling under the department's jurisdiction. Chadwick saw himself as coordinating the various activities, handling publicity, and devising new legislation—indeed a position ideally suited to his talents and temperament.[36] That he preferred such a position over the others listed is evident from his letter to Russell the following month saying that he still had heard nothing about his transfer to the Home Office as special counsel.[37] Nor would he, as the government had finally collapsed. In the ensuing election, as in the 1837 contest, Chadwick made a vain attempt to secure one of Lord Fitzwilliam's pocket boroughs.[38]

The Conservative victory put an end to all his hopes of poor-law preferment, as Graham, the new Home Secretary, was a close friend of G. C. Lewis and not disposed to alter the planned appointment of Sir Edmund Head to the commission.[39] With two hostile commissioners at Somerset House and a Home Secretary at best indifferent, he was cut off more than ever from participating in the work of the Poor Law Commission, though he continued nominally as secretary. Not only was Graham unwilling to forward Chadwick's poor-law ambitions, but he was disinclined to offer him any kind of promotion. In June of 1842, following the death of T. H. Lister, Nassau Senior urged Graham to appoint Chadwick Registrar-General, declaring that "his position as the visible organ of the Commission has loaded him with an amount of unpopularity which is not the less mischievous for being undeserved."[40] Chadwick may have asked Senior to make this request, but can hardly have been surprised when it was turned down.

In spite of these unpromising signs, Chadwick was by no means willing to give up on the Tories. Indeed, he could not afford to, as they would be the dispensers of patronage for several years at least. Moreover, his sanitary inquiry had been saved by their electoral victory in 1841. Chadwick had begun currying favor with the Conservatives even before that election, and this involved a further attenuation of his radical connections. He told J. Hill Burton, Bowring's collaborator on the collected works of Bentham, that as there was some chance of getting the *Quarterly Review* to publish an article on public health, "I would hold back as to the Westminster or any leading Radical publication that it may not tend by instinctive aversion to impel the Quarterly into any opposite course."[41] After the election he also began trying to gain Peel's attention, sending him pamphlets and other materials on such questions as education and the powers of poor-law guardians.[42]

Graham's attitude toward Chadwick was one of distaste, even contempt, for this middle-class official who would usurp the landed interest's dominance of government administration. But it was tempered by a grudging recognition of Chadwick's talents and his usefulness in undertaking protracted inquiries that could stall or undercut powerful reforming impulses. Graham, after all, had been a member of Lord Grey's cabinet when Chadwick and the Royal Commission on Factories had blunted the factory-reform movement, substituting a moderate bill for the much more sweeping measure that was demanded. Chadwick's role in reforming the poor-law system in a manner that enhanced the powers of local landed leaders was also appreciated. Once the New Poor Law was established, Chadwick earned his keep in quite another way — as the scapegoat for the law's alleged inhumanity. It was largely for this reason that he was kept on the payroll as the Secretary to the Poor Law Commissioners for years while performing relatively few duties. It also, of course, gave him the leisure to undertake investigations into social questions. But Chadwick needed very careful managing, and there must have been times when Graham and other ministers wondered whether he was worth the trouble. The man was a vain, ambitious upstart, quick to take offense and increasingly restive in his circumscribed position. He also appeared less and less inclined to accept blame for harsh policies toward the poor. The best strategy was to keep him occupied with official inquiries. During the investigation and writing of a report, Chadwick was least disposed to create difficulties. And Graham had just the job for him — a supplementary report on interments.

The dangerously overcrowded cemeteries of London and other large towns emerged as a major public-health issue by the end of the 1830s, though the matter had been addressed neither by Slaney's select committee nor by Chadwick. Early in 1842, Lord Normanby pointed out to the House of Commons the need for a burial bill,[43] but the most active and persistent campaigner was W. A. Mackinnon, the Conservative M.P. for Lymington. Mackinnon, who had been a member of Slaney's committee, was by 1842 something of an expert on the evils of intramural interments. In response to his repeated demands for government action, Graham agreed to a select committee headed by Mackinnon and containing Lord Ashley. The committee recommended terminating burials in all towns with a population over fifty thousand, and empowering parishes or unions of parishes to assess a rate for the acquiring of land in the suburbs for new cemeteries. Furthermore, the report called for "some central and superintending authority to be established for that purpose."[44]

Both R. A. Lewis and Finer criticize the committee for not going beyond recommending extramural interment, ignoring the report's call for a new central agency.[45] The committee's recommendations were far-reaching and viable in relation to interments. Moreover, Mackinnon recognized the potential of his proposed central agency for directing other areas of public health. Introducing his burial bill in August 1842, he declared that the proposed new board "could also superintend the drainage and ventilation in large towns."[46]

At this juncture Graham, loath to stir up the opposition of undertakers, burial clubs, clergy, and others with a vested interest in the existing system, turned to Chadwick. A protracted inquiry would consume the rest of the 1842 parliamentary session and, with a bit of luck, the 1843 session as well. Thus when Mackinnon reintroduced his burial bill in February 1843, Graham was able to declare that an official investigation was under way and hinted at the possibility of a government measure before the session ended.[47] The matter was raised again a few months later by Lord Robert Grosvenor, but this time Graham, while alluding again to "a very elaborate report" that was in progress, declared there would be no bill this session and gave a far more negative assessment of the whole issue than heretofore: "He was not satisfied that the practice of interment within the metropolis was inconsistent with the health of the inhabitants—that fact was by no means demonstrated."[48] The hardening of the Home Secretary's attitude may have resulted from learning of Chadwick's intended proposals, which were bolder and more sweeping than Mackinnon's.

Although the investigation had been underway since August 1842,

Graham probably had little idea of Chadwick's likely recommendations until the following June.[49] By that time, Chadwick had completed his investigation and was writing his report. With typical
thoroughness, he had examined not only a large number of laborers,
undertakers, doctors, and officers of burial clubs, but also the systems
of interment practiced in Germany, France, Austria, and the United
States. The Interment Report[50] was published in December 1843, and
like the Sanitary Report to which it was a supplement, caused a
considerable stir. As he had done in the earlier report, Chadwick
skillfully wove together the testimony of his witnesses to present
shocking revelations on the state of interments in large towns. He
detailed the loathsome conditions of many metropolitan burial grounds
and the serious health hazards posed by their "fetid effluvia" and
"noxious ooze." The modern town had been presented as a vast
dung-heap in the Sanitary Report; now it was made to seem more like
a charnel house. Unlike the Mackinnon committee, Chadwick did
not confine himself to the sanitary side of urban burial, but examined
many of the sharp practices of undertakers and burial clubs: wasteful
extravagance, exorbitant prices, and the mercenary exploitation of
the bereaved. Most ghastly of all was Chadwick's revelation of the
inducement to infanticide represented by the financial structure of
the burial-club system.

Having demonstrated the utter incompetence of the parochial
authorities and the utter rapacity of the undertakers, it is not surprising that Chadwick recommended a comprehensive nationalized system of interment.[51] Most intramural burial was to be abolished and
new national cemeteries built beyond the confines of the towns. They
would be not merely sanitary places of interment, but would provide
funerals and materials at reasonable cost. Chadwick reckoned the
saving to the poor would be no less than 50 percent. Properly qualified officers of health were to verify the fact and cause of death before
interment. Finally, recognizing the existence of powerful vested
interests, Chadwick recommended that the burial fees should defray
not only the costs of acquiring and operating the cemeteries but also
that of compensating "such existing interests as it may be necessary to
disturb. . . . "[52] While such interests were not identified in the enumer-
ated recommendations, it is clear from the body of the report that he
had chiefly in mind the clergy of the established church. Noting the

importance of burial fees to many urban ministers, he suggested that the compensation be determined by the "adjudication and examination" of each parish by the Tithe Commissioners.[53] Since this particular recommendation was likely to alienate many Dissenters, Chadwick tried his best to placate them by appealing to the influential editor (of the *Leeds Mercury*) and M.P. Edward Baines, stressing the secularizing features of the plan.[54] But he told Bishop Blomfield, whose major concern was to secure compensation for his clergy, that the report would find "no favour" with the Dissenters.[55]

Chadwick was as unsuccessful in abating the hostility of *The Times* as he was with Baines and the Dissenters. He sent a copy of the report to Walter, stressing that he had not volunteered for the assignment. Furthermore, he urged Walter not to assume that the report had anything to do "with the new poor law or the poor law commissioners or has any tendency in the measure proposed to give them any new powers or to connect them with it in any way."[56] Walter was unimpressed, and *The Times* responded with several critical leading articles. The most comprehensive critique appeared on December 30, and was a well-argued, point-by-point rebuttal of the Interment Report, free of the sarcasm and high-flown rhetoric *The Times* usually employed in discussing Chadwick's schemes. It was argued that the creation of suburban cemeteries and reform of parochial administration were sufficient remedies for the admitted evils of the present system, and *The Times* predicted that the proposed national sepulture would be rejected:

> The unpopularity and dislike which Mr. Chadwick charges against parish funerals would hold tenfold against funerals performed by a public officer, and by a Government establishment. Mr. Chadwick is at great pains to expose the evils of the uniform contract system, when only carried to the length of the *parish* funeral; what will it be under the magnified uniformity of a central commission?[57]

The opposition of the country's most influential newspaper was not Chadwick's only worry. For several years he had been investing in securities in the United States, possibly on the advice of his father, who had emigrated there at the end of the 1830s. He had recently suffered financial reverses on these American investments to the extent, as he claimed to one of his German acquaintances, "of nearly the whole of my private fortune. . . . "[58] Chadwick's "private fortune" is unlikely to have been very extensive if it was based on investments paid for out of his rather modest salary and small annuity from Bentham's estate. However, it seems quite possible that by his marriage in 1839 to Rachel Kennedy he may have received a sizeable dowry and promptly invested it as well. The Kennedys were a prominent Manchester textile family, and Chadwick's social position was clearly enhanced by the match. Rachel's father, John Kennedy (1769–1855), was a friend of James Watt and an important innovator in the textile industry as well as a leading figure in the Manchester Literary and Philosophical Society. But while the marriage represented a social advance, it also created new demands. Setting up and maintaining a suitable domestic establishment was a major expense, which of course increased with the birth of their son Osbert in 1842 and daughter Marion two years later. When we also consider the added pressure of trying to keep up appearances with his affluent in-laws, Chadwick's deep anxiety over his stock-market losses becomes understandable.

The gloom over his financial prospects was compounded by the realization that the government was unlikely to embrace his interment proposals. As he lamented to Lord Ashley:

> It was the most difficult and the most painful of the painful investigations which I have been called upon to conduct, and unless it be followed by some better and more complete adoption of the measures recommended than is usual, I intend that so far as I am concerned it shall be the last that I conduct. . . . I confess however that I have little hope of anything being done without a strong expression of public opinion from without and especially of the religious public.[59]

The hoped-for public outcry failed to develop, and when Parliament resumed Graham quickly scotched all hope of reform by his curt statement "that it was not the intention of Government to prohibit interment in towns in ancient churchyards where the ancestors of those who had the right of interment there had been buried."[60]

Disgusted as he was at this outright repudiation of his labors, Chadwick was still unwilling to give up completely on Peel's government. The reason was that a royal commission on the health of towns had been at work since the early months of 1843 and was drafting its first report in the spring of 1844. The origins of this commission go back to the spirited demands in Parliament for sanitary reform during the 1842 and 1843 sessions. Graham's strategy was to fragment the question into building regulation, interment, and drainage. In February 1843 he announced that only the first of these was to be a subject of government action, while interment was to be studied by Chadwick and drainage was to be investigated by a royal commission.[61] A month before this, Graham had been approached by a deputation from some of the metropolitan commissions of sewers asking for an inquiry. Chadwick, who had sharply criticized the commissions of sewers in his Sanitary Report, not only urged the appointment of a royal commission but sent along a list of names.[62] Of the ten men suggested, Graham appointed five and added eight of his own, a course of action that hardly justifies Finer's assertion that Graham simply followed Chadwick's advice.[63] And the omission of Chadwick himself from the commission was hardly the result of a "strange whim of Graham's," as R. A. Lewis paraphrases Chadwick's later charge.[64] No "strange whim" is needed to account for the Home Secretary's reluctance to appoint a man who was heavily engaged in the interment inquiry and who was, after all, still employed as Secretary to the Poor Law Commissioners. Moreover, since the royal commission would be investigating the viability of a number of the proposals made in the Sanitary Report, the commission's impartiality would have been compromised by Chadwick's appointment. Finally, the government was becoming increasingly exasperated with Chadwick over his attempts to enlarge the scope of the metropolitan survey and map that were being undertaken in relation to Lord Lincoln's Building Bill. Bypassing Graham, Chadwick appealed directly to Peel to expand the survey to include drainage and sewerage, and also to include other great towns. While replying politely and noncommittally to Chadwick, the Prime Minister wrote angrily to Lincoln that such an expansion of the survey would "lead to endless controversy." Lincoln agreed that it would be "necessary to discard all or nearly all of Mr. Chadwick's suggestions. . . . "[65]

The government did, of course, accept some of Chadwick's suggested royal commissioners, and this provided him with a fair measure of influence. Both of the civil engineers on his list, Sir Henry de la Beche and Captain Denison, were appointed, as were the railway engineer Robert Stephenson junior and the expert on land drainage and manure James Smith of Deanston.[66] Chadwick fared less well with the medical members of the commission, getting Professor Richard Owen, the physiologist, but neither Sir James Clark nor Neil Arnott. Clark, the Queen's physician, was very likely excluded because of the odium he had incurred during the Lady Flora Hastings affair. In the case of Arnott, his intimacy with Chadwick was probably a liability. Perhaps most interesting of those not appointed was a man Chadwick had not even recommended, in spite of his obvious qualifications — Thomas Southwood Smith. The latter had indeed written to Chadwick in March 1843:

> If there is really to be a Commission for improving the Health of the Metropolis do you not think that I ought in justice to be put upon it? . . . I have no means of access to any of the present men, nor have I any reason to suppose that they regard me with a favourable disposition.[67]

Chadwick's failure to include Southwood Smith on his list was no accident. Out of his personal jealousy and fear of a medical "take-over" of the sanitary movement there was developing a powerful rivalry between the two men, not the less real for being obscured by the appearance of cooperation.[68]

The eight members of the royal commission chosen by the cabinet were its chairman, the Duke of Buccleuch, Lord Lincoln, R. A. Slaney, George Graham, the chemist Lyon Playfair, and the medical doctors D. B. Reid and J. R. Martin. The Health of Towns Commission, as it came to be called, began its labors on June 1, 1843, at Gwydyr House. During the next year and a half, the commissioners took the testimony of sixty-five engineers, architects, registrars, poor-law officials, and doctors, issuing their first report in July 1845. While lacking a set of formal recommendations, the tenor of the first report strongly supported Chadwick's Sanitary Report. There is a question as to the degree of Chadwick's involvement in the inquiry and in the writing of the report of the Health of Towns Commission. A month after the first report was issued, he recommended it to Macvey Napier, editor of the *Edinburgh Review,* with the observation that "it is in all important points, indeed on every point confirmatory of the view taken in the sanitary report. . . ."[69] It should be noted that Chadwick at this point made no claim to have written any of the report. It certainly would have served his interests to do so, as he was trying to interest Napier in publishing an article linking the Sanitary Report to the Health of Towns Commission report, and the connection would have been stronger if accompanied by a claim of authorship.[70]

It was not for another two months that Chadwick made the claim, echoed by his biographers, that he wrote most of the report. In a letter to Macvey Napier on October 12, he claimed that, since the commissioners had had little time to devote to the task of writing, most of it had devolved upon him, for which he was "to get only posthumous credit, if at all."[71] The next day he made a similar assertion to John Forster, the friend and later biographer of Dickens:

> My name is not upon the commission, by some caprice of Sir James Graham, but the commissioners are all men engaged in active pursuits and could only give incidental attention to the enquiry. I was compelled to attend as Amicus Curiae and conduct the examinations, instruct the local commissioners, and write the report. I have no objection to all this, if we succeed in getting anything carried out into actual practice.[72]

In escalating his claim to include writing the report, Chadwick was trying to strengthen his appeal for an article to Napier, who seemed disinclined to publish one.[73] In making the same assertion to Forster, he was of course trying to impress Dickens. Neither Napier nor Forster was in a position to know the truth of the matter. The Duke of Buccleuch clearly was in such a position, and it is noteworthy that Chadwick, in asking the Duke for some recognition of his contributions, moderated his claim. The Duke replied by giving "full and willing testimony to your great exertions, constant attendance, and most valuable information and assistance which you rendered to the Commission."[74] This is probably an accurate characterization of Chadwick's role. He did help direct the inquiry, select the witnesses, and coach his friends on the commission. He perhaps even wrote portions of the report, but not to the extent that he and his biographers have claimed.

If Chadwick's role in the making of the first report of the Health of Towns Commission was somewhat more modest than is generally supposed, it was considerably less in the writing of the second report. This was probably the result of the commissioners becoming more confident about completing the task without Chadwick's direction, or perhaps resentful at his attempt to dictate their recommendations. In December 1844 Chadwick sent the Duke of Buccleuch a memorandum on the report complete with a draft of clauses for a bill. Finer considers this memorandum to have been accepted *in toto* by the commission for its report,[75] but there are crucial differences. Perhaps the most important relates to Chadwick's call for a judicial committee of the Privy Council under the direction of a single officer to be the central agency, rather than a board. This new departure by Chadwick has been interpreted as growing out of his bitter experience of ten years of the Poor Law Commission, and his longing for a role analogous to that of James Kay, secretary to the Educational Committee of the Privy Council.[76] But there was another reason of equal importance —Chadwick's growing anxiety over the ambitions of the engineers and doctors, especially Southwood Smith. The latter, though he had been kept off the commission, had appeared as a principal witness, and his testimony must have alarmed Chadwick. When questioned about the constitution of his proposed central agency, Southwood Smith replied that it should consist of a doctor, a civil engineer, and an architect, a far cry from the subsidiary, advisory role envisaged for such professionals by Chadwick.[77]

Seen in this light, the failure of the royal commission to include Chadwick's Privy Council scheme in its recommendations[78] assumes greater significance. This impression is reinforced by the rest of the report and the other recommendations. In discussing the precursors of the Health of Towns Commission, for example, Southwood Smith's report to the Poor Law Commissioners in 1839 and Slaney's select committee of 1840 are specifically cited, followed by a brief mention of "subsequent reports."[79] Such cavalier treatment of the Sanitary Report itself testifies to the absence of Chadwick's hand. Recently, Anthony Wohl has pointed out the great attention paid in the report to crowded housing and other insalubrious domestic conditions along with a call for a central inspector of housing, concerns which he rightly considers un-Chadwickian.[80] A final piece of evidence is a letter from Chadwick to Slaney in March 1845, a month after the appearance of the commission's second report: "The report has attracted very little notice I am sorry to say. I have heard from two quarters that persons who had attended to the subject and read the former report considered this greatly below the evidence."[81] Had Chadwick exercised any control over the shaping of the second report, he would never have characterized it as "greatly below the evidence."

Thus while Chadwick clearly played an important role in the earlier phases of the Health of Towns Commission and the writing of the first report, he had far less influence in the second report. It is true that, since both reports treated water supply, sewerage, and drainage as parts of a single system to be applied within natural drainage areas determined by careful surveys, they did confirm Chadwick's basic tenets. But in failing to endorse his Privy Council proposal and by stressing the improvement of workers' dwellings through design changes and compulsory maintenance and cleansing by landlords, the reports made Chadwick a less likely choice to direct any new government measure. His disappointment was sharpened by the fact that Southwood Smith's prospects seemed even brighter as a result of the Health of Towns Commission. The development of their rivalry, felt much more acutely by Chadwick than by Southwood Smith, needs to be examined more closely.

Southwood Smith began the decade without any of Chadwick's liabilities. His entire public career had been devoted to such measures as sanitation and protection of factory children, while Chadwick was burdened by his close association with repressive measures like the New Poor Law and police reform. The contrast can be seen in the reaction of Charles Dickens when each man sought to gain his attention and approval. Dickens, whose social novels were a powerful factor in the sharpened public consciousness of the "condition-of-England" question, was obviously an attractive conquest. Southwood Smith's initial approach was received warmly. In December 1840 he sent Dickens the Instructions of the Children's Employment Commission, to which he had just been appointed. He also sent a pamphlet on a benevolent institution he had co-founded — the Sanatorium, a middle-class health-care facility funded by a combination of a guinea-a-year fee and charitable donations. Dickens, in a very cordial reply, stressed his support of both enterprises and his desire to meet Southwood Smith.[82] The two men became good friends, Southwood Smith participating in Dickens's amateur theatricals, and Dickens actively supporting the Sanatorium. Dickens was in the chair and delivered a lengthy speech on behalf of the Sanatorium at its anniversary festival in 1844 at the London Tavern. The next year, as the Sanatorium faltered because of financial problems, Dickens organized a fund-raising production of *Every Man in His Humour* at the St. James Theater. Though a theatrical success, it failed to save the Sanatorium.[83]

Chadwick's first approach to Dickens, an indirect one, came two years after Southwood Smith's. The intermediary was Dickens's brother-in-law Henry Austin, a young engineer who had written a report for Chadwick. Dickens's response, after perusing the copy of the Sanitary Report given him by Austin, was guarded and skeptical: "Pray tell Mr. Chadwick that I am greatly obliged for his remembrance of me, and that I heartily concur with him in the great importance and interest of the subject—though I do differ from him, to the death, on his crack topic, the new Poor Law."[84] Chadwick did not manage to meet Dickens for another two years, and then it was only by means of an invitation to dinner at the home of Southwood Smith. A week before the dinner, Chadwick sent Dickens a letter along with some of the minutes of evidence of the Health of Towns Commission, which he claimed showed the importance of "fresh air in your room and the public importance of keeping yourself in good health and spirits."[85] The meeting was apparently not a complete success, for several months later Chadwick was trying to convince John Forster of the unfairness of his reputation for harsh measures, even alleging that indoor relief to the aged was a blessing because of their deplorable dwellings.[86]

It is also evident that Chadwick, while in alliance with Southwood Smith on the broad principles of the sanitary movement, was quick to criticize his views and activities. In a paper read before the Statistical Society in December 1843, Chadwick pointed out Southwood Smith's uncritical acceptance (in his *Philosophy of Health*) of a major error in statistical theory.[87] In 1844 Chadwick turned a caustic eye on another of Southwood Smith's enterprises, the Metropolitan Association for the Improvement of the Dwellings of the Labouring Classes, a "four percent philanthropy" scheme. Having initially expressed an interest in the organization, Chadwick wrote to Southwood Smith on June 25 that, as he was not "satisfied as to its course," he wanted his name removed from the provisional committee.[88] A week later he expressed a more fundamental objection to any reliance on the "principle of benevolence."[89] Then he wrote to Lord Ashley, who was actively involved in the organization, not only arguing against the "benevolent" interest rates but registering contempt for his rival: "There are one or two men of business on the committee but Dr. Southwood Smith who is a man of benevolence only and who has mismanaged the Sanatorium took the leading part."[90]

Another organization in which Southwood Smith took an active part was the Health of Towns Association, founded in December 1844. The most important of the pressure groups working to promote the sanitary idea, it coordinated a network of provincial associations through a central committee in London. Chadwick, while refusing to become a member on the grounds of his official position, did take an active part. It would not do to leave the organization to Southwood Smith, a prominent member of the central committee. Besides, there were a number of influential members of the association whom Chadwick wished to cultivate—Whig politicians like Lords Normanby and Morpeth, Young Englanders Disraeli and Lord John Manners, and of course the great Ashley himself.[91] Indeed, the latter became Chadwick's greatest conquest, in a complete about-face from his resentment of Chadwick's role in trimming the factory-reform measure in 1833. Disraeli, however, remained cool, and when he researched the "condition-of-England" question for the writing of *Sybil,* his major source was not any of Chadwick's publications but rather Southwood Smith's report of the Children's Employment Commission.[92]

If Chadwick had drawn up a balance sheet in 1845 on his achievements and prospects, the most optimistic assessment he could have made was that he was barely holding his own in his quest to lead the sanitary movement. There was still considerable skepticism regarding him among the leading literary figures with an interest in social questions. Dickens would not overcome his misgivings until the end of the decade. Chadwick entertained some hope of winning over Thomas

Carlyle, despite the latter's sarcastic treatment of the Benthamite calculus in the chapter on "Statistics" in *Chartism* (1840). However, as Gertrude Himmelfarb has shown,[93] Carlyle was not an out-and-out opponent of the New Poor Law, and Chadwick sent him a copy of the final proofs of the Sanitary Report in 1842, asking him to make "annotations." Pleading the unexpected death of his mother-in-law, Carlyle begged off, but at least did not adopt a hostile attitude.[94] Chadwick was even less successful when he tried to enlist the support of Thomas Babington Macaulay for his interment proposals in 1845.[95] Macaulay expressed his wholehearted opposition to involving the central government in burials, especially since the strong public opposition to it was likely to impede other sanitary reforms.[96]

Finally, whatever shred of hope remained about Peel's government taking action was destroyed early in the 1845 session. Questioned about interment, Graham replied that "any prohibition of interment within the walls of a city would not be in harmony with the feelings of a great body of the people."[97] Stung to fury, Chadwick drew up a spirited attack cast in the form of a parliamentary question.[98] This was clearly the basis of Mackinnon's speech of April 8 moving a resolution against intramural interments.[99] In seconding the motion, Joseph Hume praised Chadwick's Interment Report, but Graham, while admitting the report was "most laborious, able, and comprehensive, as to the evils described," denounced Chadwick's proposed remedies.[100] Mackinnon's motion passed by a vote of 66 to 49, but the government refused to consider this defeat an important matter. And while Lord Lincoln did introduce a comprehensive measure based on the Health of Towns Commission report, it soon became evident that there was no serious intention of passing it.[101]

Chadwick was furious but hardly surprised. He had come to realize that there were some differences between Whigs and Tories after all. The latter now appeared obstinately determined to do nothing. And since it seemed unlikely they would be dislodged from power in the near future, Chadwick turned in a bold new direction — the pursuit of sanitary reform, as well as wealth and renown, through private enterprise.

6   Capitalism to the Rescue: The Towns Improvement Company

By the end of 1843, the manifest unwillingness of Peel's government to adopt major sanitary reforms and a hostile regime at Somerset House had rendered Chadwick's official career bleak and unpromising. Even if significant legislation were to be passed, it was far from certain that Chadwick would be given a major role in its implementation. The financial reverse he had suffered in his American investments was giving him "sleepless nights,"[1] and he was depressed and ill through the early months of 1844. To his American brother-in-law, Andrew Boardman, he complained bitterly that the poor law had only been carried out "by halves" due to the "intense latent jealousy of my superiors." But for his stock-market losses, he would have "given up office and gone to the public."[2] Such a claim must be treated with caution. Chadwick was always threatening to "go public" with his grievances, but such a course would have cut him off permanently from all chance of official preferment. Furthermore, it would have been hard to abandon his £1,200 a year as Poor Law Commission Secretary even if he had not sustained losses in the stock market. His financial reverses gave him a convenient excuse to maintain his position as well as his silence while he hurled himself into the exciting world of capitalist enterprise.

Very little attention has been given to Chadwick's Towns Improvement Company scheme, even though it dominated his life from late 1844 through 1845. His biographers are inclined to neglect this episode or to treat it as an embarrassing aberration. Finer devotes only two pages to it, and treats it as "a novel thought" that came to Chadwick quite suddenly in November 1844.[3] Such a belittling of this episode has tended to promote a misleading picture of Chadwick as consistently devoted to an ever-expanding array of government services. In fact he was considerably more flexible, and if his powerful ambitions were thwarted in one direction, he was willing to try another, even if this meant abandoning government service altogether. He also counted many men of business among his associates and, through his marriage in 1839 to Rachel Kennedy, was related to a prominent family of Lancashire textile manufacturers.

Money for Chadwick was not an end in itself, nor was its appeal based on his desire for more creature comforts. Rather it represented status and an immunity from the kind of humiliating insults that had been his lot as a public official, beginning with the denial of a Poor Law Commissionership because he was not a man of "rank or station." As he explained to Andrew Boardman: "In such a country as this, with a position to maintain amongst public men of aristocratical connexions, it is not easy to contend without pecuniary resources. . . ."[4] Chadwick read a paper to the Statistical Society in December 1843 that nicely illustrates the difference between an impecunious civil servant and an independent capitalist, both of whom attempted to promote sanitary improvements. He cited the case of Dr. Griscom, New York inspector of interments, who tried to save lives and public money by getting the city to adopt Joseph Whitworth's street-cleaning machine. The hapless Griscom, at the mercy of shifting political winds, was "swept away from his office by change of parties. . . ." Whitworth, however, "who would have been ruined by his invention if he had been a poor man," returned to England and was promoting the use of his machine through a joint-stock company.[5] It is not difficult to see the lesson Chadwick drew from this tale.

While Chadwick continued to lobby actively for an interment measure and other public-health reforms into the spring of 1845, he had begun formulating his private-enterprise schemes at least six months earlier. In a letter to Thomas Garnier in September 1844 he explained how this course of action was necessitated by the political stalemate and how it might be squared with Benthamite theory:

I have been greatly annoyed that no popular support has been given to my recommendations for the appointment of an officer of Health and the removal of the practice of burial in our town. I must own my disgust at the carelessness and selfishness of our public men. An excess of selfishness or of what Bentham calls the "self-regarding virtues" without any compensating power of the "extra-regarding virtues" is perhaps characteristic of our people. It is however to this excess, to strong stomachs and appetites that our manufacturing and commercial energy is to be ascribed. I shall try an appeal to these feelings, in the popular behalf, by a joint stock company.[6]

By the following month he had worked out a plan whereby a company, with an assured 6 or 7 percent profit, could provide the necessary services, "acting as renters or leasees for a term of years, on terms such as those on which railways have been undertaken abroad."[7] By November he told R. A. Slaney, who would himself soon be a director of the company, that he had been busy "feeling the pulse of capitalists, for the requisite enterprise and advances of money."[8]

Chadwick invested his new project with the same single-minded devotion and enthusiasm he had given to public inquiries and reform campaigns. Even a cursory look at his correspondence from this period reveals his near-total absorption in the project. By early 1845 an impressive prospectus had been prepared,[9] and a new company was born. It carried the grandiose title of "The British, Colonial, and Foreign Drainage, Water Supply, and Towns Improvement Company" —mercifully shortened to Towns Improvement Company. The prospectus claimed, somewhat hopefully, an active capital of £1,000,000, with shares at £50 each. A number of Chadwick's friends, colleagues, and parliamentary connections appeared on the sixteen-man board of directors, including Earl Fortescue, Lord Ebrington, Nassau Senior, Neil Arnott, Rowland Hill, and R. A. Slaney. On the engineering staff were men with whom Chadwick had worked previously, like James Smith of Deanston, John Roe, and Henry Austin. The Standing Counsel was composed of two dedicated Chadwickians: George Coode, assistant secretary of the Poor Law Commission, and S. H. Gael, who had served as secretary to the rural constabulary inquiry. The objects of the company, the prospectus explained, were "to supply water to towns; to effect their drainage and cleansing and to apply their refuse to agricultural production; to supply gas, and carry out any connected or similar improvements, of towns either in the British Empire or abroad, where adequate interest and security can be given for the capital invested." There was to be a guaranteed return of 6½ percent. Prospective investors were given strong arguments in favor of combined management of water supply, drainage, and cleansing, as well as the promise of such collateral benefits as better fire-fighting, the use of sewerage for agriculture, and even the application of waste heat from the gas works to operate pumps. Whatever the technological or commercial viability of this scheme, it bears the distinctive imprint of Chadwick's genius. It might be seen as a logical extension, in the realm of engineering and public works, of the principle of "combination of services" he had already developed in the area of public administration. The same rigorous utilitarian logic and passion for efficiency were at work as in his arguments for cooperation among the poor-law, factory, and prison inspectorates.[10]

By the spring of 1845, however, it was proving difficult to attract major investors. Chadwick bent every effort to bring in well-known public figures, especially those associated with the public-health campaign. One of these was the Duke of Buccleuch, but in this case Chadwick's efforts were unavailing.[11] A major problem he faced was that the sanitary movement had produced widespread expectations of government action, while the success of the company was predicated on the assumption that government would do little or nothing. This placed Chadwick in a painful conflict with his frequent pronouncements concerning the need for new public authorities, but he did not shrink from the entrepreneurial task at hand. In his new-found zeal for private enterprise, he went so far as to claim: "The evidence almost goes so far as this that the worst company would almost be better than the best corporate municipality."[12]

Along with such arguments went a mounting anxiety that Peel's government might pass significant legislation after all. As the time approached for Lord Lincoln's bill to be introduced, Chadwick expressed his concern over the government's proposals, as these would "materially affect the course of the company."[13] Two weeks later he was able to breathe more easily, as it became clear that the bill would not be proceeded with that session. Chadwick wrote to Sir

John Easthope, an M.P. and director of the Towns Improvement Company, that the government's delay would work to their advantage, "for we may in each of the towns under consideration show that the company will supply their wants much cheaper, than they will probably be supplied under the provisions of Lord Lincoln's bill."[14]

Indeed, detailed surveys of nearly a dozen towns were in process, and Chadwick was pursuing negotiations with each of them.[15] Typical of the upbeat promoters of the 1840s, he claimed there was strong interest among the stock-buying public along with enthusiastic support by local authorities.[16] Carried along by his own ardor, he indulged in grandiose fantasies of the company extending its civilizing services throughout the empire. The effect of town services in India he compared to the impact of British factory goods on traditional artisans. Chadwick asserted that once his company had extended its sway the Hindu water carrier would be in the same position as the weaver, who, upon the introduction of cheap English cloth,

> is undersold and vanquished, obliged to give up his occupation and seek service as a Sepoy, and find good pay (without plunder) such as the Mogul never gave, and glory in further extending the beneficent domination of the civilized Saxon, by whose science and capital his rude art has been eclipsed and extinguished.

By a similar application of British capital and machinery, "water may be carried night and day into every house in Calcutta and Bombay at a rate so low that no Water Carrier could compete with it however scanty his pay."[17]

Such flights of imperialist fancy were premature, to say the least. Until England was convinced of the soundness of the scheme, it was pointless to fantasize about India. The British capital market, heavily drained by the mania for railway speculation, would prove resistant to even the most imaginative sales campaign Chadwick could devise. And besides overcoming the skepticism of potential investors, there was the necessity of convincing local authorities to contract for the company's services. This involved more than getting a community to accept the principle of combination of services, and the closed loop of water supply, drainage, sewerage, and "sewer manure." It also meant confronting the competition of numerous local companies that were being formed to provide one or more services. Local companies had a significant advantage in that their directors were usually established, well-known local figures more likely to be trusted by municipal governments. In such cases the Towns Improvement Company had to negotiate with the local company, a process that was often protracted and frustrating. A good example is Leicester.

The Leicester Water Company was established in March 1845 with the sole purpose of supplying water to the town. Finding a rival to contend with, Chadwick attempted to convince the local company directors of the benefits of partnership with his enterprise. On August 11 he appeared in person, armed with copies of the Towns Improvement Company prospectus and his own report on Leicester, urging the committee to add drainage and irrigation and promising that the London company would provide the remaining necessary capital.[18] In his report, Chadwick set forth the advantage of combined services by an expanded local company called the Leicester Water and Sewerage Company, capitalized at £150,000. To the existing local directors were added two directors of the Towns Improvement Company: Sir John Easthope and Chadwick himself. Easthope was no doubt useful in reassuring the local directors, as he was one of Leicester's M.P.s. To round out the participation of the local parliamentary representatives, there were added to the committee in a revised report Easthope's liberal colleague at Leicester, Wynn Ellis, and the two Conservative M.P.s for South Leicestershire, Sir Henry Halford and Charles William Packe.[19]

It is not possible to determine the success of this ploy to win local acceptance by a political balance on the board of directors. At any rate, Chadwick's major problem lay in another quarter, namely, the civil engineer Thomas Hawkesley, one of the fastest-rising stars in his profession. Not yet forty years old, Hawkesley had already achieved a solid reputation as the engineer for a number of local water companies. Although a member of the engineering staff of the Towns Improvement Company, he was about to enter the service of the Leicester Company. As he did so, he became an outspoken critic of Chadwick's report on Leicester, which is covered with marginal comments in Hawkesley's hand.[20] Many of these challenge the accuracy of Chadwick's statements and figures. More fundamental was Hawkesley's sounding of the alarm at what he considered a takeover bid led by Chadwick:

> The foregoing report proceeds upon the supposition that the London proprietary are to supersede the Leicester proprietary —whereas the understanding at the meeting was this that the Leicester proprietary were to form a Company and obtain an act, accepting if they thought fit, upon a due consideration of Mr. Chadwick's report, the whole or any portion of the London proprietary as joint stockholders in the undertaking. I am fully persuaded that the Leicester gentlemen have never contemplated that the Water Works would be taken out of their hands and have therefore no hesitation in recommending that the Report be corrected accordingly.

In another part of the report, a vigorous Hawkesley gloss reads: "The Leicester people are the Company and at most propose to accept the proferred assistance of the London Company. ... "[21] On the basis of Hawkesley's remonstrances, the Leicester directors required revisions of the report to insure their continued control. Although Chadwick's next meeting with the local board seemed amicable and he was added to the directors, the board also confirmed Hawkesley's appointment as chief engineer.[22] Not only had Chadwick's attempt to take over the Leicester operation been effectively stymied, he had acquired in Hawkesley a powerful and determined foe, who would play an increasingly important role in thwarting his career.

The unfortunate turn of events at Leicester brought Chadwick to a realization that private enterprise meant competition, and that one's competitors were unlikely to submit quietly to a takeover or simply retire from the field. It would be necessary to stifle the competition, and to a long-time public official with many parliamentary connections, government interference seemed a natural remedy. In a memo he asked rhetorically:

> ... should not the Company, in places where it plants its foot and confers benefits, be protected from the competition of other Companies—if so, a charter will not do, as it can not give any exclusive privilege—in that case an act would be indispensable.[23]

A local act of Parliament would indeed confer monopolistic powers on the company, but there were some problems with this method: time, expense, and the distressing fact that many other companies were in the process of procuring local improvement acts. A way had to be found to streamline the local act process dramatically, so that the Towns Improvement Company could acquire monopoly powers without undue expense and delay. And the new procedure would have to be structured so that the company would have a clear edge over its rivals.

Chadwick believed he found the answer in a House of Commons Select Committee on Private Bills chaired by his old Benthamite colleague Joseph Hume during the 1846 session. While not responsible for the creation of the committee, which was a logical response to the flood of local acts that threatened to overwhelm Parliament in the 1840s, Chadwick quickly perceived its potential usefulness. He got his friend and fellow company director Lord Ebrington on the committee. Ebrington then proceeded to nominate no fewer than six of the remaining thirteen members. In forwarding Ebrington's list of names to Hume, Chadwick also tried to keep off the committee the M.P. for Tower Hamlets, Sir William Clay, who, "as the proprietor of one London Waterworks Company and as the Chairman and a large share holder of another, the Grand Junction, is deeply interested against the reform of the system of water supply."[24] In spite of Clay's presence, Chadwick had secured a friendly committee, which he intended to use for his company's benefit. As he confided to an associate:

> You will have perceived that Mr. Hume has got a committee to examine the different water bills and other private bills. I had suggested his form of resolution, and I may mention it to you confidentially shall have to work for him. In working for him or for the public I shall certainly seek extended powers for the use of the towns improvement company.[25]

The Select Committee on Private Bills met eight times between May 25 and June 29, 1846. Having secured a friendly committee, Chadwick sought to guide its labors to a conclusion beneficial to the company. Specifically, he wanted the report to mandate the combination of services, thus giving his company a clear advantage over its competitors.[26] Most of the twenty-five witnesses supported this concept, and, as usual, Chadwick himself gave the most effective (as well as the lengthiest) testimony.[27] The result of this investigation and report was the Preliminary Inquiries Act (9 & 10 Vict., c. 106), which went a long way toward meeting Chadwick's goal, though it was less explicit on combination of services than he wished. The Commissioners of Woods and Forests were required to investigate and approve all new local projects. The act proved a failure and was repealed in 1850 — not, Chadwick believed, because of any inherent defect, but because of a lack of vigorous and knowledgeable implementation by Woods and Forests.[28]

In the event, Chadwick's lobbying efforts in the House of Commons were wasted. Only a few months after the passage of the Preliminary Inquiries Act, well before it had been put to the test, he admitted to his brother-in-law that the company was failing due to the drainage of the money market by the railway mania.[29] Of course, Chadwick would never admit that the problem was due in part to the skepticism of many investors regarding him and his schemes. The most controversial of these was the use of sewer manure to fertilize arable land in the vicinity of towns served by his company. Its success was indeed critical to the company's fortunes, as the profit margins were calculated on the basis of manure sales to farmers. As with most of his other pet projects, Chadwick vastly exaggerated his own role in developing the idea.[30] But the concept had no more spirited proponent, and he continued to promote it even as he was reluctantly jettisoning the remainder of the company's operations. In June 1846 he was a most enthusiastic witness before a Select Committee on Metropolitan Sewage Manure,[31] while more than a year later he was still trying to get Sir Robert Peel to undertake a demonstration project at Drayton Manor.[32] Like Bentham's Panopticon, Chadwick's sewer-manure program was the residue of a failed commercial enterprise. But while Panopticon principles were reflected in the design of many workhouses, prisons, and other public institutions, Chadwick's plan was to be thoroughly discredited, commercially as well as scientifically.[33]

Another aspect of Chadwick's commercial venture is the link between the company and his rather sudden interest in the plight of the railway laborers in the mid-1840s. R. A. Lewis has depicted Chadwick

as the exploited workers' selfless champion, who set aside his other
concerns to reveal the brutal conditions and grisly accidents among
the railway labor gangs.[34] Without denying altogether a humane
impulse on Chadwick's part, it does seem appropriate to ask how he
managed to ignore these shocking problems for fifteen years. The
timing of his "discovery" is also of interest, coming as it did in the
midst of his most active and determined efforts to promote the Towns
Improvement Company. As we have seen, one of the principal difficulties in floating the company was the railway mania, which severely
drained the capital market. The many new lines being built or
planned were especially vulnerable to new legislation on railway
workers, since they were embarking on their most labor-intensive
phase. The sort of controls which Chadwick now began to demand, if
implemented, would certainly dampen the public enthusiasm for
investing in new railways, and thus make capital available for the
Towns Improvement Company.

The evidence for this line of reasoning is of course circumstantial,
but it is strengthened by considering the presence on the board of
directors of the Towns Improvement Company of men representing
the "old" railway interests. James Morrison and Sir George de Larpent,
Bart. were both directors of established railway companies, and thus
favored regulation of the new lines on two grounds: to free capital for
the Towns Improvement Company and to remove potential competitors to their railways. Morrison and Chadwick were in close touch
throughout 1846, and frequently discussed a number of strategies to
regulate the new railway lines. Morrison was also an M.P. and, since
1836, a persistent advocate of greater state regulation of the railways.[35]
But to pave the way for him to raise the issue of the railway laborers
in the House of Commons, Chadwick had to prepare and publicize a
report.

His paper on railway laborers was read before the Manchester
Statistical Society in January 1846, and Chadwick had two thousand
copies of it printed at his own expense.[36] Citing the Prussian Code's
protection of miners, he proposed making railway owners financially
responsible for accidents to their workers—a principle he had originally set forth in the Factory Report of 1833. But he went beyond this
in advocating that parliamentary committees examining new railway
bills should be instructed to inquire into company provisions for

housing, policing, educating, and providing medical care for workers and their families. Government inspectors were to insure that these matters were properly implemented by the companies. He ended his paper by praising the provision made by some of the "old" railways for housing their laborers. Clearly, the combined cost of employers' liability and the range of services to be provided to workers and their families would make new railway investments far less attractive. Now that the issues had been so effectively raised, it was time for parliamentary action.

Shortly after Chadwick's paper was presented, Morrison resumed his efforts for a stronger regulatory body than the Railway Department of the Board of Trade. He supported Peel's motion for a Select Committee on Railway Bills with the following declaration:

> There was too great a speculation existing as to railways, and the only way to meet the spirit of speculation which prevailed was to bring down the profits so applied to an ordinary level; and this only could be effected by fixing a much lower rate of charges upon the different lines to be constructed.[37]

A few weeks later he returned again to the same need to dampen speculation through railway regulation, as did his fellow Towns Improvement Company director, Lord Ebrington.[38] Peel's government, paralyzed by the Corn Law crisis, was unwilling to promote major legislation, but was not disposed to resist private members' initiatives. Thus, in April the House of Commons assented to E. P. Bouverie's motion for a committee to investigate Chadwick's revelations. The Select Committee on Railway Laborers, chaired by Bouverie, held eight meetings in May and July, and naturally Chadwick was the major witness.[39] This was also the period during which the Metropolitan Sewage Manure Committee and Hume's committee on private bills were holding their hearings, so Chadwick was kept busy as a witness. As if all of this were not enough, the Andover workhouse scandal (to be described in the next chapter) had broken, and he was marshalling all his efforts for a final showdown with his poor-law superiors.

Bouverie's committee endorsed Chadwick's call for applying the principle of employer's liability to railway companies, but no legislation followed. This was unfortunate for the railway laborers and their families, but probably had little effect on the establishment of new lines, as the railway mania was becoming a spent force by the end of the year. Chadwick's confederate Morrison still had hopes of achieving something by means of a stronger regulatory agency. He reported to Chadwick in June the widespread belief "that it would be advantageous to the existing lines to have such a Board...." The close connection between this campaign and the simultaneous efforts regarding railway laborers and private bill legislation is indicated by the way Morrison concluded his letter: "Bouverie's committee and Hume's committee on private bills will I expect adopt resolutions concurrent with yours."[40]

When the Whigs returned to office in July 1846, Morrison was finally able to secure the passage of an act (9 & 10 Vict., c. 105) vesting a new body known as the Commissioners of Railways with greater powers than the Board of Trade. But the success of this campaign had no more effect upon the fortunes of the Towns Improvement Company than the failure of Chadwick's attempts to impede new railway ventures through enacting employer's liability. More capital was already starting to become available thanks to the rapid cooling of railway speculation, but the simple fact is that very little of it was being invested in Chadwick's company. Thus all the elaborate parliamentary maneuvers of the 1846 session, including Hume's committee on private bills, were to no avail. Chadwick must have been disappointed, but he tried to salvage what he could. With his company in ruins and the Andover scandal breaking threateningly about him, he wrote to Morrison in an unsuccessful attempt to secure one of the paid posts on the new Railway Commission. He told Morrison that the railway position would only be attractive if he were blocked in his poor-law or public-health career. His letter ended with a characteristic threat to Russell's government: "I believe that if I leave the poor law administration it will extensively shake confidence in it and that it will not increase confidence in the Government which makes such arrangements as to prevent me going on."[41] In spite of the frustrations and dashed hopes caused by his two-year involvement in the company scheme, Chadwick was able to return to the quest for preeminence as a public official, his determination and combativeness unabated.

7 Poor-Law and Public-Health Battles

By the mid-1840s, Chadwick was simultaneously involved in a multitude of projects, both public and private. When not testifying before a parliamentary committee or delivering a paper before a learned society, he was promoting his company, revealing new social evils, or jockeying for position in the public-health movement. As we have seen, he was quite prepared to abandon an official career in favor of private enterprise. Nor were his aspirations as a government official limited to one or two fields. His attempt to secure a post on the new Railway Commission has already been described. At about the same time he applied to Ashley to become a Lunacy Commissioner (the salary for which had just been raised to £1,500) and to Graham for a place as an Enclosure Commissioner.[1] It may be wondered what effect this exhausting range of activities had on his poor-law work.

Chadwick's attendance at Somerset House had become infrequent ever since his exclusion from board meetings in 1839. Though continuing to draw his salary as Secretary, he had become completely estranged from his superiors, and frequently sniped at them for their backsliding from the "principles of 1834." He was particularly incensed when they withdrew the Consolidated Order in 1842, replacing it with a General Order that allowed no fewer than six exceptions to the prohibition of outdoor relief. He also objected to the commissioners' unwillingness to push for greater powers to dissolve Gilbert Act unions or to establish a truly independent audit of the boards of guardians.[2] This kind of criticism found no favor with Graham, who had earlier told Peel that Chadwick was "no less indiscreet in his advice than in his language. . . ."[3] In this same letter, Graham also criticized the commissioners. In spite of Chadwick's quarrelsomeness as Secretary, Graham feared that his criticisms would be much more spirited if he were dismissed. Besides, he was earning his keep not only by undertaking various health inquiries, but also by serving as a lightning rod, along with the rest of the Somerset House establishment, for the New Poor Law's opponents. As Graham expressed it to Peel: "This Poor Law Commission is a heavy Burthen to the Government: the only real use of it is as a Brake to prevent collision between the Executive and the Poor. . . ."[4]

Knowing of Graham's fixed animosity, Chadwick wrote directly to Peel that he was not behind the criticisms being leveled at the poor-law administrative structure. In April 1845 he informed Peel that he had nothing to do with the bills of 1844 and 1845 that would have extended the area of settlement from the parish to the poor-law union, nor had he pushed to abolish parochial settlement in 1834.[5] The latter assertion was untrue, since he had worked hard but unsuccessfully to insert the principle of union chargeability in the 1834 measure.[6] And he was to return to the campaign for union settlement as soon as Peel was out of office.

The only other poor-law stratagem employed by Chadwick in the mid-1840s was to continue the campaign of altering his image as an oppressor of the poor. His earlier efforts, with Dickens and others, have already been recounted, and had mixed results. In late 1844 he began to cultivate the Reverend Lord Sidney Godolphin Osborne, an author of numerous letters to *The Times* on a variety of social issues. Osborne, some of whose "S.G.O." letters called for more humane treatment of the poor, was denounced by Graham as a "popularity-hunting parson."[7] Chadwick tried to establish an alliance with Osborne on the basis of a shared persecution by the Home Secretary: "Whilst you are under condemnation as a 'popularity-hunting parson' I am under Sir James Graham's censure for having, as he says, written so harshly as to make the poor laws unpopular." He denied that the unpopular directives issuing from Somerset House were of his devising and concluded by claiming that he had his "own story to tell which must sooner or later be told, in answer to Sir James' censure."[8] It was well that Chadwick took the trouble, even during this period of his preoccupation with the Towns Improvement Company, to establish positive relations with people like Osborne. For the Andover Workhouse scandal was about to break, and he would need all the support he could muster.

From its beginnings in 1835, the Andover Union in Hampshire had developed a reputation in poor-law circles for its strict implementation of the workhouse test. It came to the attention of the general public in 1845, however, with lurid revelations in *The Times* about pauper inmates resorting to gnawing marrow and gristle from bones in the workhouse bone-crushing yard. The subsequent inquiry by Assistant Commissioner Henry Parker pointed to a host of abuses by the workhouse master and the guardians. Peel's government, tottering to its fall because of the Corn Law crisis, was unable to avoid a parliamentary inquiry, and the affair escalated to an emotionally charged struggle in the House of Commons, with the Poor Law Commission and the New Poor Law itself on trial before the nation. The Andover scandal has been well described in several places,[9] and the details need not concern us overmuch. But Chadwick's crucial if belated role in the affair is of considerable interest, since it decisively affected the administrative structure of the poor law as well as his own career.

Chadwick had taken no action at first, either regarding the initial revelations or Parker's subsequent dismissal by the commissioners. This was hardly surprising, since he had had a somewhat tenuous connection with Somerset House for many years, in spite of continuing to receive his full salary as secretary. Furthermore, he was fully absorbed in his company scheme throughout 1845 and at any rate had never developed any closeness with most of the assistant commissioners. This can be seen in his virtually ignoring the dismissal in 1843 of William Day, who was made a scapegoat for the bitter resistance to the implementation of the New Poor Law in Wales.[10]

As late as the summer of 1846, after the Andover select committee had begun its labors, Chadwick's knowledge of the case was still derived almost exclusively from the newspapers.[11] His sudden transition from the outer periphery to the very center of the crisis was due to several factors. First, he had been denounced as insubordinate and devious by Sir Edmund Head and G. C. Lewis in their testimony before the committee, and it was necessary to defend himself. Second, since considerable public interest had been aroused by Parker's vindicating pamphlet, the forum provided by the Andover committee was too good to pass up. Third, the committee had broadened its scope to include Day's dismissal, thus opening the way for a full airing of all Chadwick's pent-up grievances concerning the administrative procedures at Somerset House. Finally, with the Towns Improvement Company clearly in shambles by 1846, Chadwick was forced to turn back to a government career. If he did not publicly defend himself, this too would evaporate.

The strategy for questioning and presenting evidence was developed in a hastily convened conference between Chadwick, Parker, Assistant Poor Law Secretary George Coode, and W. D. Christie, the chairman of the House of Commons select committee. Coode whetted the public appetite for further revelations, and served as an effective warm-up act for Chadwick. The latter's four-day testimony in July was the centerpiece of the inquiry. He laid bare the unorthodox and unfair practices of the commissioners, and swayed public and press opinion in his direction. It was indeed his consummate performance, replete with numerous flattering references to John Walter of *The Times*.[12] Chadwick also demonstrated, correctly but misleadingly, that he had protested the reduction of the assistant commissioners to nine, a key point since the heavy workload of the assistants was obviously an important factor in the existence of abuses such as those at Andover. It was misleading, however, since it was Chadwick who had urged very substantial reductions in the corps of assistant commissioners to Russell in 1838.[13] He was certainly pleased when the committee's report, published in August, was roundly critical of the Poor Law Commissioners. But there were no resignations, and Sir George Grey, the new Home Secretary, announced that nothing would be done until it was time for a renewal bill in 1847.[14]

Chadwick had achieved public vindication, but at the cost of further embittering his relations with most of the cabinet as well as his superiors at Somerset House. Indeed the tightly knit and closely related Whig coterie in power, from Lord John Russell to G. C. Lewis, would not soon forget this plebeian assault upon their honor. In spite of his victory, deep uncertainties about the future of both his poor-law and public-health careers remained. In a letter to W. E. Hickson, Chadwick put his dilemma nicely: "If I am not put down three carriages must be put down which have been kept up on my labours whilst I have walked." He went on to lament the ruining of the poor law by those in power and ended by declaring that "the quantity of spoiled work is becoming so annoying and this jealousy so great and so noxious to carrying out public principles that an appeal to the public and an independent position may be necessary. . . . "[15] In a similar vein he wrote to Frederic Hill that he was "on the look out for further attacks, and prepared to expect to have to appeal to the public in vindication of the law and myself."[16]

In both of these letters, as well as in others of this period, Chadwick likened his position to that of Rowland Hill, the postal reformer. After devising the penny-postage scheme and receiving a special appointment to the Treasury to implement it, Hill found his efforts thwarted at every turn by the Post Office officials, particularly Col. William Maberly, the permanent secretary. Although Hill was able to surmount this opposition and establish the penny post on a sound footing, he lacked family background, connections, and a university education and was unceremoniously dropped from government service when his original term expired in 1842. The comparisons with his own life and career were obvious, though typically Chadwick made his persecution seem much worse by claiming, in the letter to Hickson, that he had "three Maberlys to deal with." Another interesting parallel is that Hill, after losing his government post, became chairman of the Brighton Railway from 1843 to 1846, introducing popular express and excursion train service. It is impossible to say how much Chadwick may have been influenced by Hill's successful foray into private enterprise, but it is noteworthy that he launched his own company scheme shortly after Hill took up his railway post. And when Hill left the railway to resume government service in 1846, a public testimonial to him raised £13,000. Chadwick must have reflected that no such outpouring in his behalf was likely, as long as he was tainted by the odium of the workhouse test. If Chadwick continued to follow Hill's career and compare it to his own, he could only note wistfully the other's greater measure of success—a distinguished career in the Post Office, a F.R.S., a D.C.L. from Oxford, a knighthood (thirty years before Chadwick's) and, finally, burial at Westminster Abbey.

It was clear that the Andover inquiry, however important a victory, was only one battle in an ongoing war with the government. Chadwick knew that in the next fray he would probably have to resort to the threat of revealing everything about the broken promises by Althorp and others regarding his promotion to the Poor Law Commission. During a lull in the hostilities in the early months of 1847, he was summoned as a witness before a House of Commons select committee on settlement and poor removal. This was necessitated by the effects of the "Irremovability Act" of 1846 (9 & 10 Vict., c. 66), by which a resident for at least five years in a parish other than that of his settlement was rendered irremovable. This act, passed in a turbulent session at the behest of the agricultural interest, had produced much confusion and a considerable financial hardship on certain urban parishes, hitherto able to remove their surplus population when employment slackened.[17] While it created a novel category of the "irremovable," the 1846 measure had not altered the law of settlement, which had long been the target of reformers. Hence when Russell's government appointed a select committee in 1847, it was obvious that Chadwick's testimony would be crucial. Yet, depending on whom he was addressing himself to, Chadwick made quite different recommendations. As we have seen, he had told Peel in 1845 that it was never his intention to tamper with parochial settlement.[18] In his evidence before the committee, he recommended the abolition of settlement altogether,[19] yet many of his letters from this period endorse union settlement.[20] With one of the foremost experts on the topic espousing the three principal options, it is scarcely surprising that the committee threw up its hands and simply published the evidence without specific recommendations.[21] Thanks in part to Chadwick's vacillation, reform of the law of settlement, in the form of union chargeability, was deferred until 1865.

As Chadwick anticipated, when the Poor Law Renewal Bill was brought forward, hostilities were resumed. He was vilified in the House of Commons by Russell on May 20, and by Graham the next day.[22] While caught somewhat off-guard by the suddenness of the renewal legislation's introduction, Chadwick had been busily preparing a Vindicating Letter, in which all the broken promises, injustices, and indignities he had suffered since 1834 were detailed. He hoped that the threat of publishing this document would be sufficient to pressure the government into major concessions, but just what should these be? He could hardly expect a position in the amended poor-law system, after all that had been revealed about the poisonous atmosphere at Somerset House—not without Russell utterly repudiating the three commissioners, and that was simply not in the cards. Nor could he expect to alter the new administrative structure (a Poor Law Board of four plus a parliamentary secretary who would be the effective head), much as he disapproved. What he could hope to achieve was preventing the reappointment of Lewis or Head. Beyond this, the essential thing was to use the Vindicating Letter to force the government into appointing him to a new post, preferably in the field of public health.

The strategy had its desired effect. The government, after showing every sign of planning to appoint Lewis to the Poor Law Board, was forced to back down. This was largely the result of pressure brought by Chadwick's parliamentary friends, including Brougham and Bishop Blomfield in the House of Lords. One of the tactics used to marshal this support reveals the lengths Chadwick was willing to go when everything was on the line. It concerns his use of a belated letter from E. C. Tufnell, one of the assistant commissioners with close family connections to the Whig leadership. This important document arrived at the last minute, after Chadwick's request to various other of the assistant commissioners for support had been turned down.[23] Tufnell's letter contained powerful supporting material but ended with the request that it be used privately. When the letter was quoted to great effect by Brougham in the House of Lords, Chadwick answered the ensuing complaints about the document's misuse by claiming that he had indeed sent the letter to Brougham, but "as luck would have it" the last page (containing Tufnell's restriction on its use) was omitted.[24] Whether this wholly implausible explanation convinced Tufnell or his friends is unknown, but the ploy succeeded brilliantly with the public.

Chadwick also skillfully utilized his ultimate weapon, the Vindicating Letter. He sent a printed version of it to Sir George Grey, containing all but the most damaging evidence against the Ministers, threatening to include this material in a subsequent edition of the letter and to make it public. He also circulated the letter among key M.P.s, thus producing a body of supporters and sympathizers whom

Russell dared not challenge. The Prime Minister retreated, sending word through Sir George Grey that Chadwick would have the paid post on the General Board of Health that would be created when the Health of Towns Bill was finally passed. Chadwick, delighted, prepared to put away his Vindicating Letter and at last assume an executive post. But the health bill, battered by the determined opposition of vested interests and the divisive politics of the post-corn-law repeal era, was emasculated and finally stalled. At the end of the 1847 session and on the eve of a general election, Chadwick found himself about to lose government employment altogether, as his poor-law secretaryship would expire with the Poor Law Commission. A threat to revive the Vindicating Letter brought a firm promise from Russell that Chadwick would have the paid post when the health bill passed in the 1848 session. To tide him over till then, he was made the paid member of a new royal commission on the sanitation of the metropolis.[25] Thus ended for Chadwick a fifteen-year career in the poor law that had started with his appointment as an assistant commissioner for the royal commission in 1832. There remained to him but seven years as a public official, all of them in the field of public health.

While Russell's hand had been largely forced on this appointment, there was a more positive reason. The public-health movement was, if anything, stronger than ever, and it is arguable that the Health of Towns Association was the most powerful pressure group in the country in 1847, the Anti–Corn Law League having accomplished its mission. It was therefore important for the Ministry to appear to be committed in this area, especially going into the general election of 1847. In the event, while the Whigs did improve their position slightly, they remained dependent on the Peelites. Since the government had to demonstrate its willingness to act on the sanitary issue, a place would have to be found for Chadwick, still widely esteemed as one of the movement's guiding lights. As his supporter, the Reverend Sidney Godolphin Osborne put it in a letter to *The Times* in April 1847:

> There is one public man living and in full force, known for a perseverance nothing can tire—a patience that seems to be soothed by abuse—a zeal that will admit of no hindrance—a power of acquiring and condensing and popularizing the

result of statistical inquiry almost marvellous—who is for-
ever pulling forth from all the odd corners and recesses of
human life its most hidden sores—where can any moral filth
be discovered, and my worthy friend Edwin Chadwick is not
found stirring it, turning it over, analysing its pernicious
power, proving the source whence it has arisen?—he is, indeed,
the great moral scavenger of the age.[26]

And editorially *The Times,* which had swung around to his side
during the Andover crisis, welcomed his accession to the health
commission.[27] Unfortunately for Chadwick, this was to be a brief
interlude, *The Times* resuming its critical stance as he became
embroiled in the stormy politics of London sanitary reform.

The metropolis having been defined, for the purposes of the inquiry,
as those districts lying within a twelve-mile radius of Charing Cross,
there remained only the necessity of appointing the other royal
commissioners. As was the case with his recommendations for the
Health of Towns Commission in 1843, Chadwick had very limited
success. Only one of the twelve names he sent to Russell was added to
the commission—Thomas Southwood Smith.[28] The government added
Richard Owen; Richard Lambert Jones, a strident member of the
London Common Council; and Lord Robert Grosvenor, son of the
Duke of Westminster, the major property owner in the metropolis.
While the commission supposedly started with a series of questions
regarding drainage, cleansing, paving, and water supply, Chadwick
began with all the answers. His engineering nostrums were unchanged
since the Health of Towns Commission, and had hardened into
dogma. Administratively he was equally clear on the necessity of
abolishing the confusing and overlapping welter of vestries, sewers
commissioners, and other local authorities, some of them corrupt,
most of them inefficient, and all of them fiercely determined to
defend themselves.

The deliberations of the Metropolitan Sanitary Commission, as the
royal commission was called, lasted about nine months. The commissioners were forced to pay a good deal of attention to the dreaded
cholera, about to make a return visit after an absence of sixteen years.
Nevertheless, in the three reports issued by the commission between
November 1847 and July 1848, there is every sign that Chadwick had

been able to convince his colleagues of the value of much of his program. In the passages disparaging the existing local bodies and calling for government by officials and experts, there is a decided Chadwickian ring:

> The more the investigation advances, the more it is apparent that the progressive improvement and proper execution of this class of public works together with the appliances of hydraulic engineering, cannot reasonably be expected to be dealt with incidentally, or collaterally to ordinary occupation, or even to connected professional pursuits, but require a degree of special study which not only place them beyond the sphere of the discussion of popular administrative bodies, but beyond that of ordinary professional engineering and architectural practice.[29]

Still, many important issues were ignored or glossed over, Chadwick telling Lord Ebrington: "To get the vote of Mr. Lambert Jones and an unanimous report required much concession and management."[30]

Actually, this particular royal commission was not as vital to Chadwick's purpose as those in previous inquiries. While he certainly sought to use it to publicize glaring public-health evils and endorse his solutions, it was not the essential vehicle of reform. Of equal or greater importance was the Consolidated Metropolitan Commission of Sewers, created in November 1847. This twenty-three-member body, which superseded six separate sewer commissions containing nearly seven hundred members, was to undertake the design and construction of a modern, efficient system of sewers and to consolidate water supplies for the metropolis. It was clear that having a secure majority on this body would be essential, and Chadwick bent every effort to this end, and even urged Russell to appoint members who would be content "to do as little as possible, and not impede the more successful and experienced of the paid officers." Their aim, he went on, should be "to emancipate those officers who have given their whole time for years to the subjects, and who have introduced successful improvements in spite of obstacles."[31] Considering these views, it is hardly surprising that Chadwick's reform program, indeed his very career, was to be destroyed by metropolitan opposition forces.

Chadwick disliked any kind of board, with appointive ones being the least obnoxious and democratically elected ones the worst. Most London vestries and other authorities were characterized by a distinctive and truculent radicalism, and were bound to take offense at his disdainful elitism. Nor would his call for increasing the power of permanent officials necessarily find favor with such functionaries in London, for Chadwick sought to destroy most of the local authorities that employed them. More fundamentally, as the report of the Metropolitan Sanitary Commission had made clear, mere technical competence or professional standing was not enough. Only a person who had devoted years to studying the particular subject—in short, someone like Chadwick—could pass muster.

The man who above all others recognized the potential for disaster in Chadwick's policy and personality was Viscount Morpeth, heir of the Earl of Carlisle and First Commissioner of Woods and Forests. In this post, he had special cognizance of all public-health legislation, for which his role as a prominent and effective member of the Health of Towns Association well qualified him. Finer describes him aptly as "one of the most able, the most disinterested and the most popular of the Whig connexion."[32] A skilled and sensitive parliamentary manager, Morpeth was the architect of the stalled 1847 general public-health bill, and would successfully guide a similar measure to victory in the 1848 session. His chief concern in the autumn of 1847 was to insure that the new Metropolitan Commission of Sewers, on which he served alongside Chadwick, did not founder on the anti-centralization cry of the vestries and water companies. This involved a frequent gentle cajoling of Chadwick to moderate his stance or soften his tone; yet Morpeth also deeply admired Chadwick and accepted the soundness of his engineering and administrative program.

One of the earliest problems to arise was over the inclusion of the City of London, whose Corporation was the proudest and most powerful in the capital. Part of Morpeth's strategy to lull the Corporation was to add to the Metropolitan Sanitary Commission Common Councillor Richard Lambert Jones, and this seemed to pay off when Lambert Jones did not resist the commission's call for a single London sanitary authority. But when the Corporation nonetheless began to maneuver in Parliament to retain a measure of independence, Chadwick leapt in by instigating a Health of Towns Association report highly critical of the Corporation.[33] Chadwick's ham-fisted foray further alienated the City of London, one of whose M.P.s was the Prime Minister himself. While Russell reluctantly accepted Chadwick's insistence that the City had to be included, he clearly favored some kind of compromise. Characteristically, it was Morpeth who devised one: the City was permitted to keep its own sewer commission provided that it sent four representatives to the Consolidated Metropolitan Commission whenever main drainage was discussed, and agreed to abide by a majority decision.[34]

A more serious crisis emerged on the Consolidated Metropolitan Sewers Commission. While the great majority of its twenty-three members were staunch supporters of Chadwick and his program, there was a small but noisy opposition party led by John Leslie, of St. George's, Hanover Square, a key figure on the Westminster Sewers Commission. Morpeth had included Leslie and a few other vestry representatives in order to give them a forum for their concerns and to avoid the sort of outraged opposition to the commission he knew would result if they had been excluded. But Chadwick, as we have seen, believed that it was the function of non-expert commissioners to be seen and not heard. Determined to brook no opposition, Chadwick made two fatal missteps: he convinced Morpeth that when the Metropolitan Sewers Commission was reconstituted in 1848 it should continue to be an appointive body; and he also attempted to exclude Leslie from it. The first proved a serious error because it helped insure that London would remain a separate entity when the public-health act was passed. Had Morpeth insisted on a Metropolitan Sewers Commission at least partly elective, it would have facilitated its control by the General Board of Health, while a crown-appointed body was very likely to remain independent. Chadwick of course realized this, but regarded it as relatively unimportant since he anticipated controlling both boards. What he failed to reckon with was the force of metropolitan radicalism, already deeply alarmed by the nonrepresentative character of the interim Metropolitan Sewers Commission. When Chadwick insisted on keeping it appointive, and tried to exclude Leslie in the bargain, it became clear to concerned Londoners that he aimed at nothing less than a sanitary dictatorship.

At this juncture, Morpeth, who had so far let Chadwick have his way, balked on removing Leslie, fully realizing that to make a martyr of this obstreperous vestryman would doom all efforts to reform London. But the damage was already done, and was compounded when Chadwick responded to Leslie's continued needling on the reconstituted commission by resorting to a series of elaborate expedients to keep Leslie at arm's length and off the key committees. These extravagant tyrannical tactics angered not only all the major London interests, but the one man whom Chadwick could ill afford to alienate — John Walter III of *The Times.* Having taken over the proprietorship of the newspaper from his father in 1847, he had so far been well-disposed to Chadwick and his program, but henceforth swung around to a tone of sarcastic disdain, at least on matters relating to the Metropolitan Commission of Sewers.[35] There were targets aplenty for such journalistic sniping, for the Leslie faction had succeeded in winning over many of the permanent officers of the commission, partly by pushing for increased salaries for them. The resulting factiousness among the officials brought forth a number of rancorous, far from private disputes about the proper methods and principles of drainage, sewerage, and water supply. With such major technical squabbles laid before the public, it was only a matter of time before Chadwick's own engineering dogmas became the center of dispute. Although this did not develop fully until after the General Board of Health had commenced, it would make Chadwick's position on the Metropolitan Commission untenable, and result in his removal from that body in 1849.

Before turning to the passage of the Public Health Act and the creation of the General Board of Health, it is necessary to consider another enemy created by Chadwick in the early part of 1848. Joshua Toulmin Smith, a publicist and constitutional lawyer, was both a committed sanitary reformer and a passionate partisan of parochial self-government. As a vigorous defender of local government, he was of course the darling of the London vestries, making it difficult to ignore him during the inquiry and subsequent attempt to reform the metropolis. Indeed, it became impossible to ignore Toulmin Smith after his two letters in the *Morning Chronicle* attacking a Health of Towns Association subcommittee report for its "blatant lies" about the sanitary condition of Highgate. He also accused the Metropolitan Commission of Sewers of using the cholera scare to destroy local self-government in London.[36] The *Morning Chronicle,* hitherto a source of unfailing support for Chadwick, had been recently acquired by a Peelite syndicate and henceforth served as a sounding board for Toulmin Smith and other opponents of Chadwick's program. Indeed the leading article on April 28, criticizing the procedures of the royal commission, reads as though it was written by Toulmin Smith himself:

> Once for all, there is no opinion, however absurd, no scheme, however mischievous, — we might almost add, no "fact," however fictitious, for which you could not make up a fair-looking case, on the *ex-parte* principle. No achievement in this line can be said to be beyond the capabilities of a homogeneous body of inquirers, framing their own queries, and choosing their own "trustworthy persons," and, it may be doing all this without the smallest conscious departure from the rules of good faith.

The very day this leader appeared, the Metropolitan Sanitary Commission examined Toulmin Smith for over five hours. Chadwick's report of the encounter to Morpeth was guarded: "I endeavoured to confine him to the Metropolitan Bill. I had a stout cross examination. How it may read I can hardly say."[37] Toulmin Smith's account was not only more fulsome and forceful, but was made public in his *Letter to the Metropolitan Sanitary Commissioners,* which he later quoted in his book *Government by Commissions:*

> The determined attempt, from beginning to end, was to extract admissions in support of the *ex-parte* case eagerly sought to be made out. I was stopped, rudely and peremptorily, when I sought to explain points on which artfully framed questions would necessarily lead to a misunderstanding of my reply without explanation.[38]

He went on to explain his difficulties in getting proof sheets of his evidence, which he finally procured only by writing directly to Lord Morpeth. When these proved to be full of errors, he sent back corrections and asked to receive a revised copy, but none ever came. There was only one conclusion he could draw: "As my evidence . . . will by no means suit the object of this Commission, it is not very likely that it will ever be honoured with a place in their 'Minutes of Evidence.' "[39] This was an accurate prediction. Chadwick solved the problem of Toulmin Smith's testimony by simply omitting the entire Minutes of Evidence from the third report of the Metropolitan Sanitary Commission.[40] Such cavalier treatment of one of the foremost champions of metropolitan local government did little to enhance the credibility of the royal commission's report in London. It was almost certainly a factor in arousing opposition to the Metropolitan Sewers Commission as well. Thus two of the public-health bodies dominated by Chadwick in 1848 were at least partially discredited, just as the general bill was being passed.

Our chief concern with this important measure is its constitutional provisions and the politics of its passage and implementation. In these matters Chadwick displayed his characteristic antipathy to popularly elected local boards and his preference for a one-man central authority, preferably under the aegis of the Privy Council. When the original general bill was before Parliament, Chadwick urged Russell to avoid direct election of the local boards. He suggested that town councils should nominate the members of the local authorities, with the poor-law union chairman and vice chairman ("who are certainly the most respectable of locally elected administrators") having ex-officio seats.[41] In a letter to his American brother-in-law, Andrew Boardman, he deplored Russell's 1854 bill to reduce the parliamentary franchise to £5, claiming that this class of voters offered "the greatest opposition to measures of sanitary improvement, specially directed to the improvement of their own dwellings and in reduction of existing charges."[42] In another letter to Boardman he expressed his wish to apply to parliamentary elections the system of voting papers filled out at home, "which I got introduced into Poor Law administration with the view of retaining the more educated and respectable class of voters." Following this opinion is one of those rare passages in which Chadwick revealed something of his inner political passions and prejudices. Deploring the "violent disruption of the Anglo-Saxon race," he expressed a "family feeling" for the United States. He went on: "I entertain a respect for its backwoodsmen and have an indulgent view for their Lynch Law." Approving the driving back of the "Spanish" in North America, he expressed his desire that the "Anglo-Saxons" take over all of South

America, "to the ultimate advancement of civilization and human happiness."[43]

There was scant time for such imperialist fantasizing in 1848. When not occupied with the royal commission or the Metropolitan Sewers Commission, Chadwick was laboring to fashion the general bill to his taste. One strategy was to urge the government to use the emergency powers conferred by a cholera bill to create, by an order in council, entirely appointive local health bodies. Once these were in operation, it might prove possible to forestall the creation of elective boards altogether. They would also be useful in his campaign against the existing boards, especially in London. As he wrote to Morpeth: "I should aim at turning these new local Boards to account as allies, as against the local paving Boards and other interests averse to sanitary improvement, and the health of the population."[44] Morpeth replied unsympathetically that "it is hardly opportune to organise an extensive temporary machinery" since the general bill would soon create permanent local authorities.[45]

It was evident that Chadwick would have to accept a network of elective local boards. The franchise by which they were elected and the powers they could exercise became the critical factors, along with something even more fundamental—the terms under which they were to be created. When Morpeth introduced the bill early in 1848, boards were to be created upon a petition of 2 percent of the local inhabitants. Since the "clean party" in any town usually numbered at least this many, there was every prospect of bringing all the worst places quickly under the act. But the "dirty party" mustered powerful support in Parliament, transforming the 2 percent into 10 percent. As Chadwick complained to Lord Lansdowne, the Lord President of the Council, with the amendment there was "no probability of the introduction of the measure into the most important places."[46] Lansdowne agreed that the amendment was unfortunate, but replied that "it would have been impossible to get it thru' without making some concessions to the prevailing jealousy of central government."[47] It was Bishop Blomfield who came up with an alternate mode of bringing the act into operation in a locality—tying it to the local death rate. Blomfield's death-rate formula was unduly complicated, and was simplified by Morpeth to a figure of 23 per 1,000 over the previous seven years.[48] In the event this was to prove effective, although probably not as effective as the simple 2 percent petition would have been.

Another useful amendment to come out of the House of Lords concerned the local boards' power of sanctioning loans. The Commons had removed the central agency's control over the local boards' power to borrow money and spread the charges over a thirty-year period. As Chadwick told Blomfield, this opened the way for ill-conceived schemes and wholesale jobbery by town councils, "which I entirely distrust."[49] And he expressed to Morpeth his fear that this provision jeopardized the entire bill: "I am apprehensive that you will find proprietors in the Lords sufficiently aware of the damage which the local boards may do to property, with the unlimited powers of spreading charges over long periods, or of imposing rent charges, to be disposed to resist the measure."[50] It was Lord Ellenborough, recently Governor-General of India and First Lord of the Admiralty, who carried an amendment in the House of Lords restoring the central agency's control over loans.[51] Thus some of the teeth were restored to the measure, partly by Chadwick's assiduous lobbying. The victories were partially offset by the government's dropping the interment clauses and relegating the anti-cholera provisions to a separate Nuisance Removal Bill.[52]

Another matter of the greatest concern to Chadwick was the constitution of the new central authority. His animus against administrative boards was of long standing and had become even more intense since the Andover scandal. He realized there was little chance of getting what he called "the principle of single-seatedness" in the form of a committee of Privy Council with himself as secretary, or in any other form for that matter.[53] Nonetheless, he urged the scheme on Russell again even as the bill was receiving its second reading. He pointed out to the Prime Minister that the Privy Council had long exercised public-health functions anyway, and that vesting executive authority in the secretary would be much more efficient than the board provided for in the bill.[54] To Morpeth he exclaimed: "Depend upon it—your present arrangement will never work satisfactorily to anyone, and that you yourself will eventually have large cause to be dissatisfied with it."[55] Since it proved impossible to avoid a board, Chadwick found himself in the position of supporting the parliamentary opposition's efforts to cut it from five to three, of which only one instead of two would be paid members. He presented this strategy to Joseph Hume as simply a compromise to save the bill: "From the position in which parties stand, I believe that if you support Mr. Miles and Mr. Henley's view as to a single paid Commissioner, that measure will stand a fair chance of being carried."[56] But it is clear that such a course recommended itself on two other grounds: it would result in an administrative structure more akin to his Privy Council scheme, and it would eliminate the necessity of having to share power with Thomas Southwood Smith, the likely candidate for the second paid post.

As the time approached for the government to make appointments to the General Board of Health, Chadwick's sense of rivalry with Southwood Smith, so evident a few years before, was rekindled. Writing to Lord Ashley to stress the widespread support for Miles's and Henley's reduction of the size of the board, he included a subtle innuendo against Southwood Smith: "If in the House there were a chance of replacing the two paid Commissioners that would be desirable; but as you are aware many have a most unjust prejudice against Medical Commissionerships."[57] Chadwick's strategy throughout was to appear as Southwood Smith's advocate, while strongly suggesting that it would be quite impossible to procure the doctor's appointment. To Sir George de Larpent, for example, he insisted that all his influence was being exerted for Southwood Smith, "who has labored at the cause from the commencement, and yet I regret that for him, I see no chance of his obtaining the position due to him and to his further services."[58]

The reason Chadwick stressed the impossibility of Southwood Smith's appointment is that it was far from impossible, even with only a single paid commissionership. The doctor was widely regarded as a leading light of the sanitary movement, had many influential friends, and was not completely dependent on Chadwick's good offices. During the passage of the general bill in the 1847 session, he got his good friend Charles Dickens to write Lords Lansdowne and Normanby on his behalf.[59] Chadwick's anxiety became acute at the end of June when several articles appeared in the *Examiner* expressing dismay regarding the rumor that Southwood Smith would not receive the paid post under the act. The doctor was extolled as the real founder of the public-health movement, and it was asserted that it was his early seminal reports "which led to Mr. Chadwick's well-known general report on the sanitary condition of the labouring population."[60] Trying to control his fury, Chadwick wrote to Southwood Smith protesting "such a course of writing and misstatement" and promising a fuller criticism to follow.[61] A few days later, Chadwick angrily asserted that the sanitary movement had grown out of his own labors in the poor law. Moreover, Southwood Smith owed his reputation to Chadwick:

> I believe that in every instance in which you have been engaged on similar public service, it has been on my recommendation. I am unaware of having received any suggestion or testimony from you, to which your name does not appear, and your friends will find no ground for accusing me of indisposition to do justice to your own labour, or those of others.[62]

Chadwick's touchy sense of his one preeminence had been thoroughly roused, and the incident would not soon be forgotten, but Southwood Smith persisted in his quest for a position. When he suggested his appointment as secretary to the board, or as head of a medical department, Chadwick fired back a remarkably vituperative letter unmentioned by Finer and only briefly alluded to by R. A. Lewis. After castigating the distortions being bandied about by the doctor's friends and by the press, Chadwick launched his direct attack:

> . . . I think the position is one incompatible with your habits and that you would fail in it. I must say that in pressing you as I have done from time to time for public employment I have had much to bear up against. One point which I would allude to has been slowness, or as it is expressed, dilatoriness in the disposal of business. . . . The towns will get greatly impatient if immediate attention be not given to them. I am apprehensive of the excess of work that may be brought upon the commission and whensoever that came, I am quite sure you would be harassed with conflicting claims beyond anything you have hitherto experienced, and would be driven from your position.

While this may have been a brutally accurate characterization of Southwood Smith's qualifications for the secretaryship, Chadwick's rejection of the proposed medical department grew out of his own anti-medical bias: "The immediate and pressing need will be for engineering. The medical demand seems to be collateral." Finally, admitting himself to be "anxious and harassed in relation to yourself," Chadwick grudgingly held out the offer of a post as medical inspector.[63] Jealous and angry as he was, there was no intention of excluding Southwood Smith altogether. The latter's talents and public standing would be quite useful to the board. Moreover, even Chadwick realized that with the impending onslaught of cholera the medical demand could hardly be considered "collateral." Southwood Smith would soon enter through a side door—a provision in the Nuisances Removal Act permitting the appointment of a medical member of the board.

8 The Frustrations and Illusions of Power: The General Board of Health

With the passage of the Public Health Act of 1848 (11 & 12 Vict., c. 63), Chadwick entered upon an executive position for the first time in his sixteen-year career as a public official. It is true that the board had been stripped of some of its vital coercive powers and, like the Poor Law Commission in 1834, its life span was confined to five years. But thanks in part to Chadwick's lobbying, it still possessed sufficient authority to begin the reformation of England's sanitary institutions. Some of his enemies were hopeful that he and the board would be powerless. G. C. Lewis wrote to Sir Edmund Head that Chadwick was the paid commissioner, "where I hope he may remain quiet." Lewis went on to speculate that the board "was so emasculated by Henley in Committee that its powers will not amount to much in practice."[1] This was wishful thinking—the board still possessed some teeth, and these would not go unused, particularly when directed by a man who was never content to remain quiet for long.

As to his unpaid colleagues on the board, Chadwick knew that Lord Morpeth would be one, since the act assigned the First Commissioner of Woods and Forests the presidency of the board ex-officio. Hoping the other appointment would go to someone accustomed to accepting his directions, he pushed for Bishop Blomfield. This was vetoed by Morpeth, who told Chadwick that Blomfield could devote little time to the board and "just possibly we might have some hitch about Dissenting cooperation."[2] The government's surprise choice was Lord Ashley, who anticipated in his diary the tribulations of the post with great accuracy: "It will involve trouble, anxiety, reproach, abuse, unpopularity; I shall become a target for private assault and the Public Press; but how could I refuse?"[3] Chadwick's reaction may have been mixed, since Ashley, while a close ally in public-health matters during the past several years, was as proud, blunt, and opinionated as Chadwick himself, with a strong dose of moral unctiousness thrown in for good measure. At any rate, Chadwick sent a long letter expressing his unqualified delight at the appointment, and the partnership was to prove remarkably smooth. With the naming of that reliable Chadwickian Henry Austin as secretary and Alexander Bain as assistant secretary, the General Board of Health, headquartered at Gwydyr House, was ready to commence operations.

Since Ashley was unable to attend for the first two months, Chadwick and Morpeth opened proceedings officially at the end of September. At that first meeting, the appearance of cholera at Hull was reported, and the board asked the government to invoke sections 9 and 10 of the Nuisances Removal and Disease Prevention Act.[4] This act permitted the adding of a medical member to the board, and Southwood Smith took his seat a week later.[5] For the next year, the bulk of the board's time and energy would be taken up with the epidemic, with the consequence that from the outset England's thinly manned new central sanitary administration was overworked, harried, and prone to physical collapse. Chadwick was no exception, and Lord Ebrington soon had to warn him to "take more care of your own health and that of your officers or you will get the name of the Board of Ill Health."[6] Even the "dilatory" Southwood Smith worked extremely hard, though Chadwick was at first disposed to maintain his highly critical stance. The earliest criticism came five days before Southwood Smith's appointment and concerned the draft circular of instructions to local authorities for dealing with cholera. In the section on diet, the doctor had recommended wine, which Chadwick complained to Morpeth was "contrary to the best medical opinion."[7]

Such paltry matters were soon overshadowed by events. The seriousness of the epidemic and the opposition to the board's methods of dealing with it produced a siege mentality at Gwydyr House, with Chadwick increasingly appreciative of having the steady and faithful

Southwood Smith at his side. When the latter's circular was sent out to the boards of guardians at the end of October, it produced sarcastic criticism from the medical professionals and foot-dragging by local authorities. Informed by the "miasma" theory of disease propagation, the circular called on guardians to identify and cleanse the worst places, provide house-to-house visitation, remove the unafflicted to houses of refuge, and administer constipative drugs to prevent "premonitory diarrhoea." In the host of conflicting theories about the origin and spread of cholera, any set of procedures was bound to arouse opposition. Where the procedures were followed, they were accompanied by some reduction of the incidence of the disease, and Finer is no doubt correct that the board did "some of the right things for reasons mostly wrong."[8]

The chief problem was that many boards of guardians, always chary of incurring expense and sensitive to being controlled, refused to act. Without coercive powers, the board could do little but urge and cajole. By the start of 1849, the epidemic seemed to peter out, leaving fewer than one thousand dead throughout the country, far from the fearsome toll that had been anticipated. But the full fury of the cholera struck with the warmth of spring and continued unabated through the summer. This time, thirty-five thousand died, fifteen thousand in London alone. Chadwick's response, on the Metropolitan Commission of Sewers, was to insist on flushing all "miasmatic" deposits into the Thames, thereby rapidly spreading the disease and earning him some of the strongest rebukes he ever received from *The Times*.[9] A measure of control over the contagion was achieved by Ashley, who pushed through an amended Nuisances Removal Act giving the board new powers to appoint medical inspectors and to compel the guardians to appoint medical visitors. But the board was checked in its attempt to close down, by special orders, the worst metropolitan burial grounds. The vestries won a signal legal victory in September, the court ruling that the board lacked the authority to close the cemeteries.[10] In one sense the point was moot, for the death rate had begun to fall off very sharply, and by November the visitation was over, not to reappear until 1853. In a more important sense, however, it was not a moot point, for London's burial grounds continued to be one of the most pressing of the major sanitary problems, cholera or no cholera. Moreover, the struggle had further exacerbated the strained relationship between the London vestries and the two Chadwick-dominated boards. Chadwick became, if possible, even more obsessive about forcing his program on London, and Ashley shared this obsession. The struggle was to be fought over the issues of water supply and interment, and was to result in the destruction of the board.

Before turning to these issues, it would be well to consider the policies and actions of Lord Morpeth, the president of the General Board of Health. Morpeth, who became the Earl of Carlisle on his father's death in October 1848, has been depicted by both Finer and R. A. Lewis as genial, competent, and well-meaning, but always prepared to allow Chadwick to control the board.[11] But their relationship was a good deal more complex. Morpeth was a knowledgeable and self-assured Whig nobleman who did not shrink from frequent rebukes of his strong-willed colleague. As we have seen, he rejected Chadwick's suggestion to appoint Blomfield to the board. Before the board even commenced its labors, Morpeth warned that he would not always go along with Chadwick because of his greater sense "of the most practicable modes of dealing successfully with Parliaments and Bodies of men."[12] Such political sagacity was a vitally important quality if the Public Health Act were to succeed. To the extent that it did succeed it is chiefly Morpeth who should get the credit. He did much to appease opponents of the measure in Parliament, and in this respect his move to the House of Lords as Earl of Carlisle in October 1848 was unfortunate. He also insisted on a conciliatory tone in official communications, such as the first circular sent to boards of guardians, which Chadwick had drafted in his usual peremptory style:

> With respect to the spirit of the whole—I imagine the regulations are for the most part very sound and judicious, but it is quite manifest that they will be very partially obeyed; this could no more be looked to be otherwise, than in the case of a sermon which gave strict rules for the conduct and conscience, could we hope that the congregation at large would go away and forthwith comply with all the admonitions given to them. I think it therefore most desirable that we should make the regulations more in the form of indication and recommendation than of unequivocal and universal command.

Lest Chadwick should be prone to consider this merely advisory, Carlisle concluded: "I am sorry for any delay this may occasion, but I consider it absolutely essential."[13]

Carlisle had to throttle Chadwick not only on the board but also on the Metropolitan Commission of Sewers. On the latter body, as we have seen, Chadwick allowed himself to be needled by the obstructionist tactics of John Leslie, one of the London vestrymen appointed by Carlisle to placate the opposition. Upon the reconstitution of the commission in October 1848, Chadwick tried to exclude Leslie, but Carlisle was adamant and attempted to instill some sense of political reality into Chadwick:

> I am entirely convinced of the thoroughly public-motivated spirit of all you do, and I can quite understand how particular people may thwart, annoy, offend, obstruct; but where is the work we can expect to do without a mixture of these elements. I sometimes think that people who have not been in Parliament are more intolerant of this species of opposition and obstruction than we who are seasoned to it.[14]

This sage advice fell, as usual, on deaf ears. Chadwick's obsession with the Leslie faction intensified, and there was little Carlisle could do beyond the sort of rebuke he administered in December 1848 when an intemperate article appeared in the *Observer* and he suspected that Chadwick had written it: "We have difficulties enough on our hands with protracted polemics, and there is no good to be gained from keeping up embittering enmities."[15] Chadwick replied combatively that the article would be unpleasant to those attacked, "but as they are trying to raise enmities by delusion, to remove the delusion is to diminish and allay the enmities. . . . "[16]

If Chadwick had confined his attacks to Leslie and his cronies, he might have succeeded. But he also criticized the permanent officials of the Metropolitan Commission of Sewers, thus alienating many engineers and allowing Leslie to pose as their champion. This dispute became particularly bitter when Chadwick sought to prevent staff pay raises. It also left him open to the charge of hypocrisy, since he was lobbying assiduously to raise his own salary as a paid member of the General Board of Health. During the bill's passage, the paid commissionership was first announced at £1,000, then changed to £1,500, and ended up at £1,200. This was the same salary Chadwick had been receiving as secretary to the Poor Law Commission, and he groused to Carlisle about the need for a "market rate of payment" and the indignities he suffered when having to deal with local officials who made as much as or more than he. Carlisle had in fact already secured from Russell an increase to £1,500, but warned Chadwick that the old officers of the sewers commission with augmented duties would also receive raises and that he must not protest.[17]

The breach with Leslie and the officials widened even further in January 1849 when Roe retired as chief consulting engineer for the Metropolitan Commission of Sewers. It was widely expected that Phillips, the other surveyor for the commission, would be appointed, but Chadwick gave it instead to his protégé, Henry Austin. Apart from his closeness to Austin (who was also secretary to the General Board of Health), Chadwick much preferred Austin's plan for the drainage of London to that of Phillips. It provided for steam-pumping of sewerage, extensive use of glazed, small-bore earthenware pipes, and made use of sewer manure.[18] There were many perfectly valid reasons for preferring Austin's plan, but given the prevailing spirit in the commission, Chadwick's act was seen as blatantly and outrageously partisan. The aggrieved Phillips brought charges before the commission and in the pages of *The Times,* and the whole affair became a lurid sideshow to the raging cholera epidemic of 1849. Throughout this incident, Carlisle seems to have supported Chadwick, doubtless because he too believed Austin's plan to be superior. Carlisle, it must be stressed, did not automatically accept Chadwick's sanitary dogma, and read widely in the technical literature of the day. On one occasion he sent along a paper challenging Chadwick's deeply held anti-contagionist views: "Here you will read a very contagionist paper. I am not clear that we have been quite ingenuous on that head, as we have seemed to infer that all the evidence was against contagion."[19]

The strategy Chadwick devised for dealing with the opposition was to divide up the commission into committees, isolating Leslie and his supporters on the relatively powerless finance committee, while the totally Chadwickian works committee exercised the real authority. This high-handed procedure infuriated the vestries and London opinion in general. It also brought from Carlisle an expression of exasperation and a threat to quit, for "I cannot endure bad blood and squabbles among ourselves, and if they go on I shall run away from both Boards, they (the Boards) being the only things which have retained me hitherto in my present office."[20] The affair escalated into an appeal by the opposition to the law-officers for an opinion, and to farcical maneuvers by Chadwick, who had the opposition misinformed as to the time and place of commission meetings. All of this occurred while Phillips was insistently bringing his rejected drainage plan before the public, *The Times* was thundering against Chadwick, and the cholera was raging.[21] This unseemly squabble, while thousands were dying each week, finally brought a measure of reason back to the proceedings of the commission, and the excluding of the opposition from the works committee was ended. Carlisle, who had never been happy with Chadwick's strategy, wrote soothingly: "I think under all the circumstances of the time, the throwing open of the Works Committee may have been a prudent step. We are sure of so many difficulties and perplexities, that the more we can diffuse the responsibility the better it may turn out."[22]

But it was too late. The Prime Minister had seen quite enough and was convinced that the Metropolitan Commission of Sewers, as constituted, was at a complete standstill and likely to bring odium upon the government. He agreed to renew the commission, but only with the provision that Chadwick, Leslie, and most of the other commissioners be removed. Carlisle, no doubt relieved at this withdrawal from the hornet's nest, told Chadwick that "the course decided upon is under present circumstances the most prudent for the Government, for the Board of Health, and for yourself."[23] But he was soon disabused of the hope that Chadwick would put the unhappy metropolitan-commission episode behind him and devote himself wholeheartedly to the labors of the General Board of Health. Chadwick continued to intrigue against the new Metropolitan Commission of Sewers, now dominated by a hostile faction of engineers. He complained of sleepless nights over the new commission's abandoning of the doctrine that house drainage and main drainage were part of the same system. Carlisle urged him not to waste time and energy, but simply to "embody your views in a temperate statement, and to hold yourself ready to impart any information that may be requested."[24]

Not only was Chadwick's feuding obsessive, he was unreconciled to losing control over London drainage. Yet this was largely due to his insistence that the Metropolitan Commission of Sewers remain appointive, making everything hinge on retaining a majority of the seats on that body. When Chadwick and his supporters were removed, he was reduced to a foolish and impotent attempt to subjugate London from Gwydyr House, issuing orders to the commission that were deeply resented and incurring another rebuke from Carlisle:

> They will give you any information you wish that they can supply, but they cannot have their officers imperiously summoned. I think they are quite right in this, and you may depend upon it no coordinate body will bear it. . . . I think it is essential to keep in mind that our inquiry is limited to water supply; sewage and drainage is their exclusive juris-diction. Only pray remember in connection with that subject that water runs best in smooth channels.[25]

A bit later, Carlisle delivered his final warning: "Pray do not be blowing sparks into flames, or I shall cut and run."[26] Shortly afterwards, utterly despairing of moderating Chadwick's course, he resigned from the General Board of Health. If anything was capable of shock-ing Chadwick into a sense of political reality and an awareness of how his behavior was undermining the sanitary cause, this should have been it. The departure of a most able, genial, loyal, and effective colleague was a major blow, but Chadwick's reply was that Carlisle "should have seen us thro' the wood" and that his "kindness was in excess for the rudeness, bad passion, and sinister interests which were opposed to us."[27]

Chadwick's ignorance of and disdain for the arts of political nego-tiation and compromise are evident, and are underscored by his frequent attempts during this period to win the support of Prince Albert. The currying of princely patronage illustrates a charge often made against him—that he would be an ideal minister to a benevo-lent despot. His first contact with the Prince Consort was in 1842, when he forwarded a copy of his Sanitary Report, pointing out the sections dealing with the town of Windsor and the drainage of the Long Walk.[28] Shortly after taking his post at the General Board of Health in 1848, he sent another letter, recommending improvements in laborers' dwellings at Osborne, which had been recently purchased by the royal couple.[29] There was a promising exchange of letters, but no commitment to allow the royal estates to be used as proving grounds for Chadwick's sanitary projects. The contact was, however, evidently responsible for his being created Companion of the Bath in 1849.[30] This honor was one of the few positive notes in Chadwick's public life during these years, and it is not surprising that he continued to exploit this favorable contact. There is a very full correspondence between Chadwick and Prince Albert (or rather with his secretary) that ended only with the prince's death in 1861. Nor is it surprising that Chadwick should have attempted to turn this contact to favorable account in his struggle with the Metropolitan Commission of Sewers. In 1851 he tried to procure the paid post on the commission for Henry Cole, the man who under the prince's direction had organized the hugely successful Great Exhibition. This was another vain attempt to gain control of the sewers commission, and Chadwick clearly hoped that with royal patronage he might get someone on the commission amenable to his control. But his own role in suggesting Cole's candidacy had to be kept secret, for reasons he explained to the prince's secretary: "I should prefer that any inquiries should be made without reference to me, unless it were necessary, for it were unnecessary to raise the jealous supposition that I suggested him to carry out some particular views of my own, of which I have none in the invidious sense."[31]

Prince Albert wisely avoided being drawn into this intrigue, which reveals Chadwick's relentless pursuit of patronage from those in exalted position as well as his ready resort to devious tactics. The episode also shows his attempt to turn the popular issues and events of the day, in this case the Great Exhibition, to his own advantage. He made similar use of the anti-Catholic hysteria that gripped the country in 1850 and 1851. This resulted from Pius IX's papal bull establishing an episcopal hierarchy in Britain, and was characterized by public demonstrations, a shrill cry of Papal Aggression from the press, and an Ecclesiastical Titles Act. Chadwick no doubt shared the average Englishman's anti-Catholic sentiments, though this had not prevented him from trying to enlist Father Matthew, the temperance reformer, as an ally in the public-health cause in 1845.[32] But in 1850, attempting to regain the favor of *The Times,* he wrote to John Delane:

> The maxim that cleanliness is next to Godliness is one which may be claimed as peculiar to the English Church. Whatever theological objections there may be to the worship of the Saints, the administrative objections which may be made to many of the Catholic Saints is, that they make filth an object of merit, as if filth were next to Godliness. Simply on civil administrative grounds I should be inclined to resist the Papal Aggression, as tending to retard the physical improvement of the population.[33]

Shortly afterwards, he wrote to the Prime Minister, stressing the important role played in the Metropolitan Sanitary Association by Church of England clergy, led by Bishop Blomfield, "whilst, although we find the Roman Catholic or Irish population of our towns, whatsoever their wages, in the lowest physical condition, yet from the Roman Catholic priests, no help is obtained to rescue them from it."[34] While anti-Catholicism was a powerful prejudice in Victorian England, even among the well-educated, it may be doubted whether Chadwick's peculiar application of it did much good, either for sanitary causes or for his own career. Ironically, his ideological enemy, Joshua Toulmin Smith, drew very different conclusions from the same prejudice:

> The Principles of Protestantism are manifestly, then, identified with the Principles of Local Self-Government; the same in idea, in spirit, in practical effect upon the life, character, and conversation. The Principles of Popery — not, necessarily, its religious faith, which is sacred to every man's soul who earnestly holds it, but its civil, social, and political pretensions — are a part of the system of Centralization, identified with every other form in which that system manifests itself in their effects on the independence and earnestness of the minds of those who bow before them.[35]

It cannot be argued that such concerns took Chadwick away from his duties at the General Board of Health. Indeed, his attendance at Gwydyr House was salutary — 1,181 meetings between September 1848 and November 1853. This compares to 1,120 for Southwood Smith and 598 for Ashley.[36] But they do reveal that alongside the steady, disciplined focus of the dedicated public official there was a certain spirit of restless, opportunistic political intrigue. It is arguable that this helped to bring discredit upon himself and the board, though certainly not to the same extent as his continuing vendetta against the Metropolitan Commission of Sewers. His growing unpopularity was also a factor in the slowing of the progress of the Public Health Act in the provinces. This was particularly unfortunate, for during the first couple of years, the board made great headway outside London. In spite of Chadwick's concerns during the bill's passage, it was frequently possible to establish a local board through the petition of 10 percent of the ratepayers. Two hundred fifteen places petitioned for the act, and the board had few occasions to resort to the death-rate clause.[37] But while the "clean party" in many towns enjoyed early victories, these were soon compromised or even reversed as the general board isolated itself through the futile efforts to conquer London.

It would be misleading to focus exclusively on Chadwick as the architect of the board's difficulties, for Ashley must bear a portion of the blame. It is difficult to imagine two individuals less suited to hold executive office, particularly in a new central agency viewed with apprehension and mistrust from the outset. Not only were both consumed with a sense of the rightness of their cause and the iniquity of their opponents, but they were woefully deficient in tact, charm, and a willingness to compromise. These qualities had been supplied at Gwydyr House by Lord Morpeth, and his departure early in 1850 left the board bereft of political skills. Things were made even worse because Morpeth's successor, Lord Seymour, seemed bent on teaching Chadwick and Ashley a lesson. Where Morpeth had quietly cajoled and soothed, Seymour provoked, challenged, and chastised his colleagues. Skeptical of the central government's role in public health, Seymour was quick to champion the cause of the London vestries and other aggrieved parties. The General Board of Health thus became a house divided. The departed Carlisle vainly appealed for conciliation: "You must take Lord Seymour quietly, and avoid occasions of clashing."[38] The most spirited clash on the board was between Ashley and Seymour, and concerned the right of the usually absent Seymour to be kept fully informed by his colleagues. Beyond this lay the constitutional question of whether Seymour, as president of the board and a cabinet minister, could be outvoted. A further issue was the degree to which the board was under the control of the Treasury. These issues are explored in depth in a frank and venomous exchange of letters in January 1851 between Ashley and Seymour, of which Chadwick received copies.[39]

To understand the constitutional issues that were raised in this dispute and why the Treasury became involved, it is necessary to examine the specific sanitary issue out of which it arose—the Interment Act of 1850. The board was able to move quickly on this issue because it already possessed, in Chadwick's Interment Report of 1843, a comprehensive analysis and a set of solutions. These, it will be recalled, would give the central government the power to forbid intramural interments as well as to provide undertaking, funeral services, and burial. All that was needed was to bring Chadwick's report up to date, and this was accomplished in the autumn of 1849 by having the board's inspectors provide supplemental illustrative material.[40] Carlisle insisted on taking on the task of convincing the cabinet of the need for such sweeping reform: "I have not I hope a high opinion of my qualifications for such a task except the single one of prudence."[41] In this instance Carlisle's prudence seems to have succeeded all too well, for the cabinet was willing to accept the plan but seems to have remained ignorant of some of its most important and controversial features. Foremost among these were the nationalization of burials and the conferring upon the General Board of Health of monopoly powers within the metropolitan area. The Treasury was also unaware of the implications of this monopoly, and it would be their reluctance to sanction loans for the general board to buy up the existing cemeteries that would touch off the most intense dispute between Ashley and Seymour.

When the provisions of the government-sponsored interment measure became known, it was clear there would be strong resistance. G. C. Lewis, informing Edmund Head of Chadwick's plan "for making the Government the universal undertaker," commented: "whatever is done, I fear that the subject will give an immensity of trouble before it is settled."[42] The trouble was not long in coming. The various affected interests as well as the defenders of local self-government began deploying their forces, though the massive public sentiment in favor of reform (including that of *The Times*) carried the bill through Parliament. The opposition could muster only sixty votes in the House of Commons,[43] but this included almost all the metropolitan M.P.s, even Chadwick's erstwhile ally Joseph Hume.[44] If the act had been a straightforward ban on intramural interment, compelling the vestries to open new graveyards in the suburbs, the London opposition would no doubt have subsided. But the radical centralizing features of the statute, especially the power vested in the General Board of Health, convinced many Londoners that this was another insidious effort by Chadwick to subjugate the capital. The opposition redoubled its efforts, lobbying assiduously in Parliament, urging the vestries to impede the act's implementation, and unleashing a flood of anti-centralizing publications.

All of this began to raise doubts about the wisdom of the enactment, but what delivered the fatal blow was the extreme fiscal conservatism of the Treasury and the skepticism of private lenders. As the full financial implications of the scheme emerged, Sir Charles Wood, the Chancellor of the Exchequer, raised a host of objections. Vast sums would have to be raised by the General Board of Health from private lenders, and these loans required Treasury sanction. Wood, surrounded by skeptical permanent officials, one of whom reportedly described Ashley and Chadwick as "no better than a couple of socialists,"[45] insisted on a piecemeal approach. He would sanction the purchase of no more than two cemeteries in the first instance, even though a government interment monopoly could not be viable without an immediate and total take-over of all the burial grounds. Chadwick made this point forcefully, but to no avail. Lord Seymour, who as first Commissioner of Woods and Forests held a position in which he was clearly subservient to the Treasury, carried the same attitude to the General Board of Health. He insisted that the board adhere to Wood's directives, and it was this issue that compounded his arguments with Ashley and raised further the issue of whether Seymour as president of the board could be outvoted by the likes of Chadwick and Southwood Smith.[46]

On top of all this, the Guardian Insurance Company, concerned that the board would expire in three years, refused to lend.[47] Typically, Chadwick lashed out at what he saw as conspiracy between the Treasury and various sinister interests. Such outbursts, coupled with the delays, the acrimonious disputes at Gwydyr House, and the mounting ideological opposition, at last turned the tide. By the end of 1851, the cabinet, thoroughly disgusted with the whole affair, determined to scrap the act. Carlisle, as usual, tried to soften the blow. He wrote to Russell that, while he was aware "that neither you or Charles Wood would much relish to see Chadwick yourselves," someone who was not ill-disposed to him should explain the cabinet's decision.[48] A new interment measure was fashioned, inherited, and enacted by Lord Derby's short-lived Conservative government in 1852, and proved much more successful. Eliminating control by the General Board of Health and the government monopoly, it simply conferred upon the Home Office the power to close down existing burial grounds. When implemented by the dedicated and skilled Lord Palmerston, who became Home Secretary in Aberdeen's government in December 1852, it provided the solution to a long-recognized evil, and without resorting to extreme and unpopular expedients.[49]

Almost simultaneously with the interment issue, Chadwick was involved in the struggle over the metropolitan water supply. His thinking had not changed since 1844—pure water must be supplied constantly and under pressure, not just for drinking and cleaning, but as the motive force for a new sewerage system composed of small-bore tubular earthenware pipes. The need for constant supply meant that virtually all the existing equipment of the eight joint-stock companies supplying London would have to be scrapped. In some of the less affluent parts of the capital, their equipment was able to provide water of appallingly bad quality only one hour per day.[50] Chadwick's grandiose scheme required vast and expensive engineering projects as well as finding new water supplies near London. Even more controversial would be the purchase or consolidation of the water companies and investing the government with extraordinary powers over water supply and drainage.

This comprehensive plan had provoked stiff opposition when Chadwick had tried to use the Metropolitan Commission of Sewers to force it on the capital. His removal from that body in September 1849 required him to implement it from Gwydyr House, just as he was doing with interments. He had been using the staff of the metropolitan commission to carry out surveys on the south bank of the Thames for new water sources, and this work, of course, ceased with his dismissal. But utilizing the data gathered up to that point, the General Board of Health prepared a report on metropolitan water supply and issued it in May 1850. Not surprisingly, this report called for consolidating the companies, providing a constant supply of water, and arterial drainage using tubular pipes. Drainage and water supply were to be administered as part of a single comprehensive system under the direction of a small professional board.[51] The most obvious targets in this report were the metropolitan commissioners and the water companies, but Chadwick also managed to antagonize many civil engineers as well. He insisted on repeatedly castigating all those who had opposed his sanitary dogma, naming such influential figures as Thomas Cubitt and Thomas Hawkesley, the latter of whom he had already locked horns with on the Towns Improvement Company. Such gratuitous attacks only multiplied Chadwick's enemies and strengthened their resolve. The engineers in particular became the mainstay of the opposition and were to play a key part in the demise of the General Board of Health.

In spite of this opposition, there were promising signs in 1850 that a water bill could be carried. Public opinion seemed to favor it, *The Times* was supportive, and Ashley secured Russell's pledge to introduce a measure in the next session. As with interments, therefore, 1850 seemed a propitious year for water reform. But delay played into the hands of the bill's opponents, who were even more powerful than those opposed to burial reform. To begin with, the eight water companies were capitalized at £5,000,000 and, it was believed, could muster nearly one hundred votes in the House of Commons.[52] Moreover, the vestries were waging a quite separate struggle to bring the companies under parochial control, and had no taste for Chadwick's centralizing solutions. The opponents created enough doubts in Russell's mind to cause him to order an independent investigation into the amount of available pure south-bank water, and the report cast some doubts on Chadwick's optimistic figures.[53] Chadwick went on the offensive by having his protégé, F. O. Ward, write an article on centralization and local government for the *Quarterly Review*. Ward, a surgeon turned journalist, had served as secretary to Joseph Hume, who evidently introduced him to Chadwick. Ward's lengthy article was ostensibly a review of the general board's annual report and special report on metropolitan water, Henry Austin's engineering report, Dr. John Simon's annual report on the sanitary state of the

City of London, the 1846 Select Committee Report on Private Bills, and Joshua Toulmin Smith's *The Laws of England Relating to Public Health*.[54] Not surprisingly, the latter publication was savaged, and defense of local government was held to be nothing but a screen for waste, corruption, and mismanagement. As the center of Empire, London was declared to be of vital importance to all citizens, and therefore "the future sanitary rulers of London should be responsible to the ratepayers through Parliament." This was an endorsement of Chadwick's small, expert, Crown-appointed body to rule London. The vestries' alternative of a popularly elected assembly to manage metropolitan sanitary affairs was held up to ridicule. A "municipal parliament" representing 176 parishes would be huge, unwieldy, inefficient, and corrupt. And might not such a body, Ward asked, "in periods of political excitement, exert a most inconvenient and unconstitutional pressure on the counsels of the Queen's Government?"[55]

Chadwick was delighted with Ward's essay and sent it along to Carlisle with the request that he show it to Russell and Sir George Grey.[56] He had good reason to be concerned about the government's commitment to water reform, for Russell had entrusted the drawing up of the bill to none other than Lord Seymour. This was yet another of the many adverse effects of the Seymour-Ashley conflict. Since Seymour, a cabinet minister, had become a minority of one on the board over which he ostensibly presided, the Prime Minister would have deeply offended him by asking the board to draw up the bill. Besides, Chadwick was more unpopular than ever, the interment act was foundering, and the water companies and vestries were making their respective cases forcefully. And since Seymour was the skeptic at Gwydyr House concerning centralized schemes, a bill fostered by him would stand a better chance of success. Russell's decision was politically judicious, but Chadwick was naturally apprehensive, particularly when Seymour turned to Sir William Clay for assistance. Clay, a Tower Hamlets M.P. and water-company owner, had served on Hume's select committee on private bills in 1846, although Chadwick had tried to keep him off. In spite of his pecuniary interest in London water, Clay was an honest and respected M.P. He was willing to promote significant reform, and had shown himself not averse to negotiation, even with Chadwick.[57] But when Grey introduced the Seymour-Clay bill as a government measure on April 29, Chadwick condemned it out of hand. It proposed to amalgamate the water companies under government control and to give the Home Secretary powers to order the use of new sources as well as water for sewering or cleansing. With amendments, it might have proved a substantial and workable first installment of metropolitan water reform, but Chadwick chose to join and even help orchestrate the chorus of abuse that greeted it. Ward was feeding Delane with material hostile to the bill, and *The Times* obligingly chimed in. The vestries had their own separate axe to grind, since the representative municipal sanitary assembly they wanted was nowhere to be found in the bill.

Battered from all sides, the water bill barely passed its second reading. Chadwick's gamble that the mounting tide of criticism would compel the cabinet to accept his measure did not pay off. Delane, finally aware that Ward was Chadwick's puppet, shifted the support of *The Times* to the vestries' measure. In the confusion, the bill had to be postponed until the next session of Parliament. But in 1852 Derby's Conservative government brought in and enacted a far worse bill. It left the separate companies, prohibited drawing Thames water from below Teddington Lock, and required filtering and the covering of reservoirs. But there was no effective control, and constant supply was all but abandoned—four-fifths of the customers in any area had to petition before it could be required.[58] Oddly, there was very little activity at Gwydyr House to oppose this disastrous bill. Having helped insure that the "half a loaf" measure of 1851 did not pass, Chadwick seems almost to have washed his hands of the water question. Indeed, as early as June 1851, Chadwick had told Ward that he would have to shoulder the burden of the water campaign, since the crisis in interments required all of his attention.

Ward, along with the leaders of the Metropolitan Sanitary Association, did what he could to agitate for meaningful water legislation, while Chadwick not only remained aloof but cast a critical eye on his allies. When Ward dutifully sent an article of Chadwick's to the *Chronicle* for publication, he included a cover letter describing Chadwick as "one of the ablest of the sanitary party." Someone in his beleaguered position should have been gratified by such positive public notice, but Chadwick's response was stiff and indignant: "To this I reply that for myself as a public officer, I must belong to no party, that socially I may move amongst a party but not be of them."

He even prevented the clerks and inspectors of the General Board of Health from attending Metropolitan Sanitary Association meetings, "and have endeavoured to keep at a distance from them myself." But, he admitted, even Shaftesbury (as Ashley had become after succeeding to the earldom in 1851) chided him for his "purism."[59] Few incidents reveal so well Chadwick's tendency to distance himself, at critical moments in his career, from movements that might have brought him success. At this juncture, his aloofness seems to be combined with almost a sense of fatalism, as if there were nothing he could do to salvage his program. After the Derby government's interment and water measures passed, he mused about the impending "close of my labours in sanitary works."[60]

This spell of paralysis proved temporary, and Chadwick's customary combativeness was much in evidence during the final two years of the General Board of Health. His chief antagonists during this period were the engineers who controlled the Metropolitan Commission of Sewers. They had won control of London with Chadwick's exclusion from the commission and his reverses on water and interment legislation. At stake was Chadwickian dogma on house and main drainage, which the engineers held to be erroneous. Their opposition was based partly on differences of sanitary theory, but more on professional pique—the resentment of a group of proud, self-assured men at being dictated to in their area of expertise by a lawyer-administrator. If they could succeed in discrediting Chadwick's tubular drainage system, the progress of the Public Health Act in the provinces might be slowed or even reversed. Beyond a powerful desire to strike any blows they could at their enemy, the engineers had a more immediate reason for concerning themselves with the operation of the local boards. Chadwick was using the 119th clause of the Public Health Act, requiring General Board of Health sanction for the loans on any projects undertaken by local boards, to strike at his opponents. The local boards tended to take the path of least resistance by simply hiring the general board's inspectors as their consulting engineers, a dubious practice that Chadwick accepted and even encouraged. Thus a large amount of patronage at the disposal of local boards was being denied to the metropolitan commission engineers, their allies, and friends.

Chadwick was especially vindictive in regard to his old nemesis,

Thomas Hawkesley, driving him from one position at Coventry and harrying him in others.[61] This vendetta was particularly ill-advised, for Hawkesley, the most respected waterworks engineer of the day, devoted himself to Chadwick's overthrow. He published a long, sarcastic critique of the General Board of Health's *Minutes on House Drainage* and circulated it throughout the country. He encouraged the metropolitan commission in a campaign to pull up some of the tubular drains that had been installed in London. When some of these proved to be cracked and clogged, this was widely trumpeted as a refutation of Chadwick's system. The same "lesson" was drawn from a serious outbreak of fever at Croydon, a town that had been sewered by a Chadwickian local board.[62] The struggle wore on, with ever more strident reports and counter-reports. In the end, Chadwick's basic system was largely vindicated, and the great majority of the local boards expressed satisfaction. No doubt this was due in part to the fact that it cost only one-third as much to sewer a town with the new than with the old system. But even the most cheeseparing local authority would not have persisted unless there were positive results, and by 1851 some twenty-six hundred miles of the new tubular pipe had been produced.[63]

It might seem that, having surmounted this challenge by the engineers to the soundness of the tubular drainage system, the General Board of Health could anticipate the renewal of its powers at the expiration of its five-year term. But this was far from the case. Much damage had been done by the controversy, and the "dirty party" had everywhere taken heart from the vigor of the engineers' assault. Moreover, while Seymour did not return to Gwydyr House when the Aberdeen government came to power in December 1852, the new president, Sir William Molesworth, was almost as bad. This was a great shock to Chadwick, for Molesworth was an old Philosophic Radical and an erstwhile friend from *London Review* days. Molesworth announced publicly that he would not apply the Public Health Act where a majority of the ratepayers opposed it—a statement that made nonsense of the one-tenth petition clause.[64] Fortunately for the board, Molesworth's presence was largely offset by the vigor and support of Lord Palmerston at the Home Office. In addition to being Shaftesbury's father-in-law, Palmerston was an able and effective Home Secretary who, among other things, took the initiative in sending out questionnaires to the local boards to determine the effectiveness of tubular drains.[65] Ebrington, who had been forced out of his position as head of the Metropolitan Sanitary Commission, told Chadwick that he wished Palmerston instead of Molesworth was president of the General Board of Health, "indeed we want him at the head of any department almost foreign and domestic—or better still at the head of all as Prime Minister."[66]

For all his helpfulness to the board and commitment to sanitary improvement, however, Palmerston was a political realist who recognized that the board as constituted and staffed stood little chance of renewal. He did manage to secure a one-year extension in 1853, and then set about in earnest to devise a more workable and acceptable structure of central sanitary administration. Russell, who after a brief stint as Foreign Secretary was now a Minister without Office in Aberdeen's cabinet, suggested replacing the board by a president with a seat in Parliament assisted by two paid secretaries.[67] Shaftesbury, who was also consulted about the impending change, replied to Palmerston:

> I should have no hesitation in giving an equally decided opinion that, for the Public Service, the Board should remain as it is. We shall never find men to replace Chadwick and Southwood, in whom great knowledge, experience, and indefatigable zeal are so combined; and the service of a President, changeable on every change of Government, aided by two secretaries, will give a very different result from the continuous and undivided attention of men such as those whom I have mentioned.[68]

In spite of his son-in-law's plea, Palmerston proceeded with working up a bill that would place the board firmly under the Home Secretary. Even the legislative draftsman queried him on how the removal of the board's independence would be interpreted: "Will not this be in the nature of a censure upon the present Board? Unless it has been found by experience that they have abused this power, why should the new board be placed under the absolute control of the Secretary of State?" Palmerston replied curtly: "Everybody agrees that the Board must be reconstructed and represented by some responsible organ in Parliament."[69] Sending a copy of his bill to Russell, Palmerston expressed a distaste for independent boards and stressed his belief that the Home Secretary should watch over the health of the country.[70]

In preparation for the parliamentary campaign, Chadwick worked up a vindicating report in May 1854 which, as expected, excoriated all the board's enemies. Some four thousand copies of this highly charged political document were circulated throughout the country, and only served to increase the opposition's resolve.[71] A quiet lobbying effort was also undertaken, but with little success. One of those approached was C. N. Newdegate, a Tory M.P. for North Warwickshire and a leading figure in the anti-Catholic movement. While Chadwick shared Newdegate's religious prejudices, it was clear that Newdegate had no enthusiasm for Chadwick's centralizing ideas:

> I think it destroys self-reliance and prevents individuals of good capacity in their several spheres exercising that amount of independent authority, subject of course to the law and public opinion of their localities, which affords the only inducement to persons in the middle classes to act upon some more generous principles than those of mere self-interest; I fear nothing more than the loss of public spirit, and this is the effect of centralization.[72]

Such an ardently held belief in the virtues of local self-government was a powerful force opposing the bill. So was the more direct and personal opposition based on a dislike of the members of the General Board of Health. This was expressed curtly by Macaulay, to whom Chadwick was simply a "knave," and Shaftesbury "one of the tools that knaves do work with."[73] These privately expressed views were echoed many times over by the public clamor. Chadwick's enemies pulled out all the stops, and *The Times* indulged in some of its most scathing rebukes.[74] It is small wonder that Chadwick's health broke down once again, to the extent that his friend Dr. Hodgson advised him "to seek some alteration in his position which would relieve him from part of his constant and laborious exertions in the public service. . . ."[75]

The breakdown in Chadwick's health offered, if not a graceful exit, at least a face-saving expedient. Palmerston was able to go into the second reading with Chadwick's resignation in his pocket—in fact with Shaftesbury's and Southwood Smith's as well.[76] Thus armed, Palmerston was confident of carrying the bill, but he had failed to measure the depth and intensity of metropolitan opposition. After several delays, the second reading took place on July 31. With a nod toward the anti-centralizing mood of the House, Palmerston declared that the purpose of the General Board of Health

> was to create in towns and in districts local boards, self-governing, composed of persons belonging to the respective towns or districts, who, by their knowledge of the particular condition, and by the information they might acquire themselves, or obtain from the General Board, might be in a position to make effectual those arrangements, and to adopt those precautions, necessary for securing, as far as human relations may do it, the health of the quarter committed to their charge.[77]

To further mollify opponents, he pointed out that the board was to be renewed for only two years, or one if the House preferred, and would be firmly under the Home Office. Finally, Palmerston announced that all three board members had offered to resign.[78] The most effective speech opposing the bill was, predictably, from Lord Seymour, who accused the board of arrogance, extravagance, and a lust for power.[79] Russell, in defending the bill, actually agreed with Seymour on the board's "exaggerated views on the subject of central powers, and on the mode in which those powers could be used in this country." With respect to Chadwick, whose name had already come up several times in the debate, Russell told the House that he had warned him twenty years before "that he did not take sufficiently into account the habits of self-government of this country, and the desire there was in all local bodies to continue that government in their own hands."[80]

With cabinet ministers defending their own bill in terms such as these, it is not surprising that the opposition redoubled its efforts. The House had been thin at the start of the morning session, but during the debate one metropolitan M.P. after another took his seat. Whether or not this was the result of a London plot to overturn the board[81] is open to question, but Chadwick's supporters now sought in vain to stave off defeat. James Heywood, a Liberal M.P. from north Lancashire and a distant relative, announced that Chadwick had authorized him to state that his doctors "had recommended him not to continue in the Board."[82] But iron-clad guarantees were demanded, and by none other than Chadwick's long-time ally Joseph Hume, who, "before giving his vote, wished to know whether, if this Bill was read a second time, the Government would undertake as soon as possible to remove Mr. Chadwick, and to reform the constitution of the Board." Palmerston, who never dreamed he would be pressed so hard, was forced to reply that, after his own speech and Heywood's statement, "there need be no longer any question about that gentleman."[83] Even this failed to assuage the aroused opposition, and the bill went down to defeat by a vote of 74 to 65.

Having flexed its muscle so dramatically, the opposition was content to allow the board, stripped of many of its powers and of course its old members, to be renewed on a year-by-year basis. They also relented sufficiently to vote Chadwick a pension of £1,000 a year. But nothing could mask the magnitude of the defeat. His enemy Sir Benjamin Hall was the new president of the board, and the vestries and engineers exulted. So, too, did much of the press. Always an avid and anxious newspaper reader, Chadwick kept a clipping from a Manchester paper that gleefully pointed out the key role played by Hume in his downfall.[84] *The Times,* beside itself with joy, indulged in extravagant mockery of the fallen official.[85] Among the more perceptive leading articles was one that appeared in the *Economist* and was added to his collection of clippings: "We know scarcely any public man to whom the country has been more indebted. His industry is something frightful. His pertinacity is something more terrible still." Then, however, after enumerating the great services he had performed as an investigator, the editorial continued:

> These services are vast; — but there Mr. Chadwick's powers of usefulness end. In spite of his extensive information, in spite of his great sagacity, in spite of his wonderful and unwearied industry, in spite of his sincere benevolence, he has one mental peculiarity which utterly disqualifies him for the executive services of his country. He is essentially a despot and a bureaucrat. He thinks that people ought to be well

> governed, but does not believe in the possibility of their governing themselves well. He would coerce them to their own good.

The perfect place for a man of his genius, the editorial concluded, would be Russia, where self-government was completely unknown. Upon that country's certain defeat in the Crimean War, Britain should send Chadwick there "to preside over and reform her corrupt but far stretching bureaucracy."[86]

9   After the Fall: Chadwick's Legacy

I n spite of the magnitude of the victory of the engineers, vestries, and anti-centralizers in 1854, it was not
clear for many years that it marked the termination of Chadwick's
career as a public official. Never content to remain idle, he spent a
good deal of his time writing articles and delivering papers before
learned societies. He also continued to struggle for the next quarter
of a century to re-acquire authority and influence, either as an official
or as a member of Parliament. Before these often frustrating public
activities are recounted, it should be noted that Chadwick's private life
continued to prove deeply satisfying. His marriage was a happy one,
Rachel supplying in full measure the wit, charm, and spontaneity he
lacked. While his personality and obsessive work habits must have
made him a sometimes difficult husband and father, it is clear that he
was devoted to his family. His children were certainly a source of
satisfaction. Osbert, who died in 1913, became an eminent civil
engineer, while Marion (died 1928) took an active role in the women's
rights movement, a cause which her father strongly supported. There
were no financial worries, and life seems to have been serene, comfortable, and happy at Park Cottage, East Sheen, Surrey. But it was
Chadwick's nature that, despite this domestic tranquility, he continued
to strive for power or at least vindication in the public arena.

In the immediate aftermath of his fall from power, Chadwick felt
considerable bitterness at the sight of his triumphant enemies in

control of both the General Board of Health and the new Metropolitan Board of Works. But neither of these bodies functioned as disastrously as he anticipated, thanks in part to the continuity of some of the permanent staff and in part to some excellent appointments, like that of Dr. John Simon, who was created medical officer of the General Board of Health (Southwood Smith's old post) in 1855. Simon had proved an extremely effective medical officer for the City of London, and his zeal for public health was matched by his tact, discretion, and persuasiveness. These distinctly un-Chadwickian qualities had converted or neutralized many enemies to the cause. He was on cordial terms with the management of *The Times,* which sang his praises as it denounced Chadwick. Simon was frequently cited as an example of how much progress could be achieved by non-doctrinaire officials of local government in contrast to the overbearing bureaucrats of central government.[1] His conciliatory manner extended to Chadwick, but there is no evidence that Chadwick reciprocated the kind message Simon sent to him as he assumed his new post at the general board in 1855: "I wish I could flatter myself that the news would be received by you with *unmixed* satisfaction: for I have always so unfeignedly considered you the father of our sanitary party in England, that I should greatly have valued your *entire* approval of my appointment."[2]

When the General Board of Health was at length dismantled in 1858, its functions were divided among the Privy Council, the Home Office, and the Poor Law Board, seemingly a further victory for the anti-centralizers.[3] But since Simon moved on to the post of medical officer of the Privy Council, significant advances continued to be made. In fact, as Anthony Wohl points out, the Privy Council Medical Department proved to be a more effective organ of central power than the General Board of Health.[4] The irony of this situation for Chadwick was that for many years he had been calling for a public-health executive under the Privy Council. But the arrangement after 1858, with its emphasis on the medical aspects and control by a doctor, was also a repudiation of Chadwick's idea. In spite of Chadwick's persistent efforts to keep the medical side of public health "collateral" (as he had expressed it to Southwood Smith in 1848), the doctors had emerged at the forefront of the movement. This was symbolized by the formation in 1856 of the Metropolitan Association of Medical

Officers of Health, a highly influential body that eventually included half the MOHs in the country. While Chadwick was granted honorary membership, the organization steadfastly refused to change its name to the Society for the Promotion of Public Health.[5] Even the much maligned Metropolitan Board of Works, one of the fruits of the anti-centralizers' victory in 1855, was a more effective body than Chadwick and other detractors would acknowledge, as a masterful study by the late David Owen has shown.[6]

There was more to Chadwick's opposition to the new central and metropolitan sanitary organs than their domination by his enemies or their alleged inefficiency. Structurally they represented a chaotic patchwork of authorities, with duplication of some services and gaps in others, but few outside his own circle seemed to share his contempt for this lack of system and symmetry. Lovers of "traditional English liberties" tended rather to boast of this state of affairs, and Parliament had vindicated this widespread sentiment. Chadwick, unable to mobilize support under the banner of centralization and tidiness, turned instead to the powerful movement for civil-service reform. This had sprung to life with the revelations of massive incompetence in both the military and the civil service during the opening year of the Crimean War. The leaders of the newly formed Administrative Reform Association were middle-class businessmen disgusted with the ineptitude and inefficiency of the bureaucracy, and Chadwick played no part in its early stages. But he was quick to appreciate the usefulness of the organization and was soon enlisted as their chief publicist and pamphleteer. His participation was not without a measure of discomfort and irony, as R. A. Lewis notes: "Chadwick himself was a somewhat strange ally for a businessman's league, and he must have listened with a mixture of feelings when Samuel Morley, voicing the creed of the self-reliant capitalist, asserted that 'the only true theory of Reform was this—to seek to have less rather than more government'."[7] Actually Chadwick himself had displayed, as will be recalled, a rather anti-government view during his involvement with the Towns Improvement Company. Yet his pamphlets for the association were ardently pro-government. They were also perfect opportunities for getting back at his enemies, and he could not resist using George Cornewall Lewis and Lord Seymour as glaring examples of the need for reform.[8]

Chadwick was also active in promoting the reforming impulses that grew out of the Northcote-Trevelyan report, even though, as with the Administrative Reform Association, he had nothing to do with its inception. Sir Charles Trevelyan, permanent assistant secretary to the Treasury, was in 1848 given the task of inquiring into the internal operations of the Treasury and instituting reforms. These were successfully initiated the next year, and by the early 1850s Trevelyan had expanded his investigation to other departments. Sir Stafford Northcote, formerly Gladstone's private secretary, was brought in as his partner in the inquiry. Their report, issued in 1853, recommended civil-service exams for entry and promotion, with a demarcation between those grades requiring only a "mechanical" clerical ability and the higher reaches of the service, where intellectual prowess was desirable.[9] In July 1854, as Chadwick's own administrative career was in its terminal phase, he submitted a couple of papers to Trevelyan on the need for civil-service reform, calling for a special committee of Privy Councillors "selected for their interest in the subject and their known superiority to common party motives" to supervise the reform.[10] While this idea and the strongly pro-government tone of Chadwick's paper were compatible with the Northcote-Trevelyan report, Trevelyan had little use for Chadwick, who had carried out a protracted struggle with the Treasury over money for the interment measure. The irascible, hard-working Trevelyan, temperamentally very similar to Chadwick,[11] had written disparagingly of him as a reckless spendthrift who "had never shown any feeling about the public money except to get as much as he could of it," which alone "disqualified him from holding office."[12] Moreover, Trevelyan was the brother-in-law of Macaulay, whose contempt for Chadwick was noted in the last chapter.

Chadwick was aware of Trevelyan's antipathy, but this did not discourage his attempt to co-opt the reform movement, especially the insistence on competitive examinations. Benjamin Jowett, an eminent Oxford classicist and later Master of Balliol College, had been brought into the Northcote-Trevelyan inquiry to advise on the type of examinations that should be required for the higher levels of the civil service, and not surprisingly the recommendations favored candidates with a strong background in classics. Trevelyan approved this approach as a way to strengthen what he called "our aristocratic institutions."[13] Chadwick was aware that Gladstone and other reformers supported the movement because they believed it would have precisely this result, and in one of the Administrative Reform Association pamphlets he even employed a similar argument:

> The fact is, that at present only a small proportion of the whole mass of patronage has been obtained by the representatives of the county constituencies or by persons of high position, and that a larger and increasing proportion has been obtained for the constituencies of the smaller boroughs by persons of the lowest condition; and however high the present social position of the Service, I should say that the proposed measures might be supported as being needed, and as calculated to check its downward social tendency produced by the present system of patronage.[14]

These sentiments, however, were only superficially like those of Jowett or Trevelyan, for Chadwick wanted the examinations for the higher ranks to test for the kind of expertise relevant to the department in question, rather than for general intellectual development. This opened up the possibility of government by a meritocracy of specialists selected without regard to social background, a system which Chadwick believed would have permitted him to rise to the top.

Aside from the generalist versus specialist dimension of the issue was the question of social standing, and its relationship to character. Many of the Whigs, imbued with the ideal of the "gentleman" exercising authority by virtue of breeding, education, and character, were disquieted by Chadwick's version of civil-service reform. That very Whiggish inspector of mines H. S. Tremenheere[15] warned him:

> Take care in your (if it is your) proposed new mode of appointing civil servants to offices of Trust, that you do not get uncommon clever fellows from some third rate place of Education, who will sell public documents to the first newspaper that offers a good price, just at the moment when nobody ought to know anything about them. It is not now

done by Mr. Octavius Fifthursulinus, who goes to Almacks' on £90 a year, because if he did he would never appear there again and his Father would blow his brains out.[16]

The fear that the "aristocratical institutions" Trevelyan sought to bolster would be jeopardized should the system develop in a Chadwickian direction led Russell and the other Whig ministers to oppose the reform.[17] Accordingly, the examination system of the Civil Service Commission, established by an order-in-Council in May 1855, was only voluntary and advisory; the basic patronage system remained intact. The reformers kept up the pressure against a most reluctant Palmerston to make the system truly open and competitive. An advisory motion to this effect was passed in the House of Commons in 1856, to Chadwick's particular delight, since it had been stoutly resisted by his old nemesis George Cornewall Lewis, the Chancellor of the Exchequer.[18] This turned out to be a hollow victory, however, as the government took no steps to implement the motion. In fact, the momentum of the reform movement had already begun to wane with the concluding of the war, and the Administrative Reform Association fell into disarray. With it went Chadwick's hope of riding the crest of the movement back into a position of authority.

Even before the civil-service reform movement showed signs of flagging, Chadwick had been trying to get something going on another front—the revival of interest in police reform. As we have seen, he always claimed that the 1839 constabulary report was only a first installment and was meant to be followed by an inquiry directed to methods of prevention rather than repression. The Melbourne ministry had bungled the 1839 act, but he hoped that Palmerston might prove willing to set things right. Shortly before Chadwick's ouster from the General Board of Health, he was trying to interest Palmerston in fresh police reforms.[19] Following his dismissal, he drafted instructions for a new royal commission on the subject with himself as chief commissioner, assisted by Shaftesbury and Ebrington, and sent them to Palmerston.[20] Shaftesbury, however, counseled Chadwick that his timing was bad, for "with the prospective change of the Minister at the Home Office there is little hope of gaining attention to your plans for the Constabulary."[21] This referred to Palmerston's assuming the premiership on the break-up of Aberdeen's ministry, a change that put Sir George Grey back at the Home Office. Chadwick tried his best to stir up interest, sending off copies of the 1839 report to influential persons and insisting that the dire state of affairs he described then was still uncorrected. He dispatched one to Lord Brougham with the alarming message: "Wrecking still prevails on part of our coast, there are numerous towns where farmers return home in company for safety, and places where it is dangerous for labouring men to have a watch, or silver spoons, and where the barbarous insecurity is amazing."[22] Palmerston's government did sponsor and enact a police bill in 1856, but it was based on a select-committee report of 1853 rather than on a royal-commission inquiry, as urged by Chadwick. Nor did it incorporate his schemes for preventing crime; in essence it was a mandatory version of the 1839 measure, with the addition of a Treasury grant to the county forces and provision for central inspection. The "unfinished business" of police reform remained something of an obsession with Chadwick. As late as 1867, disturbed by the overpowering of police by rioters at Oxford and Exeter as well as by "union outrages," he wrote to Samuel Redgrave that it was "time to bring our constabulary force commission and its work under notice."[23]

Chadwick also tried to interest Prince Albert in police reform, sending him a copy of the 1839 report along with the usual frightening description of the persistence of crime.[24] This represented a revival of the attempts he had made during the public-health campaign to cultivate the favor of the prince. The immediate aim in the 1850s was to secure Albert's support in his quest for a knighthood. On April 25, 1857, Chadwick sent the prince a very lengthy letter enumerating his services.[25] He followed this up two days later with an ecstatic proposal for elevating the moral condition of the people through cheap, mass-produced works of art:

> It may be anticipated that Claudes and Turners and Landseers will be multiplied by thousands in color, and with such execution, that only experienced eyes will distinguish between the copy and the original. Artists and art possessors dislike the prospect of this mechanical invasion, as they dislike the progress of photography but it will come and it will enable remote populations, Australians or others, to obtain concep-

tions of the works of great masters of which they would otherwise be deprived.[26]

This and other letters in which Chadwick expressed his bitterness about being passed over by government ministers in their honors list were laid before the prince. Albert's response was markedly cooler than it had been ten years earlier, when he had helped procure a C.B. for Chadwick. On this occasion he replied curtly that all honors recommendations must come from the cabinet and that it would be "inadvisable" for him to comment further.[27]

Chadwick's currying favor with royalty was not confined to the British monarchy. He was greatly interested in the French administrative and sanitary systems, particularly the urban renewal of Paris undertaken by Napoleon III. When it was reported that the Empress Eugénie was to visit Queen Victoria at Windsor in 1860, Chadwick urged Florence Nightingale to acquaint the Empress with his sanitary reforms. The aristocratic Nightingale, who was definitely not dazzled by royalty, especially the Bonapartist variety, replied that a change of schedule in the visit relieved her from having to communicate with Eugénie, "who was born to be a dress-maker and married to the wickedest man in Europe to be made an Empress."[28] This was no doubt intended as a criticism of Chadwick's adulation of royalty (and parvenu royalty at that), but it did not deter his continuing search for monarchical patronage. In 1874 he again used Nightingale as an intermediary, this time with more success. The quarry was the Prince Royal of Germany, who invited Chadwick to dinner on the Isle of Wight and seemed to find the topic of sanitary science most engaging, especially its military applications:

> I was particularly impressed with his emphatic declaration of approval of the policy of increasing the strength of populations for war by sanitary measures rather than by the commonplace military policy. When I told him that with us "our losses from preventible disease are upwards of a hundred thousand a year but with you the deathrate being higher, your losses must be much greater," he received the statement with a deep expression of concern as if he felt "that indeed is the enemy to be seriously encountered."[29]

Chadwick's emphasis on the military aspect of public health that evening was more than a matter of obliging a Prussian prince with a particular interest. Chadwick himself had a deep interest in military affairs and technology, which is revealed in a letter to Florence Nightingale in 1858:

> I am glad to find improvements going on rapidly in the arts of war, which will necessitate, or give the victory to more respectable men in the ranks of war. The profligate, the passionate, and the low will in general be bad shots. The more educated soldiers, are I am assured actually beating largely, the inferior sort, as shots. What think you of new cannon, Whitworth's or Armstrong's, sending shot accurately four miles distances?[30]

Joseph Whitworth, a former associate from the Towns Improvement Company, had made a very profitable transition from street-sweeping machines to artillery, and kept Chadwick informed of the latest improvements.[31] Nightingale encouraged his interest in the sanitary arrangements of the military and pointed out the great obstacles that still had to be overcome in British India. He agreed that improved sanitary measures were needed for the army there, and deemed this a matter "essential to the dominion of Anglo-Saxon Race in India." On another occasion he thanked her for drawing his attention to India, declaring that if he were "twenty years younger you might have driven me amidst the jungles and the marshes there."[32]

If public health was closely bound up with military and imperial matters in Chadwick's mind, so was education. Curiously, for a Benthamite reformer he had shown only intermittent interest in the question during his long years of government service. True, he had inserted an education clause in the Factory Act of 1833, but this was more to prevent children working two jobs than to instruct them. He showed some interest in the education of pauper children, but was largely content to leave this question to Assistant Poor Law Commissioners E. C. Tufnell and James Kay.[33] When Kay moved to the newly formed Privy Council Committee on Education in 1839, Chadwick's interest centered more on the enviable "single-seated" authority of Kay (later Sir James Kay-Shuttleworth) under the aegis of the Privy

Council than it did on education. Chadwick's full-fledged interest in the subject developed after his removal from the General Board of Health and was chosen, like civil-service reform, partly because it was topical and offered a potential vehicle for returning to power. In 1857 he sent Russell a letter reiterating his earlier interest in factory and poor-law schools and calling for a royal commission on popular education. He even included a draft of a proclamation for creating such an inquiry, with the clear intention that he should be appointed.[34] The government did institute an inquiry on the education of the working class, the Newcastle Commission, but he was not made a member of it.

The Newcastle Commission did ask Chadwick to testify, and what he delivered was his novel scheme of "half-time" education, which he had first raised in his 1857 proposal to Russell. Advocating a marked reduction in the hours of schooling, he argued that the effectiveness of part-time factory schools was as high as that of most full-time institutions, a consequence of the fact that the attention span of most children was limited to three hours. The extra time could be spent on drill and gymnastics, which would markedly improve the children's health.[35] The Newcastle Commission ignored his recommendations, choosing instead to focus on the issue of accountability by advocating "payment by results." This system was fully established by Robert Lowe's Revised Code in 1862, and the physical education of school-children was largely neglected for the next thirty years. Chadwick protested this short-sightedness and reiterated his scheme to Russell, this time promoting it as a virtual "child's bill of rights":

> But every minute of detention beyond a child's capacity of attention, under the best method of teaching, is an injury and a torment, from which the child has a right to be preserved; five or six hours of sedentary constraint, two or three hours beyond the receptive power which lasts for only three, is the reverse of a blessing, and is a violation of the laws of *psychology*. Prolonged sedentary constraint, confinement in the infantile stage, in closely crowded school rooms, without proper bodily exercise is a violation of the laws of *physiology*. Violations of these laws such as are perpetrated, throughout the country, are violations of the rights of children. The right of the child

in the infantile stage may be defined to be in respect to education that he shall have just as much of lesson, as will enable him to relish his play, and just as much of play, as will enable him to relish his lesson. A Minister of Public Instruction might be well sworn to respect, and promote these rights of children.[36]

The idealistic-sounding sentiments with which he couched his proposal probably account for S. E. Finer's description of this episode as "a good campaign to have fought, and one of Chadwick's most attractive."[37] There is no doubt that Chadwick, whose own childhood was free of the constraints of any educational institutions, genuinely saw himself as crusading against oppressive practices. But there is a darker side to his proposal, and it concerns the use of the time not spent in the classroom. He described the non-academic pursuits variously as "play," "gymnastics," or "drill," but it is the latter which is the most accurate. In 1859 he sent a printed proof of his proposal to Florence Nightingale under the title *Education—Heads of a Paper on the expediency of measures for reducing the hours of instruction and for the general introduction of the Naval and Military Drill systematised as Gymnastic Exercise as parts of any national system of Education.*[38] The alleged benefits of the system were classified under several headings, the most interesting of which are "Military," "Economical," and "Moral." The military benefits were said to be the employment of retired drill sergeants and officers to run the program. The "economical" benefits were described as a "Better disciplined and more productive work force." The "moral" category is the most revealing of all: "For giving an early initiation to all that is implied in the term discipline, viz.: —Duty, Order, Obedience to Command, Self-restraint, Punctuality, Patience." Thus the idealistic rhetoric of his letter to Russell, with its tender regard for children's "play" time, masked a rigidly authoritarian program with militaristic overtones. The social-control aspect of Chadwick's thinking was never more evident than in his educational scheme.

As for the repressive measure his name was first associated with— the New Poor Law—time had not abated his enthusiasm for the severe doctrines of 1834. Chadwick had quit Somerset House in 1847 despairing of the law ever being put on a sound footing. Toleration of outdoor relief as the dominant mode of relieving the poor had become institutionalized at both the national and local levels.[39] The "crusade against outdoor relief," which is usually taken to start with the policies of G. J. Goschen, president of the New Poor Law Board from 1868 to 1871, encouraged Chadwick to get into the campaign, even though he was now in his seventies. He wrote to several of his old colleagues among the original corps of assistant commissioners to solicit advice and offer encouragement. Edward Gulson was in accord with Chadwick on the urgency of reform, declaring that "everything has been going down hill, till another Commission of Enquiry has become as necessary as before the law of 1834." Robert Weale agreed with Chadwick on the continued validity of the workhouse test, while W. H. T. Hawley approved of his suggestion that the policies of "model poor law unions" should be publicized to encourage others to emulate their strictness.[40] Even *The Times* had swung around to supporting the campaign, and Chadwick was deeply gratified by a leading article in 1872: "The change . . . introduced five-and-thirty years ago was so radical that it was not to be expected it should at once be successfully applied or adequately appreciated. But experience has more and more justified the results of that inquiry, and even now the facts thus collected afford the most practical instruction available to Poor Law Administrators."[41] Chadwick was still at it in 1877, conferring closely with Albert Pell, the leading figure in the anti-outdoor-relief movement.[42] The crusade ultimately foundered, however, largely as a result of the extension of democracy for both parliamentary and local elections. For the poor law, this came four years after Chadwick's death in 1890, with the introduction of democratic elections for poor-law guardians,[43] a change he would have regarded with horror.

Chadwick's own political ambitions were far from dormant. In 1837 he had come close to a safe seat at Earl Fitzwilliam's borough of Malton. There was also talk of his standing for election in 1841 and 1847, the latter of which would have pitted him against Macaulay at Edinburgh.[44] In 1857 he tried to get Earl Carlisle to find him a seat for some "protestant place" in Ireland so he could further the cause of public health in the House of Commons.[45] Two years later he was at last a candidate—as a "Liberal-Conservative" for the borough of Evesham in Worcestershire. This small constituency, with fewer than four hundred voters, was slated to lose its representatives in the various reform proposals of the period. Chadwick chose to appeal to the fear of Evesham electors, who until a few years before had been noted for their venality:

> You are threatened with disfranchisement! Your privileges, equally with those of others of the smaller Boroughs, are defended on the grounds that they serve to introduce to the representation men of eminent talent who would not seek admission to Parliament through the new and more populous constituencies. At this crisis especially it behoves you to sustain this defense, and vindicate yourselves, by obtaining a Representative of well-known public position whose long-tried ability will be recognized throughout the country.[46]

In spite of this anti-reform appeal he ended up with only 49 votes, the victors, a Conservative and a Liberal, emerging with 188 and 149 votes respectively. When the Conservative, Sir Henry Willoughby, declared handsomely that he wished there had been three seats, Chadwick's churlish reply was that he "must upon the facts question the results of the poll as being in this particular case expressions of the real sense of the electors."[47] He even went so far as to call for a parliamentary inquiry, alleging that he had been cajoled into standing by a fraudulent petition. This document, with two-fifths of the electors' names, he claimed had actually been prepared by some tavern keepers for another candidate two years before. Believing himself defrauded, he refused to pay some of his expenses and was sued in 1860 by his election agent.[48]

In spite of the Evesham fiasco, Chadwick's parliamentary ambition continued to burn brightly. The general election of 1865 offered another opportunity—this time at Westminster, which sent John Stuart Mill to Parliament that year. Mill wanted Chadwick to run as well, and wrote in his behalf to the chairman of the Westminster selection committee, declaring he "would be one of the most valuable members who could be chosen by any constituency." Chadwick stressed his own long-standing radical associations, back to the days of Bentham.[49] He felt sufficiently hopeful of securing the candidacy to request a campaign donation from Florence Nightingale, who refused.[50] In the event, he withdrew his candidacy, claiming he did not wish to hurt Mill's chances but also blaming "sanitary adherents on whom I thought I might have counted for some exertions and sacrifice."[51] In 1867, again with Mill's support, he planned to stand for the University of London against Robert Lowe. He withdrew when it appeared he had no chance of success, searched desperately for another constituency, but missed out on opportunities at Maldon and Falmouth.[52] This was to be his last chance before the Second Reform Act, and in the general election of 1868 he had to face a democratic electorate—at the Kilmarnock Boroughs in Scotland. In this contest he stood as an "advanced Liberal" and stalwart Gladstonian against the rather Whiggish M.P. Edward Pleydell-Bouverie. The latter had held himself aloof from Gladstone, so Chadwick underscored his own support of all the Prime Minister's programs, including disestablishment of the Church of Ireland. John Stuart Mill was once again his outspoken advocate—in fact it was this that made the Kilmarnock contest the *cause célèbre* of the election. A heated exchange between Mill and Bouverie was printed in *The Times,* which strongly supported Bouverie's charge that Mill's intervention was ill-considered and unwarranted, and described Chadwick as "an elderly civil servant not at all in the political line."[53] When he lost the election by a margin of almost twelve thousand votes, *The Times* could not resist reporting that "Mr. Chadwick, that person of universal genius was literally 'nowhere' in the race, Mr. Bouverie beating him in the proportion of five to two."[54]

Probably the only safe conclusion to draw from Chadwick's defeats is that he was a remarkably unattractive candidate. His repudiation by a large democratic electorate at Kilmarnock cannot necessarily be taken as evidence of rejection of his reforms, programs, and ideas, because these do not seem to have been raised much in the campaign. Nonetheless, it is hard to avoid the impression that most Victorians were left cold or positively repelled by the type of government he espoused. The tight controls and tidy centralization which characterized even his most ameliorative measures were apt to seem claustrophobic, while the repressive social control that accompanied them united voters of all classes in a defense of traditional liberties. This may well help explain, as A. P. Donajgrodzki claims, the retardation of socialism and social reform for the rest of the century:

It was not only Lord John Russell who noticed the Prussian element in the thought of men like Chadwick. Recognition of its tutelary nature may account, in part, for the tenacity of liberalism in the mid-Victorian working class, and the intense suspicion of the state evinced by many working men even in late Victorian Britain.[55]

It is important to note that when the banner of Benthamism was again raised in behalf of a reform program, as it was during the last five years of Chadwick's life by the Fabian Society, its tone and content were substantially different from his peculiar brand. Elitist the Fabians certainly were, and possessed of a fondness for social engineering, yet they also saw the necessity of developing and implementing their policies within the context of mass politics. They saw the need for slow, unspectacular progress, the pace of which would be determined by the advance of public opinion. They also recognized that, where public enterprise was deemed necessary, its organizational basis—national, county, or municipal—should be judged on purely pragmatic grounds and not according to a master blueprint. The Fabian Society, and the Labor Party to which it attached itself, represents one of the major revisionist tendencies in the modern socialist movement. It should also be considered revisionist in relation to Benthamism, or rather to Benthamism as filtered through the autocratic mind and temperament of Edwin Chadwick. The vast civil service of today's welfare state certainly has its unresponsive, supercilious, and arrogant elements. Yet, on the whole, the services organized and provided by government are popular. There is, to be sure, a persistent measure of alienation in working-class attitudes toward the state. But among the various pejoratives that might be used against the welfare state or its administrators, the term "Prussian" is one of the least likely.

The knighthood which was at last bestowed on Chadwick in 1889 was a belated recognition of his many important contributions. It was not, however, a vindication of his concept of the role and structure of government, for his autocratic, highly centralized approach had been repudiated decades before. Sir Edwin Chadwick died a year later at the age of ninety. In addition to providing for his family, he left the considerable sum of £47,000 in trust to be awarded annually to the civil and military authorities achieving the greatest reduction in the death rate. Poor-law district schools with the best records as well as teachers with the greatest success implementing his half-time educational scheme were also to be rewarded.

His funeral, utterly unlike that of his master Bentham, was a quiet, conventional affair attended by family members, friends, and professional colleagues. Instead of a dissection of the corpse accompanied by an anatomy lesson, interment followed the reading of the service by the vicar of Mortlake. Instead of a legion of eager young intellectuals determined to transform the world, there were representatives of the Association of Public Sanitary Inspectors, an organization that Chadwick had chaired. Instead of a fervid celebration of the achievements of a departed sage and architect of an anticipated new order, there were altogether unexceptionable last rites for a retired civil servant.[56]

Between 1832 and 1890 Benthamism lost its excitement and sense of mission or, more accurately, had its less controversial elements absorbed into the governmental mechanism. The result was a growing network of services administered by experts operating according to a fixed routine and in subordination to their political superiors—in a word, bureaucracy. Chadwick's government career fell in that exciting period that Kitson Clark has called "the heroic age of the civil servant,"[57] when regularity and routine had not yet developed. Bureaucratic routine emerged partly as a response to Chadwick's excesses, but was also a natural outgrowth of the Benthamism he espoused and the reforms he instigated. Ironically, both his triumphs and his reverses helped insure there would be no more Chadwicks.

Notes

Note: Citations that do not mention a specific manuscript collection are to the Chadwick Papers, University College, London. In other citations, the following abbreviations are used:

B.L.—British Library
BPP—British Parliamentary Papers (House of Commons Sessional Papers)
P.R.O.—Public Record Office

Chapter 1

1. The major contributors to this debate are A. V. Dicey, J. B. Brebner, S. E. Finer, Oliver MacDonagh, David Roberts, Henry Parris, George Kitson Clark, Jenifer Hart, L. J. Hume, Robert Gutchen, William C. Lubenow, and D. G. Paz, whose works are listed in the bibliography.

2. S. E. Finer, *The Life and Times of Sir Edwin Chadwick* (London: Methuen, 1952), and R. A. Lewis, *Edwin Chadwick and the Public Health Movement 1834–1854* (London: Longmans, 1952). Hereafter cited as Finer, *Life,* and Lewis, *Chadwick.*

3. William Thomas, *The Philosophical Radicals. Nine Studies in Theory and Practice* (Oxford: Clarendon Press, 1979).

4. Ibid., 12.

5. Ursula Henriques, "Jeremy Bentham and the Machinery of Social Reform," in *British Government and Administration: Studies Presented to S. B. Chrimes,*

ed. H. Hearder and H. R. Loyn (Cardiff: University of Wales Press, 1974), 180.

6. Fragment in Chadwick's hand on his family background, Item 131.

7. For Chadwick's early years, I have relied chiefly on Finer, *Life*, 6–37.

8. *Westminster Review* IX (1828): 384–421.

9. Ibid., 385.

10. Ibid., 392.

11. *London Review*, no. 1 (1829): 252–308.

12. Ibid., 271.

13. Ibid., 307.

14. Francis Place to EC, 21 June 1829. Chadwick had earlier asked Place for advice about books on the history of crime in London. EC to Place, n.d. [1829], Place Papers, B.L. ADD. MSS. 37,949, fo. 240.

15. Joseph Hamburger, *Intellectuals in Politics: John Stuart Mill and the Philosophic Radicals* (New Haven: Yale University Press, 1956), 19n.

16. Joseph Hume to J. Andrew, 15 January 1831.

17. Finer, *Life*, 33–34.

18. Helen Benyon, "Mighty Bentham," *Journal of Legal History* 2 (1981): 62–76.

19. Ibid., 69.

20. Henriques, "Jeremy Bentham and the Machinery of Social Reform," 186.

21. Ibid., 181.

22. L. J. Hume, *Bentham and Bureaucracy* (Cambridge: Cambridge University Press, 1981), 180.

23. Henriques, "Jeremy Bentham and the Machinery of Social Reform," 186.

24. Hume, *Bentham and Bureaucracy*, 176.

25. John Roach, *Social Reform in England 1780–1880* (London: Batsford, 1978), 110.

26. Gertrude Himmelfarb, "The Haunted House of Jeremy Bentham," in *Victorian Minds* (New York: Alfred A. Knopf, 1968), 32–81. See also Charles Bahmueller, *The National Charity Company: Jeremy Bentham's Silent Revolution* (Berkeley: University of California Press, 1981).

27. Thomas Southwood Smith, *A Lecture Delivered over the Remains of Jeremy Bentham, Esq., in the Webb Street School of Anatomy and Medicine on the 9th of June, 1832* (London: Effingham Wilson, 1832), 49.

Chapter 2

1. David Roberts, *Victorian Origins of the British Welfare State* (New Haven: Yale University Press, 1960), 25.

2. Finer, "The Transmission of Benthamite Ideas, 1820–50," in *Studies in the Growth of Nineteenth-Century Government*, ed. Gillian Sutherland (London: Routledge and Kegan Paul, 1972), 16–17.

3. Hamburger, *Intellectuals in Politics*, 11–14.

4. Finer, "The Transmission of Benthamite Ideas, 1820–50," 19.

5. David Roberts, *Paternalism in Early Victorian England* (New Brunswick: Rutgers University Press, 1979), 8.

6. Peter Mandler, "Cain and Abel: Two Aristocrats and the Early Victorian Factory Acts," *Historical Journal* 27, no. 1 (1984): 105.

7. Roberts, *Paternalism in Early Victorian England*, 8.

8. Elie Halévy, *The Triumph of Reform 1830–1841*, 2nd ed. (London: Benn, 1950), 19.

9. 3 Hansard IV, cc. 261–65 (23 June 1831).

10. Anthony Brundage, *The Making of the New Poor Law. The Politics of Inquiry, Enactment, and Implementation, 1832–1839* (New Brunswick, N.J.: Rutgers University Press, 1978), 18.

11. H. M. Clokie and J. W. Robinson, *Royal Commissions of Inquiry* (Stanford: Stanford University Press, 1937), 74.

12. Sidney and Beatrice Webb, *English Poor Law History: Part II, The Last Hundred Years* (London: Longmans, 1929), 48n.

13. Graham to Peel, 17 September 1842, Peel Papers, B.L. ADD. MSS. 40,447, fo. 163.

14. Landsdowne to Brougham, 18 October 1833, Brougham Papers, 38,923.

15. Brundage, *The Making of the New Poor Law*, 19–20.

16. Finer, *Life*, 39.

17. Lewis, *Chadwick*, 10.

18. Report of His Majesty's Commissioners for inquiry into the Administration and Practical Operation of the Poor Laws, BPP 1834, XXVII, 156.

19. Senior to Brougham, 16 December 1832, Brougham Papers, 44,440.

20. *Extracts from the Information Received by His Majesty's Commissioners as to the Administration and Operation of the Poor Laws* (London: B. Fellows, 1833), 201–339.

21. Ibid., 338–39.

22. Senior to Denis LeMarchant, 1 April 1833, Brougham Papers, 43,840.

23. Mandler, "Cain and Abel," 94.

24. 3 Hansard XVII, c. 106 (3 April 1833).

25. Cecil Driver, *Tory Radical. The Life of Richard Oastler* (New York: Oxford University Press, 1946), 222–36.

26. *The Times*, 3 June 1833.

27. Finer, *Life*, 56.

28. Ibid., 55.

29. First Report of the Central Board of His Majesty's Commissioners appointed to collect Information in the Manufacturing Districts as to the Employment of Children in Factories, and as to the Propriety and Means of Curtailing the Hours of the Labour, BPP 1833, XX, 15–16.

30. Ibid., 24.

31. Ibid., 31–32.

32. Ibid., 58–62.

33. Ibid., 44, 47.

34. Ibid., 62–63.

35. Finer, *Life,* 123–24.

36. 3 Hansard XVIII, cc. 914–15 (17 June 1833).

37. 3 Hansard XIX, cc. 913–14 (18 July 1833).

38. BPP 1833, XX, 69–71.

39. M. W. Thomas, *The Early Factory Legislation: A Study in Legislative and Administrative Evolution* (Leigh-on-Sea: Thames Bank Publishing Co., 1948), 64–65.

40. Ibid., 72.

41. Tooke to EC, 15 November 1841.

42. EC to Peel, 16 May 1846, Peel Papers, B.L. ADD. MSS. 40,592, ff. 6–7.

43. EC to Denis LeMarchant, 9 May 1833, Brougham Papers, 10,835.

44. J. M. White to EC, 25 May 1833.

45. EC to Denis LeMarchant, November 1833, Brougham Papers, 19,798.

46. S. Leon Levy, *Nassau W. Senior, 1790–1864* (Newton Abbot: David and Charles, 1970), 255–62.

47. Brundage, *The Making of the New Poor Law,* 24–25.

48. EC to Lord John Russell, n.d. [1841].

49. EC to Russell, 2 July 1866.

50. Finer, *Life,* 79.

51. Power to EC, 31 March 1833.

52. Day to EC, n.d., Box 18.

53. Mott to EC, 27 April 1833.

54. The various versions of Chadwick's poor-law bill are in Box 18.

55. Brundage, *The Making of the New Poor Law,* 35, 62.

56. Finer, *Life,* 78.

57. Ibid., 96.

58. J. M. White to EC, 9 April 1834.

59. BPP 1834, XXIX, 420.

60. EC to Denis LeMarchant [January 1834], Brougham Papers, 27,618.

61. Ibid.

Chapter 3

1. Senior to Tocqueville, 18 March 1835, quoted in Webb, *Last Hundred Years,* I, 56.

2. EC to LeMarchant, n.d. [December 1833], Brougham Papers, 27,617.

3. Finer, *Life*, 86.

4. Raymond G. Cowherd, *Political Economists and the English Poor Laws* (Athens: Ohio University Press, 1977), 191.

5. Nassau Senior's MS Diary on the Passing of the Poor Law Amendment Act, MS Diary 173, Goldsmith's Library, University of London.

6. Brundage, *The Making of the New Poor Law*, 47–57.

7. Ibid., 55–73.

8. Salisbury to EC, 6 July 1834.

9. EC to LeMarchant, May 1834 and July 1834, Brougham Papers, 27,620 and 10,837.

10. BPP 1834, XXVII, 132.

11. EC to LeMarchant, n.d. [December 1833], Brougham Papers, 27,617.

12. A. P. Donajgrodzki, " 'Social Police' and the Bureaucratic Elite: A Vision of Order in the Age of Reform," in *Social Control in Nineteenth Century Britain*, ed. A. P. Donajgrodzki (London: Croom Helm, 1977), 57–76.

13. Finer, *Life*, 69–70.

14. BPP 1834, VIII, 361–62.

15. Whately to Brougham, 3 August 1834, Brougham Papers, 27,557.

16. Place to Harriet Martineau, 31 March 1834, Place Papers, B.L. ADD. MSS. 35,149, fo. 279.

17. Albany Fonblanque to Place, 22 October 1834, Place Papers, B.L. ADD. MSS. 37,949, fo. 321.

18. Senior to Melbourne, 30 June 1834.

19. Finer, *Life*, 105–11.

20. Place to EC, 26 August 1834; Mill to EC, May 1841.

21. Thomas, *The Philosophical Radicals*, 329–30.

22. Hume to EC, 17 December 1836.

23. Ibid., 2 June 1836.

24. Ibid., 3 November and 9 December 1836.

25. Place to EC, 21 April 1835.

26. *The Times*, 13 November 1834.

27. Hume to EC, 22 November 1841.

28. Richard Hall to EC, 10 July 1835.

29. Power to EC, 12 September 1835.

30. First Annual Report of the Poor Law Commissioners, BPP 1835, XXXV, 131; John Knott, *Popular Opposition to the 1834 Poor Law* (New York: St. Martin's Press, 1986), 252–56.

31. Poor Law Commissioners' Minute Book, 9 October 1835, P.R.O. MH 1/3.

32. EC to Brougham, 2 April 1835, Brougham Papers, 10,793.

33. *Quarterly Review* LIII (April 1835): 473–539.

34. EC to Napier, 17 December 1835, Macvey Napier MSS., B.L. ADD. MSS. 34,617, ff. 288–89.

35. Ibid., 26 May 1836, ff. 439–40.

36. *Edinburgh Review* (July 1836): 487–537.

37. BPP 1837–38, XXIII, 275.

38. Ibid., 306.

39. EC to Russell, 12 July 1838.

40. See Russell's important statement in reply to John Walter's motion for a select committee on the poor laws. 3 Hansard XXXVI, cc. 1032–34 (24 February 1837).

41. BPP 1837–38, XXIII, 306.

42. Finer, *Life,* 109.

43. Spencer to Russell, 28 April 1838, Russell Correspondence, P.R.O. 30/22/3A, ff. 395–96.

44. First Annual Report of the Poor Law Commissioners, BPP 1835, XXXV, 122.

45. Second Annual Report of the Poor Law Commissioners, BPP 1836, XXIX, 8.

46. Webb, *Last Hundred Years,* I, 149.

47. J. G. Shaw Lefevre to William Heathcote, 21 November 1835, Shaw Lefevre MSS.

48. Finer, *Life,* 115–23.

49. Poor Law Commissioners' Minute Book, 3 November 1835, P.R.O. MH 1/3.

50. T. F. Lewis to Earl Fitzwilliam, 22 March 1836, Fitzwilliam MSS., Bundle AF.

51. M. A. Crowther, *The Workhouse System, 1834–1929* (Athens: University of Georgia Press, 1982), 38.

52. Finer, *Life,* 115.

53. James Kay to T. F. Lewis, 3 July 1836, P.R.O. MH 32/48.

54. For details of the northern opposition, see Nicholas C. Edsall, *The Anti-Poor Law Movement 1834–44* (Manchester: Manchester University Press, 1971); Cecil Driver, *Tory Radical: The Life of Richard Oastler* (New York: Oxford University Press, 1946); and Knott, *Popular Opposition to the 1834 Poor Law.*

55. Russell to the Poor Law Commissioners, 26 June 1837, P.R.O. HO 73/52.

56. Knott, *Popular Opposition to the 1834 Poor Law,* 203.

57. Ibid., 238–39.

58. Crowther, *The Workhouse System, 1834–1929,* 49.

59. Power to EC, 19 and 21 March 1835.

60. Russell to Lord Howick, 16 August 1837, Grey of Howick MSS.

61. Russell to EC, 16 October 1837.

62. Power to George Nicholls, 27 July 1837, P.R.O. MH 32/63.

63. 3 Hansard XXXVI, c. 1034 (24 February 1837).

64. Brundage, *The Making of the New Poor Law,* 161–75.

65. EC to Lord Howick, 28 March 1837, Grey of Howick MSS; Howick to EC, 31 March 1837.

66. *The Times,* 25 July 1837.

67. EC to Russell, 12 October 1837.

68. Report from the Select Committee on the Poor Law Amendment Act, BPP 1837, XVII, pt. 1, 11.

69. EC to Lord Howick, 7 September 1837, Grey of Howick MSS.

70. EC to the Duke of Richmond, 4 September 1837, Goodwood MSS. 1585, fo. 72.

71. Poor Law Commission Minute Book, 16 August 1837, P.R.O. MH 1/12.

72. Robert Weale to EC, 4 June 1837.

73. Undated memo by EC, P.R.O. HO 73/53.

74. Poor Law Commission Minute Book, 6 November 1837, P.R.O. MH 1/13.

75. Report of the Select Committee on the Poor Law Amendment Act, BPP 1837–38, XVIII, pt. 1, 11–40.

76. EC to Russell, 27 July 1838, Russell Correspondence, P.R.O. 30/22/3B, ff. 217–22.

77. EC to Russell, 2 and 10 July 1838.

78. Russell to the Poor Law Commissioners, 11 August 1838.

79. EC to Russell, 5 February 1840.

80. EC to Russell, 19 June 1841.

81. Graham to EC, 14 October 1841.

82. Brundage, *The Making of the New Poor Law*, 176–79.

83. John Stuart Mill to Charles Dupont-White, 6 April 1860, *The Later Letters of John Stuart Mill*, ed. Francis E. Mineka and Dwight N. Lindley, *The Collected Works of John Stuart Mill*, Vol. XV (Toronto: Toronto University Press, 1972), 691–92. "You believe perhaps that the administration of poor relief has been truly centralized here since the law of 1834. Well, it is not. The enormous abuses of local power had so horrified the public that it became possible to pass this law, but it did not prove possible to execute it; local authority ended up by regaining its predominance over central authority; and the latter has been able to retain its powers only by exercising them with a reserve so excessive that they have remained a resource resorted to only in extreme cases rather than a regular feature of the administrative system. It will be all that can be pointed to here in the way of centralization for a long time. The intervention of central authority will be allowed only as a temporary heroic remedy; it will not be allowed as a regime."

Chapter 4

1. *London Review*, no. 1 (February 1829), 291.

2. Leon Radzinowicz, *A History of English Criminal Law and Its Administration from 1750*, 4 vols. (London: Stevens and Sons, 1948–68), III, 445–47.

3. Finer, *Life*, 165.

4. Jenifer Hart, "Reform of the Borough Police, 1835–56," *English Historical Review* 70 (1955): 411–27; F. C. Mather, *Public Order in the Age of the Chartists* (Manchester: Manchester University Press, 1959), 128. E. C. Midwinter warns against exaggerating the Chartist factor in his *Social Administration in Lancashire, 1830–1860. Poor Law, Public Health and Police* (Manchester: Manchester University Press, 1969), 138–42.

5. Finer, *Life,* 164–80.

6. Charles Reith, *A New Study of Police History* (Edinburgh: Oliver and Boyd, 1956), 201.

7. Jenifer Hart, "Police," in *Crime and Law in the Nineteenth Century* (Dublin: Irish University Press, 1978), 177–219.

8. EC to Russell, August 1836.

9. Russell to EC, 1 September 1836.

10. C. S. Lefevre to Russell, 11 September 1836, Russell Correspondence, P.R.O. 30/22/2C, ff. 89–90.

11. EC to Russell, 15 September 1836.

12. Russell to EC, 16 September 1836.

13. EC to Russell, 17 September 1836.

14. C. S. Lefevre to Russell, 22 September 1836, Russell Correspondence, P.R.O. 30/22/2C, ff. 154–56.

15. Russell to EC, 30 September and 9 October 1836.

16. S. H. Gael to EC, 13 July 1836.

17. EC to Russell, 10 October 1836.

18. Russell to EC, 11 October 1836.

19. S. H. Gael to EC, 28 October 1836. Gael in fact continued to perform unpaid secretarial duties for Chadwick and the royal commission. Gael to EC, 30 October 1836.

20. Russell to EC, 9 October 1836.

21. C. S. Lefevre to EC, n.d. [1836].

22. Ibid., 20 October 1836.

23. Ibid., 14 December 1836.

24. Rowan to Richmond, 22 November 1836, Goodwood MSS. 1876, fo. 1837.

25. Ibid., January 1837, Goodwood MSS. 1589, fo. 1148.

26. Ibid., 11 May 1837, Goodwood MSS. 1589, fo. 1220.

27. Lefevre to Rowan, 18 September 1837, Letters and Papers of the Constabulary Force Commission, P.R.O. HO 73/3.

28. BPP 1836, XXVII, 50.

29. Hume to EC, 21 September 1836.

30. James Kay to the Poor Law Commissioners, 9 January 1836, Letters and Papers of the Constabulary Force Commission, P.R.O. HO 73/4, Part I.

31. Report by W. J. Voules, n.d., Letters and Papers of the Constabulary Force Commission, P.R.O. HO 73/4, Part I.

32. Gulson to EC, October 1836.

33. Constabulary Force Commission, Letters and Accounts Book, 1 July 1838.

34. W. A. Miles to EC, 23 January 1837.

35. R. Digby Neave to EC, 28 April 1838, Letters and Papers of the Constabulary Force Commission, P.R.O. HO 73/3.

36. W. A. Miles to EC, 9 October 1836.

37. W. A. Miles to Constabulary Force Commission, 12 July 1837.

38. EC to R. H. Grey, 20 November 1838, Constabulary Force Commission, Letters and Accounts Book. Also EC to Ashworth, 21 November 1838, and EC to Horner and Saunders, n.d.

39. Letters and Papers of the Constabulary Force Commission, P.R.O. HO 73/2.

40. C. S. Lefevre to EC, 1838.

41. EC to Russell, 3 May 1838.

42. Russell to EC, 4 May 1838.

43. Brundage, *The Making of the New Poor Law,* 161–62.

44. Redgrave to EC, 22 January 1839, Letters and Papers of the Constabulary Force Commission, P.R.O. HO 73/2.

45. Draft report in Chadwick's hand, Letters and Papers of the Constabulary Force Commission, P.R.O. HO 73/4, Part I.

46. C. S. Lefevre to EC, 2 March 1839.

47. EC to Russell, 4 March 1839.

48. EC and Rowan to Russell, 5 March 1839, Constabulary Force Commission, Letters and Accounts Book.

49. Lefevre to EC, 27 March 1839. Charles Reith's contention that Lefevre "was never more than a figurehead in this Royal Commission" is obviously incorrect. *A New Study of Police History,* 201.

50. Draft report in Chadwick's hand, Letters and Papers of the Constabulary Force Commission, P.R.O. HO 73/4, Part I.

51. Report of the Commissioners appointed to inquire as to the best means of establishing an efficient Constabulary Force in the Counties of England and Wales, BPP 1839, XIX, 181–82.

52. BPP 1839, XLVII, 517.

53. Ibid., 518–22.

54. Redgrave to EC, 23 March 1839.

55. Rowan to Richmond, 2 April 1839, Goodwood MSS. 1605, fo. 1692.

56. Rowan to EC, 26 April 1839.

57. Ibid., 13 April 1839.

58. EC to Brougham, 22 April 1839, Brougham Papers, 10,798.

59. Finer, *Life,* 172.

60. Redgrave to EC, 13 April 1839.

61. Finer, *Life,* 176–78.

62. Redgrave to EC, 10 June 1839.

63. Dr. John Simon to EC, 21 October 1850.

64. EC to Florence Nightingale, 28 August 1860, Nightingale MSS., B.L. ADD. MSS. 45,770, fo. 151.

65. BPP 1839, XIX, 73.

66. EC to Macvey Napier, 2 March 1845, Napier MSS., B.L. ADD. MSS. 34,625, fo. 70.

67. Chadwick's original draft had called for one-third of the expense to be paid by the Treasury. Russell had him reduce it to one-fourth, the same proportion as that received by the Metropolitan Police. Russell to EC, 6 March 1839.

68. 3 Hansard XLIX, cc. 731–32 (24 July 1839), and L, cc. 356–58 (15 August 1839).

69. 3 Hansard L, cc. 6–8 (7 August 1839).

70. Ibid., cc. 435–36 (20 August 1839).

71. Item 5.

72. EC to Jelinger Symons, 18 July 1844, Copybook 3.

73. EC to Eversley, 25 May 1859; Eversley to EC, 27 May 1859.

74. Finer, *Life*, 165–67.

75. 3 Hansard LIII, cc. 20–21 (24 March 1840).

76. In the 1853 inquiry that preceded the Police Act of 1856 (which mandated the creation of county forces) even Chadwick had to admit that "the working of the fragmentitious county forces has, on the whole, been much more satisfactory than we anticipated." BPP 1852–53, XXXVI, 254.

Chapter 5

1. Lewis, *Chadwick*, 33.

2. Finer, *Life*, 154–55.

3. M. J. Cullen, "The Making of the Civil Registration Act of 1836," *Journal of Ecclesiastical History* 25 (1974): 39–59.

4. Ibid., 55–56. A similar view is found in C. Fraser Brockington, "Public Health and the Privy Council, 1831–4," *Journal of the History of Medicine* 16 (1961): 161–85. After reviewing the significant measures (including an active though temporary central board) adopted to deal with the cholera epidemic of 1831, Brockington asks whether Chadwick "may have been building more on what had gone before than some of his biographers and historians have given us to believe?" (p. 185).

5. See above, 45–46.

6. Cullen, "The Making of the Civil Registration Act of 1836," 57–58.

7. Ibid., 59.

8. M. W. Flinn, introduction to Edwin Chadwick, *Report on the Sanitary Condition of the Labouring Population of Great Britain* (Edinburgh: At the University Press, 1965), 43–44.

9. BPP 1837–38, XXVIII, 210–36.

10. *Report on the Prevalence of Fever in Twenty Metropolitan Unions or Parishes, during the Year ended 20 March 1838,* BPP 1839, XX, 112–18.

11. *The Times,* 20 August 1839. Hansard did not mention Blomfield's motion, though it did report the speech he gave on the first of August. 3 Hansard XLIX, cc. 1056–58 (1 August 1839).

12. Southwood Smith to EC, 23 July 1839.

13. 3 Hansard LI, c. 1234 (4 February 1840).

14. Ibid., c. 1246.

15. BPP 1840, XI, 277.

16. BPP 1839, XX, 118.

17. Finer, *Life,* 221–22.

18. Ibid., 211–12.

19. Lewis, *Chadwick,* 37–39.

20. Finer, *Life,* 212.

21. John Stuart Mill to EC, April 1842.

22. Ibid., 8 June 1842.

23. Lewis, *Chadwick,* 60.

24. *Report on the Sanitary Condition of the Labouring Population of Great Britain,* 120–24. All references to this report are to the M. W. Flinn edition cited in note 8. It is hereafter cited as *Sanitary Report.*

25. Ibid., 214.

26. Ibid., 396.

27. EC to Napier, 11 October 1842, Macvey Napier Papers, B.L. ADD. MSS. 34,626, ff. 175–76.

28. *Sanitary Report,* 424.

29. Ibid., 425.

30. Ibid.

31. Lord Melbourne to EC, 5 February 1840, Melbourne Papers, Royal Archives, RA MP 53/45.

32. EC to Russell, 5 February 1840.

33. EC to Russell, n.d.

34. EC to Normanby, 7 May 1841.

35. EC to Normanby, 12 May 1841.

36. Finer, while alluding briefly to this letter, mentions only the suggested supervision of the factory inspectors. Finer, *Life,* 200.

37. EC to Russell, 17 June 1841. In this same letter, he suggested that, since he was considered too unpopular for the Poor Law Commission in England, Nicholls could be brought home from Ireland and Chadwick could take his place there.

38. Finer, *Life,* 205.

39. Graham to EC, 14 October 1841.

40. Senior to Graham, 6 June 1842.

41. EC to Burton, 16 February 1841. In the event, an article by R. Head very

favorable to the *Sanitary Report* was published in the *Quarterly Review* LXXI (March 1843): 417–53.

42. EC to Peel, 23 September 1841, Peel Papers, B.L. ADD. MSS. 40,489, ff. 321–22; EC to Peel, 23 June 1842, ADD. MSS. 40,511, ff. 32–33.

43. 3 Hansard LX, cc. 316–17 (14 February 1842).

44. BPP 1842, X, 356.

45. Lewis, *Chadwick*, 68; Finer, *Life*, 231.

46. 3 Hansard LXV, c. 1032 (4 August 1842).

47. 3 Hansard LXVI, cc. 574–77 (14 February 1843).

48. 3 Hansard LXIX, cc. 1444–45 (13 June 1843).

49. There is only one extant letter on interments to Graham from this period, in which Chadwick describes the likely opposition of the Dissenters. EC to Graham, 28 February 1843.

50. *A Supplementary Report on the Results of a Special Inquiry into the Practice of Interments in Towns* by Edwin Chadwick, BPP 1843, XII, 395.

51. Ibid., 600–604.

52. Ibid., 602.

53. Ibid., 593.

54. EC to Edward Baines, 7 December 1843.

55. EC to Blomfield, 22 December 1843.

56. EC to John Walter, 12 December 1843, Copybook 2.

57. *The Times,* 30 December 1843. Leading articles critical of the report also appeared on December 22 and 25.

58. EC to Albert G. Escher, 24 December 1843, Copybook 2.

59. EC to Ashley, 13 December 1843, Copybook 1.

60. 3 Hansard LXXIII, cc. 1304–5 (20 March 1844).

61. 3 Hansard LXVI, cc. 574–77 (14 February 1843).

62. Graham to EC, 19 January 1843.

63. Finer, *Life*, 232.

64. Lewis, *Chadwick*, 85.

65. Peel to EC, 29 May 1843, Peel Papers, B.L. ADD. MSS. 40,481, ff. 149–50; Peel to Lincoln, 29 May 1843, ff. 147–48; Lincoln to Peel, 8 June 1843, fo. 151.

66. The complete list of Chadwick's recommendations is in Finer, *Life,* 233.

67. Southwood Smith to EC, 29 March 1843.

68. Both R. A. Lewis and M. W. Flinn err in including not only Southwood Smith but also Arnott as members of the royal commission. Lewis, *Chadwick*, 85; Flinn, introduction to *Sanitary Report*, 67. This error has obscured Chadwick's role in keeping Southwood Smith off the commission as well as Graham's reluctance to appoint out-and-out "Chadwickians."

69. EC to Napier, 17 August 1844, Macvey Napier Papers, B.L. ADD. MSS. 34,624, fo. 560.

70. At the same time Chadwick, complaining that the *Sanitary Report* had been treated "rather cavalierly," sent copies of that publication to a Dr. Willis,

asking him to send them to Graham and Peel. EC to Willis, 17 August 1844.

71. EC to Napier, 12 October 1844, "Private and Confidential," Macvey Napier Papers, B.L. ADD. MSS. 34,624, fo. 629.

72. EC to John Forster, 13 October 1844, Copybook 6.

73. No article on the *Sanitary Report* or the Health of Towns Commission, by Chadwick or anyone else, appeared in the *Edinburgh Review.*

74. EC to Duke of Buccleuch, December 1844, Copybook 6; Duke of Buccleuch to EC, 17 December 1845.

75. Finer, *Life,* 236.

76. Ibid., 304–5.

77. *First Report of the Commissioners for inquiring into the State of Large Towns and Populous Districts,* BPP 1844, XVII, Q. 1025.

78. *Second Report of the Commissioners for inquiring into the State of Large Towns and Populous Districts,* BPP 1845, XVIII, 1.

79. Ibid., 2.

80. Anthony Wohl, *Endangered Lives: Public Health in Victorian Britain* (Cambridge: Harvard University Press, 1983), 308.

81. EC to Slaney, 3 March 1845, Copybook 7.

82. Dickens to Southwood Smith, 15 December 1840, *The Letters of Charles Dickens,* ed. Madeline and Graham Storey (Oxford: Clarendon Press, 1969), II, 164–66. Hereafter cited as *Letters of Dickens.*

83. *The Speeches of Charles Dickens,* ed. K. J. Fielding (Oxford: Clarendon Press, 1960), 68–72.

84. Dickens to Henry Austin, 25 September 1842, *Letters of Dickens,* III, 330.

85. EC to Dickens, 21 June 1844, Copybook 3.

86. EC to John Forster, 13 October 1844, Copybook 8.

87. "On the best modes of representing accurately by statistical returns the duration of life," *Journal of the Royal Statistical Society* VII, 2.

88. EC to Southwood Smith, 25 June 1844, Copybook 5.

89. Ibid., 1 July 1844.

90. EC to Lord Ashley, 31 July 1844, Copybook 5.

91. Finer, *Life,* 237–79.

92. Sheila M. Smith, "Willenhall and Wodgate: Disraeli's Use of Bluebook Evidence," *Review of English Studies,* n.s., 13 (1962): 368–84.

93. Gertrude Himmelfarb, *The Idea of Poverty: England in the Early Industrial Age* (New York: Alfred A. Knopf, 1984), 194–95.

94. Carlyle to EC, 23 March 1842.

95. EC to Macaulay, 18 April 1845, Copybook 9.

96. Macaulay to unidentified recipient, 30 April 1845. *The Letters of Thomas Babington Macaulay,* ed. Thomas Pinney (Cambridge: Cambridge University Press, 1974–81), IV, 253–54.

97. 3 Hansard LXXVIII, c. 325 (5 March 1845).

98. Undated [March 1845] memorandum in Chadwick's hand, Copybook 8.

99. 3 Hansard LXXIX, cc. 330–35 (8 April 1845).

100. Ibid., cc. 335–36, 341.

101. Finer, *Life,* 240.

Chapter 6

1. EC to Albert G. Escher, 24 December 1843, Copybook 2.

2. EC to Andrew Boardman, 4 February 1844, Copybook 2. Neither Finer nor Lewis mentions this letter.

3. Finer, *Life,* 240–42.

4. EC to Andrew Boardman, 3 October 1846.

5. "On the best modes of representing accurately by statistical returns the duration of life," 30.

6. EC to T. Garnier, 19 September 1844, Copybook 4.

7. EC to George Warde Norman, 26 October 1844, Copybook 5.

8. EC to Slaney, 23 November 1844, Copybook 6.

9. "First Draft, Private," Item 50.

10. Undated memorandum [1840–42] by Chadwick on combination of services, Item 71.

11. EC to Duke of Buccleuch, 23 May 1845, Copybook 10.

12. EC to J. Hodson, 10 April 1845, Copybook 10.

13. EC to James Terrell, 26 June 1845, Copybook 11.

14. EC to Sir John Easthope, 10 July 1845, Copybook 11.

15. Item 50. The towns were Bolton, Salford, Manchester, Leicester, Bristol, Loughborough, Worksop, Chorley, Kendal, Lancaster, and Clitheroe.

16. EC to R. A. Slaney, 16 September 1845.

17. "Notes on power of capital and machinery," Item 50.

18. "Minutes of the Resolution of the Company," Item 48.

19. "The Improvement of Leicester," revised edition, Item 48.

20. "The Improvement of Leicester," first draft, Item 48.

21. Original emphasis.

22. "Minutes of the Resolution of the Company," 30 September, 6 October, and 8 October 1845, Item 48.

23. Undated memo in Chadwick's hand, Item 50.

24. EC to Hume, 19 April 1846, Copybook 15.

25. EC to Philip Holland, 13 April 1846, Copybook 15.

26. Report by Edwin Chadwick on plan for company extending its powers, Item 50.

27. BPP 1846, XII, 29–49.

28. Lewis, *Chadwick,* 137.

29. EC to A. Boardman, 3 October 1846, Copybook 16.

30. In this case the originator seems to have been John Joseph Mechi

(1802–80), the son of an Italian immigrant. There were a great many early Victorians intrigued by Mechi's ideas. See Nicholas Goddard, "Nineteenth Century Recycling: The Victorians and the Agricultural Utilization of Sewage," *History Today* 31 (June 1981): 32–36.

31. BPP 1846, X, 648–62.

32. EC to Rev. A. Huxtable, 17 October 1847, Copybook 19.

33. Finer, *Life*, 300–301.

34. R. A. Lewis, "Edwin Chadwick and the Railway Labourers," *Economic History Review* 3 (1950): 107–18.

35. Henry Parris, *Government and the Railways in Nineteenth Century Britain* (London: Routledge and Kegan Paul, 1965), 21–23.

36. *Papers read before the Statistical Society of Manchester on the Demoralization and Injuries occasioned by the Want of Proper Regulations of Labourers engaged in the Construction and Working of Railways* (Manchester: Simms and Denham, n.d. [1846]).

37. 3 Hansard LXXXIII, c. 217 (26 January 1846).

38. 3 Hansard LXXXIV, cc. 1229–33, 1256–57 (19 March 1846).

39. For Chadwick's evidence, see BPP 1846, XIII, 584–91.

40. Morrison to EC, 22 June 1846.

41. EC to Morrison, 24 August 1846, Copybook 17.

Chapter 7

1. EC to Graham, 5 August 1845; EC to Ashley, 15 November 1845.

2. Finer, *Life*, 245–46.

3. Graham to Peel, 6 August 1841, Peel Papers, B.L. ADD. MSS. 40,318, fo. 294.

4. Graham to Peel, n.d. [October 1841], Peel Papers, B.L. ADD. MSS. 40,565, ff. 80–81.

5. EC to Peel, 30 April 1845, Peel Papers, B.L. ADD. MSS. 40,565, ff. 308–13.

6. Finer, *Life*, 87–88.

7. *The Times*, 16 September 1845. Reprinted in *The Letters of S.G.O.*, ed. Arnold White (London: Griffith, Farram, Okeden, and Welsh, 1888), II, 1975.

8. EC to Slaney, Lord Sidney Godolphin Osborne, 22 August 1844, Copybook 4.

9. See Finer, *Life*, 257–73; Norman Longmate, *The Workhouse* (London: Temple Smith, 1974), 119–35; Ian Anstruther, *The Scandal of the Andover Workhouse* (London: Geoffrey Bles, 1973).

10. R. A. Lewis, "William Day and the Poor Law Commissioners," *University of Birmingham Historical Journal* 9 (1964): 163–96.

11. Finer, *Life*, 261.

12. Ibid., 265–69.

13. EC to Russell, 27 July 1838, Russell Papers, P.R.O. 30/22/3B.

14. Finer, *Life*, 278.

15. EC to W. E. Hickson, n.d.

16. EC to Frederic Hill, 25 September 1846.

17. See Michael E. Rose, "Settlement, Removal and the New Poor Law," in *The New Poor Law in the Nineteenth Century*, ed. Derek Fraser (London: Macmillan, 1976).

18. See above, 114.

19. *Evidence before the House of Commons Select Committee on Settlement and Poor Removal*, BPP 1847, XI, Q. 2068.

20. See, for example, EC to Lord Grey, 14 June 1847.

21. BPP 1847, XI, 1. The only immediate fruit of this inquiry was an 1847 statute (10 & 11 Vict., c. 110) which spread the cost of the irremovable poor over the entire union.

22. Finer, *Life*, 279–80.

23. Ibid., 281.

24. EC to Viscount Ebrington, 2 July 1847.

25. Finer, *Life*, 286–91.

26. *The Letters of S.G.O.*, I, 323.

27. *The Times*, 11 September 1847.

28. EC to Russell, 4 August 1847.

29. *Report of the Metropolitan Sanitary Commissioners*, BPP 1847–48, XXXII, 55.

30. EC to Viscount Ebrington, n.d.

31. EC to Russell, 8 August 1847.

32. Finer, *Life*, 311.

33. Ibid., 328.

34. Ibid., 329.

35. Ibid., 372.

36. *Morning Chronicle*, 26 and 28 April 1848.

37. EC to Morpeth, 29 April 1848.

38. Joshua Toulmin Smith, *Government by Commissions Illegal and Pernicious. The Nature and Effects of all Commissions of Inquiry and other Crown-Appointed Commissions. The Constitutional Principles of Taxation; And the Rights, Duties, and Importance of Local Self-Government* (London: S. Sweet, 1849), 221.

39. Ibid., 225.

40. BPP 1847–48, XXXII, 1. Toulmin Smith printed extracts of his evidence in *Government by Commissions*, 359–65.

41. EC to Russell, 8 August 1847.

42. EC to Andrew Boardman, n.d.

43. EC to Andrew Boardman, n.d. This is a separate letter from the one cited in note 42.

44. EC to Morpeth, 6 January 1848.

45. Morpeth to EC, 9 January 1848. Also Morpeth to EC, 22 February 1848.

46. EC to Lansdowne, 13 July 1848.
47. Lansdowne to EC, n.d.
48. Finer, *Life*, 324–25.
49. EC to Blomfield, 16 June 1848.
50. EC to Morpeth, 11 June 1848.
51. Finer, *Life*, 324.
52. Ibid., 322.
53. EC to W. E. Hickson, 4 March 1848.
54. EC to Russell, 14 May 1848.
55. EC to Morpeth, 15 May 1848.
56. EC to Hume, n.d. ("Friday").
57. EC to Ashley, 18 May 1848.
58. EC to Sir George de Larpent, 20 June 1848.
59. Dickens to Southwood Smith, 29 June 1847; Dickens to Normanby, 1 July 1847. *Letters of Dickens,* V, 106–9.
60. *Examiner,* 24 June 1848.
61. EC to Southwood Smith, 27 June 1848.
62. Ibid., n.d. [July 1848].
63. Ibid., 11 August 1848.

Chapter 8

1. G. C. Lewis to Sir Edmund Head, 28 September 1848, *Letters of the Right Hon. Sir George Cornewall Lewis, Bart. to Various Friends,* ed. the Rev. Sir Gilbert Frankland Lewis, Bart. (London: Longman, Green & Co., 1870), 185–86.
2. Morpeth to EC, 25 January [1848].
3. Ashley's Diary, 29 September 1848, Broadlands Papers, SHA/PD/5.
4. General Board of Health, Rough Minute Book, 26 September 1848, P.R.O. MH 6/1.
5. Ibid., 2 October 1848.
6. Ebrington to EC, 25 November 1848.
7. EC to Morpeth, 30 September 1848.
8. Finer, *Life*, 343.
9. Ibid., 347.
10. Ibid., 351.
11. Finer, *Life*, 311–13; Lewis, *Chadwick*, 242.
12. Morpeth to EC, 4 September 1848.
13. Carlisle to EC, 18 October 1848.
14. Carlisle to EC, 18 October 1848 (separate letter from that cited in note 13).
15. Carlisle to EC, 4 December 1848.

16. EC to Carlisle, 5 December 1848.

17. EC to Carlisle, 22 November 1848; Carlisle to EC, 16 November 1848.

18. Finer, *Life,* 367–70.

19. Carlisle to EC, 22 December 1848.

20. Carlisle to EC, 26 January 1849.

21. Finer, *Life,* 364–76.

22. Carlisle to EC, 10 August 1849.

23. Carlisle to EC, 29 September 1849.

24. EC to Carlisle, 1 November 1849; Carlisle to EC, 2 November 1849.

25. Carlisle to EC, 12 January 1850.

26. Carlisle to EC, n.d. (marked "found after Feb. 1850").

27. EC to Carlisle, 27 March 1850.

28. George Anson to EC, 4 August 1842.

29. See, for example, Col. C. B. Phipps to EC, 8 December 1848, 26 December 1848, 1 January 1849, 13 February 1849, and 3 April 1849.

30. Finer, *Life,* 321.

31. EC to Col. C. B. Phipps, 28 July 1851.

32. EC to Father Theobald Matthew, 26 April 1845, Copybook 9.

33. EC to John Delane, 26 November 1850.

34. EC to Russell, 29 January 1851, Russell Correspondence, P.R.O. 30/22/9A, fo. 271.

35. Joshua Toulmin Smith, *Local Self-Government and Centralization,* 334.

36. Russell to Palmerston, 28 November 1853, Enclosure 3, Broadlands Papers, GC/RV/473.

37. Finer, *Life,* 431.

38. Carlisle to EC, 7 August 1850.

39. Finer, *Life,* 397–401. Copies of the letters are included in the Carlisle correspondence file in the Chadwick papers.

40. Finer, *Life,* 382.

41. Carlisle to EC, 13 December 1849.

42. G. C. Lewis to Sir Edmund Head, 25 January 1850, *Letters of the Right Hon. George Cornewall Lewis,* 186.

43. Finer, *Life,* 389.

44. See especially the spirited debate in committee led by the metropolitan M.P.s. 3 Hansard CXI, cc. 677–710 (3 June 1850).

45. Finer, *Life,* 405.

46. Ibid., 400.

47. Ibid., 405.

48. Carlisle to Russell, 4 November 1851, Russell Correspondence, P.R.O. 30/22/9H, ff. 49–50.

49. Finer, *Life,* 456–57.

50. Ibid., 391–92.

51. Ibid., 394–95.

52. Ibid., 403.

53. Ibid., 404.
54. *Quarterly Review* LXXXVIII (March 1851): 435–92.
55. Ibid., 462.
56. EC to Carlisle, 9 April 1851.
57. Finer, *Life*, 408.
58. Ibid., 412.
59. EC to S. H. Gael, 6 August 1852.
60. EC to Samuel Redgrave, 7 October 1852.
61. Finer, *Life*, 444–45.
62. Ibid., 447.
63. Ibid., 451.
64. Ibid., 455.
65. See David Roberts, "Lord Palmerston at the Home Office, 1853–1854," *Historian* 21 (November 1958): 63–81.
66. Ebrington to EC, 15 August 1853.
67. Russell to Palmerston, 28 November 1853, Broadlands Papers, GC/RV/473.
68. Shaftesbury to Palmerston, 28 January 1854, Broadlands Papers, GC/SH/26/1.
69. Minutes on New Board of Health Bills between Lord Palmerston and Mr. Waddington, Broadlands Papers, HA/F/5/5–6.
70. Palmerston to Russell, 7 July 1854, Russell Correspondence, P.R.O. 30/22/11D, ff. 185–87.
71. Finer, *Life*, 460–62.
72. C. N. Newdegate to S. H. Gael, 24 July 1854.
73. Macaulay to Thomas Flower Ellis, 4 March 1854, *The Letters of Thomas Babington Macaulay*, V, 387.
74. Finer, *Life*, 464, 467.
75. J. Hodgson to Shaftesbury, 28 July 1854.
76. Finer, *Life*, 468.
77. 3 Hansard CXXXV, cc. 969–70 (31 July 1854).
78. Ibid., c. 976.
79. Ibid., cc. 980–94.
80. Ibid., cc. 999–1000.
81. Finer, *Life*, 471.
82. 3 Hansard CXXXV, c. 1004 (31 July 1854).
83. Ibid.
84. *Manchester Weekly Advertiser*, 5 August 1854, Item 55.
85. Finer, *Life*, 472.
86. *Economist*, 5 August 1854, Item 55.

Chapter 9

1. Royston Lambert, *Sir John Simon 1816-1904 and English Social Administration* (London: MacGibbon and Kee, 1963), 139-42.

2. John Simon to EC, 28 September 1855.

3. Oliver MacDonagh, *Early Victorian Government 1830-1870* (London: Weidenfeld and Nicolson, 1977), 152-57.

4. Wohl, *Endangered Lives: Public Health in Victorian Britain*, 153-59.

5. Ibid., 196.

6. David Owen, *The Government of Victorian London 1855-1889. The Metropolitan Board of Works, the Vestries and the City Corporation*, ed. Roy McLeod (Cambridge, Mass.: Belknap Press, 1982).

7. R. A. Lewis, "Edwin Chadwick and the Administrative Reform Movement, 1854-6," *University of Birmingham Historical Journal* 2 (1950): 178-200.

8. Ibid., 195.

9. Edward Hughes, "Sir Charles Trevelyan and Civil Service Reform, 1853-5," *English Historical Review* 64 (1949): 53-88.

10. Papers on the Reorganization of the Civil Service, BPP 1854-55, XX, 219.

11. Jenifer Hart, "Sir Charles Trevelyan at the Treasury," *English Historical Review* 75 (1960): 92-110.

12. Ibid., 95.

13. Ibid., 110.

14. Administrative Reform Association, *The Devising Heads and Executive Hands of the English Government; as described by Privy Councillors and Civil Servants Themselves. Official Paper no. 2* (London: M. S. Rickerby, 1855), 16.

15. R. K. Webb, "A Whig Inspector," *Journal of Modern History* 27 (1955): 352-64.

16. H. S. Tremenheere to EC, 9 June 1854. Quoted in R. A. Lewis, "Edwin Chadwick and the Administrative Reform Movement, 1854-6," 189.

17. Hughes, "Sir Charles Trevelyan and Civil Service Reform, 1853-5," 62.

18. R. A. Lewis, "Edwin Chadwick and the Administrative Reform Movement, 1854-6," 198.

19. Samuel Redgrave to EC, 19 April 1854.

20. EC to Palmerston, 16 January 1855.

21. Shaftesbury to EC, 27 January 1855.

22. EC to Brougham, 24 June 1855, Brougham Papers, 35,346.

23. EC to Samuel Redgrave, 18 November 1867.

24. EC to Col. C. B. Phipps, n.d. [1854]. Chadwick wisely decided to delete from the draft of this letter an incredible story that just as he had finished writing the 1839 report "which was late after midnight, the servants came to me with an alarm that thieves were breaking into the house, and we succeeded in driving them off; when our secretary was conveying the report to be printed the horse of his cab ran away and he was upset and the report was thrown out and it was picked up by a delinquent."

25. EC to Prince Albert, 25 April 1857, Item 165.

26. EC to Col. Phipps, 27 April 1857, Royal Archives, RA PP 13782 (1857).

27. Col. Phipps to EC, 5 May 1857, Royal Archives, RA PP 13782 (1857).

28. EC to Florence Nightingale, 3 December 1860; Nightingale to EC, 10 December 1860, Nightingale MSS., B.L. ADD. MSS. 45,770, ff. 203–4, 210.

29. EC to Florence Nightingale, 16 August 1874.

30. EC to Florence Nightingale, 5 November 1858, Nightingale MSS., B.L. ADD. MSS. 45,770, ff. 75–76.

31. Joseph Whitworth to EC, 13 March 1859.

32. EC to Florence Nightingale, 12 July and 8 December 1858, Nightingale MSS., B.L. ADD. MSS. 45,707, ff. 18 and 89.

33. Finer, *Life*, 150–53.

34. EC to Russell, 11 August 1857, Russell Correspondence, P.R.O. 30/22/13D, ff. 76–83.

35. Finer, *Life*, 506–8.

36. EC to Russell, 29 November 1861, Russell Correspondence, P.R.O. 30/22/14C, ff. 16–17.

37. Finer, *Life*, 508.

38. Nightingale Papers, B.L. ADD. MSS. 45,770, fo. 106.

39. This view, held by virtually all historians of the subject, has been challenged by Karel Williams, *From Pauperism to Poverty* (London: Routledge and Kegan Paul, 1981). Williams argues that the workhouse was used freely against able-bodied workers from the outset, and applied readily to all classes of paupers after 1870.

40. Edward Gulson to EC, 9 May 1871; Robert Weale to EC, 6 May 1871; W. H. T. Hawley to EC, 29 April 1871.

41. *The Times*, 21 November 1872. Chadwick sent a letter of appreciation. EC to Editor of *The Times*, n.d. [1872].

42. EC to Albert Pell, 8 January 1877.

43. Anthony Brundage, "Reform of the Poor Law Electoral System, 1834–94," *Albion* 7 (Fall 1975): 201–15.

44. Finer, *Life*, 493.

45. EC to Carlisle, 9 March 1857. Olien, *Morpeth*, 525. His anti-Catholic sentiments never waned, and near the end of his life he strongly condemned Gladstone for the Home Rule Bill. EC to Earl Grey, 1 September 1886.

46. Printed election handbill. Item 83.

47. Finer, *Life*, 493.

48. Petition to the House of Commons and materials relating to lawsuit. Item 83.

49. John Stuart Mill to James Beal, 7 March 1865. Chadwick's prepared address to the electors of Westminster. Item 83.

50. EC to Florence Nightingale, 3 April and 28 April 1865, Nightingale MSS., B.L. ADD. MSS. 45,771, ff. 57–60.

51. Ibid., 7 August 1865, fo. 61.

52. Finer, *Life,* 494.

53. Ibid., 498.

54. *The Times,* 19 November 1868.

55. Donajgrodzki, " 'Social Police' and the Bureaucratic Elite," 73.

56. *The Times,* 10 July 1890.

57. George Kitson Clark, " 'Statesmen in Disguise': Reflections on the History of the Neutrality of the Civil Service," *Historical Journal* 2 (1959): 38.

Bibliography

Primary Sources

Manuscript Materials

University College, London
Chadwick Papers.
Brougham Papers.

Public Record Office
Russell Correspondence (P.R.O. 30/22).
Letters and Papers of the Constabulary Force Commission (HO 73/2–4).
Home Office Correspondence with the Poor Law Commission (HO 73/52–53).
Poor Law Commission Minute Books (MH 1/3–13).
General Board of Health Rough Minute Books (MH 6/1).
Reports of Assistant Poor Law Commissioner James Kay (MH 32/48).
Reports of Assistant Poor Law Commissioner Alfred Power (MH 32/63).

British Library
Macvey Napier Papers.
Nightingale Papers.
Peel Papers.
Place Papers.

Royal Archives, Windsor Castle
Correspondence of Prince Albert.
Melbourne MSS.

National Register of Archives
Broadlands Papers.

House of Lords Record Office
Shaw Lefevre MSS.

National Library of Wales
Harpton Court MSS.

West Sussex Record Office
Goodwood MSS.

University of Durham, Department of Palaeography and Diplomatic
Grey of Howick MSS.

University of London, Goldsmith's Library
Nassau Senior's MS Diary of the passing of the Poor Law Amendment Act.

Printed Materials

British Parliamentary Papers (Sessional Papers)

1833, XX, Report of the Central Board of His Majesty's Commissioners appointed to collect Information in the Manufacturing Districts as to the Employment of Children in Factories, as to the Propriety and Means of Curtailing the Hours of Labour.

1834, VII, Report of the House of Commons Select Committee on Drunkenness.

1834, XXVII, Report from His Majesty's Commissioners for Inquiring into the Administration and Practical Operation of the Poor Laws.

1834, XXVII–XXIX, Reports of Assistant Commissioners.

1835, XXXV, First Annual Report of the Poor Law Commissioners.

1836, XXVII, Report of the Royal Commission on County Rates.

1836, XXIX, Second Annual Report of the Poor Law Commissioners.

1837–38, XVII–XVIII, Report from the House of Commons Select Committee on the Poor Law Amendment Act.

1837–38, XXIII, Report of the House of Commons Select Committee on the Highway Acts.

1839, XIX, Report of the Commissioners appointed to inquire as to the best means of establishing an efficient Constabulary Force in the Counties of England and Wales.

1839, XX, Report on the Prevalence of Fever in Twenty Metropolitan Unions or Parishes, during the year ended 20 March 1838.

1839, XLVII, Home Office Circular of 2 February 1839 to Chairmen of Quarter Sessions.

1840, XI, Report of the House of Commons Select Committee on the Health of Towns.

1843, XII, A Supplementary Report on the Results of a Special Inquiry into the Practice of Interments in Towns.

1844, XVII, First Report of the Commissioners for inquiring into the State of Large Towns and Populous Districts.

1845, XVIII, Second Report of the Commissioners for inquiring into the State of Large Towns and Populous Districts.

1846, XII, Report of the House of Commons Select Committee on Private Bills.

1846, XIII, Report of the House of Commons Select Committee on Railway Laborers.

1847, XI, Report of the House of Commons Select Committee on Settlement and Poor Removal.

1847–48, XXXII, Report of the Metropolitan Sanitary Commissioners.

1852–53, XXXVI, Report of the House of Commons Select Committee on Police.

Miscellaneous

[Chadwick, Edwin]. "Animal Physiology." *Westminster Review* XVI (Jan. 1832): 192–203.

[Chadwick, Edwin]. "Centralization — Public Charities in France." *London Review* I (1829): 536–65.

[Chadwick, Edwin]. "Life assurances—diminution of sickness and mortality." *Westminster Review* IX (April 1828): 384–421.

[Chadwick, Edwin]. "The New Poor Law." *Edinburgh Review* LXIII (July 1836): 487–537.

[Chadwick, Edwin]. "On the Best Modes of Representing accurately by Statistical Returns the Duration of Life, Etc." *Journal of the Royal Statistical Society* VII (1843): 1–30.

Chadwick, Edwin. *Papers Read before the Statistical Society of Manchester on the Demoralisation and Injuries occasioned by the Want of Proper Regulations of Labourers engaged in the Construction and Working of Railways.* Manchester: Simms & Dinham, n.d. [1846].

[Chadwick, Edwin]. "Patronage of Commissions." *Westminster Review* XLVI (Oct. 1846): 222–45.

[Chadwick, Edwin]. "Preventive Police." *London Review,* no. 1 (Feb. 1829): 252–308.

Chadwick, Edwin. *The Sanitary Condition of the Labouring Population of Great Britain.* Edited with an introduction by M. W. Flinn. Edinburgh: At the University Press, 1965. First published in 1842.

The Devising Heads and Executive Hands of the English Government, as described by Privy Councillors and Civil Servants themselves. Official Paper No. 2 of the Administrative Reform Association. London: M. S. Rickerby, 1855.

Dickens, Charles. *The Letters of Charles Dickens.* Edited by Madeline House and Graham Storey. Oxford: Clarendon Press, 1965.

Dickens, Charles. *The Speeches of Charles Dickens.* Edited by K. J. Fielding. Oxford: Clarendon Press, 1960.

Engineers and Officials: An Historical Sketch of the Progress of "Health of Towns Works" (between 1838 and 1856) in London and the Provinces with Biographical Notes on Lord Palmerston, the Earl of Shaftesbury, Lord Ebrington, Edwin Chadwick, C.B., F. O. Ward, John Thwaites. London: Edward Stanford, 1856.

*Extracts from the Information Reserved by His Majesty's Commissioners as to the Admin-
istration and Practical Operation of the Poor Laws.* London: B. Fellows, 1833.

[Head, R.]. "Report on An Inquiry into the Sanitary Condition of the Labouring
Population of Great Britain." *Quarterly Review* LXXI (March 1843):
417–53.

[Hickson, W. E.]. "Fallacies on Poor Laws." *London and Westminster Review* IV
(Jan. 1837): 357–78.

Lewis, George Cornewall. *Letters of the Right Hon. Sir George Cornewall Lewis, Bart.
to Various Friends.* Edited by the Rev. Sir Gilbert Frankland Lewis, Bart.
London: Longman, Green and Co., 1870.

Macaulay, Thomas Babington. *The Letters of Thomas Babington Macaulay.* Edited
by Thomas Pinney. 6 vols. Cambridge: Cambridge University Press,
1974–81.

Mill, John Stuart. *Later Letters of John Stuart Mill.* Edited by Francis E. Meneka and
Dwight N. Lindley. In *The Collected Works of John Stuart Mill,* Vols.
XIV–XVII. Toronto: Toronto University Press, 1972.

Osborne, Lord Sidney. *The Letters of S.G.O.* Edited by Arnold White. 2 vols.
London: Griffith, Farran, Okeden and Welsh, 1888.

[Osborne, Rev. Sidney Godolphin]. *The Prospects and Present Condition of the
Labouring Classes, considered with respect to the Probable Operation of the
New Poor Law — together with some Practical Observations on Loan Funds,
Savings Banks, etc. etc.* By a Beneficed Clergyman of the County of Bucks.
London: T. & W. Boone, 1835.

[Osborne, Rev. Sidney Godolphin]. *A Word or Two about the New Poor Law;
Addressed to his Parishioners by a Beneficed Clergyman in Buckinghamshire.*
London: T. & W. Boone, 1835.

Playfair, Lyon. *Memoirs and Correspondence of Lyon Playfair.* Edited by Thomas
Wemyss Reid, with a new introduction by Colin Armstrong. Jemimaville,
Scotland: P. M. Pollak, 1976. First published in 1899.

Smith, Joshua Toulmin. *Government by Commissions Illegal and Pernicious. The
Nature and Effects of All Commissions of Inquiry and other Crown Appointed
Commissions. The Constitutional Principles of Taxation; And the Rights, Duties
and Importance of Local Self-Government.* London: S. Sweet, 1849.

Smith, Joshua Toulmin. *Local Self-Government and Centralization: The Characteristics
of Each; And its Practical Tendencies as Affecting Social, Moral and Political
Welfare and Progress Including Comprehensive Outlines of the English
Constitution.* London: John Chapman, 1851.

Smith, Joshua Toulmin. *Local Self-Government Un-mystified. A Vindication of Common Sense, Human Nature, and Practical Improvement against the Manifesto
of Centralism, as put forth at the Social Science Association, 1857.* London:
Edward Stanford, 1857.

Smith, Thomas Southwood. *A Lecture delivered over the Remains of Jeremy Bentham,
Esq., in the Webb Street School of Anatomy and Medicine on the 9th of June,
1832.* London: Effingham Wilson, 1832.

[Smith, Thomas Southwood]. "Medical Reform." *London and Westminster Review*
    IV (Oct. 1836): 58–92.
Stephen, Sir George. *A Letter to the Rt. Hon. Lord John Russell on the Probable
    Increase in Rural Crime in Consequence of the Introduction of the New
    Poor-Law and Railroad Systems.* London: Saunders and Ottey, 1836.
[Ward, F. O.]. Untitled review of six public-health publications. *Quarterly Review*
    LXXXVIII (March 1851): 435–92.

Secondary Works

Anstruther, Ian. *The Scandal of the Andover Workhouse.* London: Geoffrey Bles,
    1973.
Bahmueller, Charles. *The National Charity Company: Jeremy Bentham's Silent
    Revolution.* Berkeley: University of California Press, 1981.
Benyon, Helen. "Mighty Bentham." *Journal of Legal History* 2, no. 1 (May 1981):
    62–76.
Brebner, J. Bartlett. "Laissez-faire and State Intervention in Nineteenth-century
    Britain." *Journal of Economic History* 8 (1948), Supp.: 59–73.
Brockington, C. Fraser. "Public Health and the Privy Council 1831–4." *Journal of
    the History of Medicine* 16 (1961): 161–85.
Brundage, Anthony. *The Making of the New Poor Law. The Politics of Inquiry,
    Enactment, and Implementation, 1832–1839.* New Brunswick, N.J.: Rutgers
    University Press, 1978.
Brundage, Anthony. "Reform of the Poor Law Electoral System, 1834–94." *Albion*
    7 (Fall 1975): 201–15.
Clokie, H. M., and J. W. Robinson. *Royal Commissions of Inquiry.* Stanford:
    Stanford University Press, 1937.
Cooper, Robert Alan. "Jeremy Bentham, Elizabeth Fry, and English Prison Reform."
    Journal of the History of Ideas 42, no. 4 (1981): 675–90.
Cowherd, Raymond G. *Political Economists and the English Poor Laws. A Historical
    Study of the Influence of Classical Economics on the Formation of Social Welfare
    Policy.* Athens: Ohio University Press, 1977.
Critchley, T. A. *A History of Police in England and Wales.* Second edition. London:
    Constable, 1978.
Crowther, M. A. *The Workhouse System 1834–1929.* Athens: University of Georgia
    Press, 1982.
Cullen, M. J. "The Making of the Civil Registration Act of 1836." *Journal of
    Ecclesiastical History* 25 (1974): 39–59.
Cullen, M. J. *The Statistical Movement in Early Victorian Britain: The Foundations of
    Empirical Social Research.* New York: Harvester Press, 1975.
Dicey, Albert Venn. *Lectures on the Relation between Law and Public Opinion in*

England during the Nineteenth Century. London: Macmillan and Co., 1905.

Digby, Anne. *Pauper Palaces.* London: Routledge and Kegan Paul, 1978.

Donajgrodzki, A. P. " 'Social Police' and the Bureaucratic Elite: A Vision of Order in the Age of Reform." In *Social Control in Nineteenth Century Britain,* edited by A. P. Donajgrodzki, pp. 51–76. London: Croom Helm, 1977.

Driver, Cecil. *Tory Radical: The Life of Richard Oastler.* New York: Oxford University Press, 1946.

Dunkley, Peter. "Whigs and Paupers. The Reform of the English Poor Law 1830–34." *Journal of British Studies* 20 (1981): 124–49.

Edsall, Nicholas C. *The Anti-Poor Law Movement 1834-44.* Manchester: Manchester University Press, 1971.

Finer, S. E. *The Life and Times of Sir Edwin Chadwick.* London: Methuen, 1952.

Finer, S. E. "The Transmission of Benthamite Ideas 1820–50." In *Studies in the Growth of Nineteenth-century Government,* edited by Gillian Sutherland, pp. 11–32. London: Routledge and Kegan Paul, 1972.

Fraser, Derek. *The Evolution of the British Welfare State. A History of Social Policy since the Industrial Revolution.* London: Macmillan, 1973.

Goddard, Nicholas. "Nineteenth Century Recycling: The Victorians and the Agricultural Utilization of Sewage." *History Today* 31 (June 1981): 32–36.

Gutchen, Robert M. "Local Improvements and Centralization in Nineteenth Century England." *Historical Journal* 4 (1961): 85–96.

Halévy, Elie. *The Growth of Philosophic Radicalism.* Translated by Mary Morris. Revised edition. London: Faber and Faber, 1952.

Halévy, Elie. *The Triumph of Reform 1830-1841.* Second edition. London: Benn, 1950.

Hamburger, Joseph. *Intellectuals in Politics: John Stuart Mill and the Philosophic Radicals.* New Haven: Yale University Press, 1965.

Hart, Jenifer. "Nineteenth Century Social Reform: A Tory Interpretation of History." *Past and Present* 31 (July 1965): 39–61.

Hart, Jenifer. "Police." In *Crime and Law in Nineteenth Century Britain,* pp. 177–219. Dublin: Irish University Press, 1978.

Hart, Jenifer. "Reform of the Borough Police, 1835–56." *English Historical Review* 70 (1955): 411–27.

Hart, Jenifer. "Sir Charles Trevelyan at the Treasury." *English Historical Review* 75 (1960): 92–110.

Henriques, Ursula. *Before the Welfare State. Social Administration in Early Industrial Britain.* London: Longmans, 1979.

Henriques, Ursula. "Jeremy Bentham and the Machinery of Social Reform." In *British Government and Administration. Studies Presented to S. B. Chrimes,* edited by H. Hearder and H. R. Lyon, pp. 169–86. Cardiff: University of Wales Press, 1974.

Himmelfarb, Gertrude. "The Haunted House of Jeremy Bentham." In *Victorian Minds,* pp. 32–81. New York: Alfred A. Knopf, 1968.

Himmelfarb, Gertrude. *The Idea of Poverty. England in the Early Industrial Age.* New York: Alfred A. Knopf, 1984.

Hughes, Edward. "Sir Charles Trevelyan and Civil Service Reform, 1853–5." *English Historical Review* 64 (1949): 53–88.

Hume, L. J. "Jeremy Bentham and the Nineteenth Century Revolution in Government." *Historical Journal* 10 (1967): 361–75.

Hume, L. J. *Bentham and Bureaucracy.* Cambridge: Cambridge University Press, 1981.

Johnson, Richard. "Educating the Educators: 'Experts' and the State 1833–9." In *Social Control in Nineteenth Century Britain,* edited by A. P. Donajgrodzki, pp. 77–107. London: Croom Helm, 1977.

Keith-Lucas, B. "Some Influences Affecting the Development of Sanitary Legislation in England." *Economic History Review,* Second Series 6 (1954): 290–96.

Kitson Clark, George. " 'Statesmen in Disguise': Reflexions on the History of the Neutrality of the Civil Service." *Historical Journal* 2 (1959): 19–39.

Knott, John. *Popular Opposition to the 1834 Poor Law.* New York: St. Martin's Press, 1986.

Lambert, Royston. *Sir John Simon 1816–1904 and English Social Administration.* London: MacGibbon and Kee, 1963.

Levy, S. Leon. *Nassau W. Senior 1790–1864.* Newton Abbot: David and Charles, 1970.

Lewis, R. A. "Edwin Chadwick and the Administrative Reform Movement, 1854–56." *University of Birmingham Historical Journal* 2, No. 2 (1950): 178–200.

Lewis, R. A. *Edwin Chadwick and the Public Health Movement 1832–1854.* London: Longmans, 1952. Reprinted 1968.

Lewis, R. A. "Edwin Chadwick and the Railway Labourers." *Economic History Review,* Second Series 3, no. 1 (1950): 107–18.

Lewis, R. A. "William Day and the Poor Law Commissioners." *University of Birmingham Historical Journal* 9 (1964): 163–96.

Lieberman, David. "From Bentham to Benthamism." *Historical Journal* 28, no. 1 (1985): 199–224.

Longmate, Norman. *The Workhouse.* London: Temple Smith, 1974.

Lubenow, William C. *The Politics of Government Growth: Early Victorian Attitude toward State Intervention 1833–1848.* Newton Abbot: David and Charles, 1971.

MacDonagh, Oliver. *Early Victorian Government 1830–1870.* London: Weidenfeld and Nicolson, 1977.

MacDonagh, Oliver. "The Nineteenth Century Revolution in Government: A Reappraisal." *Historical Journal* 1 (1985): 52–67.

Mandler, Peter. "Cain and Abel: Two Aristocrats and the Early Victorian Factory Acts." *Historical Journal* 27, no. 1 (March 1984): 83–109.

Mather, F. C. *Public Order in the Age of the Chartists.* Manchester: Manchester University Press, 1959.

Midwinter, E. C. *Social Administration in Lancashire 1830–1860: Poor Law, Public Health and Police.* Manchester: Manchester University Press, 1969.

Olien, Diana Davids. *Morpeth. A Victorian Public Career.* Washington: University Press of America, 1983.

Owen, David. *The Government of Victorian London 1855–1889. The Metropolitan Board of Works, the Vestries, and the City Corporation.* Edited by Roy McLeod with contributions by David Reeder, Donald Olsen, and Francis Sheppard. Cambridge: Belknap Press of Harvard University Press, 1982.

Parris, Henry. *Government and the Railways in Nineteenth Century Britain.* London: Routledge and Kegan Paul, 1965.

Parris, Henry. "The Nineteenth Century Revolution in Government: A Reappraisal Reappraised." *Historical Journal* 3 (1960): 17–37.

Paz, D. G. "The Limits of Bureaucratic Autonomy in Victorian Administration." *The Historian* 49 (February 1987): 167–83.

Pelling, Margaret. *Cholera, Fever and English Medicine 1825–1865.* Oxford: Oxford University Press, 1978.

Radzinowicz, Leon. *A History of English Criminal Law and Its Administration from 1750.* 4 vols. London: Stevens and Sons, 1948–68.

Reith, Charles. *A New Study of Police History.* Edinburgh: Oliver and Boyd, 1956.

Roach, John. *Social Reform in England 1780–1880.* London: Batsford, 1978.

Roberts, David. "Jeremy Bentham and the Victorian Administrative State." *Victorian Studies* 2 (1959): 193–210.

Roberts, David. "Lord Palmerston at the Home Office, 1853–1854." *The Historian* 21 (November 1958): 63–81.

Roberts, David. *Paternalism in Early Victorian England.* New Brunswick, N.J.: Rutgers University Press, 1979.

Roberts, David. *Victorian Origins of the British Welfare State.* New Haven: Yale University Press, 1960.

Rose, Michael E. "Settlement, Removal and the New Poor Law." In *The New Poor Law in the Nineteenth Century,* edited by Derek Fraser, pp. 25–44. London: Macmillan, 1976.

Smith, Sheila M. "Willenhall and Wodgate: Disraeli's Use of Bluebook Evidence." *Review of English Studies,* New Series 13 (1962): 368–84.

Thomas, M. W. *The Early Factory Legislation, A Study in Legislative and Administrative Evolution.* Leigh-on-Sea: Thames Bank Publishing Co., 1948.

Thomas, William. *The Philosophical Radicals. Nine Studies in Theory and Practice.* Oxford: Clarendon Press, 1979.

Thompson, F. M. L. "Social Control in Victorian Britain." *Economic History Review,* Second Series 24 (1981): 189–208.

Ward, J. T. *The Factory Movement 1830–1855.* London: Macmillan, 1962.

Webb, R. K. "A Whig Inspector." *Journal of Modern History* 27 (1955): 352–64.

Webb, Sidney, and Beatrice Webb. *English Poor Law History: Part II, The Last Hundred Years.* 2 vols. London: Longmans and Co., 1929.

Williams, Karel. *From Pauperism to Poverty.* London: Routledge and Kegan Paul, 1981.
Wohl, Anthony S. *Endangered Lives. Public Health in Victorian Britain.* Cambridge: Harvard University Press, 1983.

Index